ABOUT ANTIQUITIES

ABOUT
ANTIQUITIES

POLITICS OF
ARCHAEOLOGY IN THE
OTTOMAN EMPIRE

ZEYNEP ÇELIK

UNIVERSITY OF TEXAS PRESS • AUSTIN

This book has been supported by an endowment dedicated to classics and the ancient world and funded by the Areté Foundation; the Gladys Krieble Delmas Foundation; the Dougherty Foundation; the James R. Dougherty, Jr. Foundation; the Rachael and Ben Vaughan Foundation; and the National Endowment for the Humanities.

*Requests for permission to reproduce material
from this work should be sent to:*
PERMISSIONS
UNIVERSITY OF TEXAS PRESS
P.O. BOX 7819
AUSTIN, TX 78713-7819
http://utpress.utexas.edu/index.php/rp-form

♾ The paper used in this book meets the minimum requirements of
ANSI/NISO Z39.48-1992 (R1997) (Permanence of Paper).

Library of Congress Cataloging-in-Publication Data

Names: Çelik, Zeynep, author.   Title: About antiquities : politics of archaeology in the Ottoman Empire / Zeynep Çelik.   Description: First edition. | Austin : University of Texas Press, 2016. | Includes bibliographical references and index.   Identifiers: LCCN 2016006704 | ISBN 978-1-4773-1019-9 (cloth : alk. paper) | ISBN 978-1-4773-1061-8 (pbk. : alk. paper) | ISBN 978-1-4773-1020-5 (library e-book) | ISBN 978-1-4773-1021-2 (non-library e-book)   Subjects: LCSH: Museums— Turkey—History. | Archaeological museums and collections— Turkey—History. | Archaeology—Turkey—History. | Turkey— Antiquities. | Archaeology and state—Turkey—History. | Istanbul Arkeoloji Müzeleri. | Nationalism—Turkey—History.   Classification: LCC AM79.T8 C45 2016 | DDC 069.094561/015—dc23   LC record available at http://lccn.loc.gov/2016006704   DOI:10.7560/310199

To Perry

CONTENTS

Acknowledgments • ix
Author's Note on Names, Dates, and Measurements • xi

INTRODUCTION • *1*

CHAPTER ONE
Beginnings: The Nineteenth-Century Museum • 13

CHAPTER TWO
Scholarship and the Imperial Museum • 43

CHAPTER THREE
The Imperial Museum and Its Visitors • 65

CHAPTER FOUR
The Ottoman Reading Public and Antiquities • 95

CHAPTER FIVE
The Landscape of Labor • 135

CHAPTER SIX
Dual Settlements • 175

EPILOGUE
Enduring Dilemmas • 215

Notes • 223   Bibliography • 245   Index • 255

ACKNOWLEDGMENTS

ABOUT ANTIQUITIES was researched and written with the generous support of fellowships from the American Council of Learned Societies and the National Endowment for the Humanities, a sabbatical leave from the New Jersey Institute of Technology, and a publication fund from Columbia University Seminars. I presented parts of my research at the Columbia University Seminar on Ottoman and Turkish History and Culture, Max Plank Institute in Florence, Graduate Center of the City University of New York, Swarthmore College, Technical University in Delft, Allard Piersen Museum in Amsterdam, Brown University, New York University, and University of Gent. The reactions and responses at each of these occasions made me think hard about many issues and oriented me toward others.

The research was conducted at the Istanbul Archaeological Museums Archives, Istanbul University Central Library, Pierpont Morgan Library Archives (New York), Prime Minister's Archives (Istanbul), Princeton University Archaeological Archives, and the University of Pennsylvania Museum of Archaeology and Anthropology Archives. I am grateful for the efficient and gracious cooperation I received from the directors and staff of these institutions. Zeynep Kızıltan, the director, and Havva Koç, the head librarian, of the Istanbul Archaeological Museum went out of their way to facilitate my work. I am particularly indebted to Ms. Koç for taking a personal interest in my topic and assembling documents pertinent to it. I also owe a special thank you to Sarah Horowitz, the director of Special Collections at Haverford College, for sending me a scanned copy of Joseph

Meyer's notebook on short notice. Ceyda Yüksel, my research assistant in Istanbul, offered much-needed long-distance help. Several digitized collections opened a wealth of primary sources; among them, the National Library in Ankara and the Atatürk Library in Istanbul provided convenient access to many printed Ottoman sources.

At the University of Texas Press, I thank my editor Jim Burr for his continued interest in this book from its conceptual state on and for accommodating the changes to the original proposal with flexibility and good cheer. He guided me through the production process with meticulous attention and professionalism. I appreciated Lynne Chapman's attention to the editing process, and I am indebted to Nancy Warrington for her careful copyediting.

I benefited from conversations with many friends and colleagues at different stages of research and writing. Zainab Bahrani, Edhem Eldem, Diane Favro, Susan Slyomovics, and Ayşe Yönder were particularly inspirational on many fronts. I appreciated very much the poignant comments of the anonymous readers for the University of Texas Press. My son, Ali Winston, spiced my work with his wit and sense of humor. As always, my most thorough and critical reader has been my husband, Perry Winston. His contribution to this book extends from the early conceptualization to the final selection of the images. I am most grateful to him for the open-mindedness and curiosity with which he welcomed another of my projects to our home and dinner table.

Perry passed away just as my book went into production. I had originally dedicated it to him; now, in all sadness, I dedicate it to his memory.

AUTHOR'S NOTE ON NAMES, DATES, AND MEASUREMENTS

PRIOR TO THE SURNAME LAW, passed on June 21, 1934, and put into effect in January 1935, Turkish names constituted a person's given names, sometimes followed by his or her father's name. Individuals signed their names in either way, or even simply by one given name. Furthermore, it was common to add "Bey" or "Efendi" to the end of a name, especially when only one given name was used. The inconsistencies in the Turkish/Ottoman names in this book derive from the multiplicity of the name formats before and after the Surname Law was enacted.

The Ottoman dating system is based on the Hegira (AD 622). When the dates are converted to the Western (Gregorian) calendar, the Hegirian date is given first, followed by the Gregorian one.

The sources used in this book give dimensions in metric or English systems. Rather than make all consistent, I kept the original numbers, providing conversions in parentheses.

ABOUT ANTIQUITIES

INTRODUCTION

"WHO OWNS ANTIQUITY?" is a familiar question that occupies a heated place in present-day international controversies. *About Antiquities* takes these debates to their origins, to the heyday of archaeology's establishment as an academic discipline. At the intersection of history, art, architecture, mythology, ethnography, and research in hard sciences, archaeology emerged as a dominant cultural field in the nineteenth century. Valorization of the heritage may go back to time immemorial, but its systematization is a modern phenomenon, profoundly entangled in the cultural and political developments of the past two hundred years. Antiquities, the material artifacts of the discipline, became charged with meanings associated with empire building, global relations and rivalries, power struggles, definitions of national and cultural identities, cross-cultural exchanges, cooperations, abuses, and misunderstandings — often influenced by the underlying element of money. The "tangible substance, the stuff" of built environments, that is, extensive infrastructural projects, cultural institutions, and architecture, contributed to their prominence, enhanced by technological innovations.

A few reminders will orient the reader to further articulation of the themes addressed in the book. The statue of Venus de Milo, the neatly constructed history of its dubious origins, and its shifting positions in the Louvre open a curious page about defining the identity of France, counterbalancing the appropriation of the Elgin Marbles into British culture — as provocatively discussed by Philippe Jockey.[1] The link between archaeology and the politics of imperialism is blatantly manifest in the figure of Austen Henry Layard, whose fame depended on his "discoveries" in Nineveh, but whose true career was intelligence service for the British Empire, aimed at defending British interests in the eastern Ottoman provinces.[2] The railroad network functioned as a double-edged sword in the late-nineteenth-century Ottoman Empire: In addition to serving broader economic and social functions, railroads spurred the growth of tourism and enabled the transportation of antiquities excavated from far-flung sites to the newly founded Imperial Museum in Istanbul (a common route was by rail to Beirut, from where they would be loaded on boats). Yet it also facilitated their smuggling out of the country.[3]

Nineteenth-century cultural and artistic productions appropriated antiquities in myriad ways. Poems, novels, plays, paintings, sculptures, and buildings with references to antiquity are so numerous and so familiar by now that we often do not think about them in the context of the history of archaeology. It may not even matter in the long run that Percy Bysshe Shelley's sonnet "Ozymandias" (1818) was written in the aftermath of Napoleon I's occupation of Egypt and during the publication of *Description de l'Égypte* (first volume published in 1809) or that Beethoven's *Ruins of Athens* (1811) was composed at the same time as Lord Elgin's men were chipping away the Parthenon "Marbles." Or that Lord Byron published *Sardanapalus* only one decade after Claudius James Rich, one of the early travelers to Mesopotamia, had recorded his observations of his 1811 expedition in *Memoir on the Ruins of Babylon*, which included Nineveh, the site of Byron's play, and that Eugène Delacroix's painting on the fall of Sardanapalus dates only a few years after Lord Byron's play. Nonetheless, a contextual history of antiquities is enriched by such connections.

About Antiquities is an inquiry into the history of archaeology. As Margarita Diaz-Andreu asserts, "There are many possible histories of archaeology, as many as understandings of what archaeology is."[4] My book is one of these. I hope to open several perspectives that have been lost between the lines of the literature on the topic, which includes the original documents and the vast scholarship that scrutinized the field. As will be obvious from my analyses, the stories I attempt to bring to life are eminently detectable in the documents, although they often demand a reading "against the grain," sometimes taking methodological risks. The geography is that of the Ottoman Empire, with its capital, Istanbul, playing a key role as the seat of the Imperial Museum of Antiquities and as the administrative center where the antiquities laws were written and from where government officials were delegated to enforce their application. Nevertheless, the book is not only about the Ottoman Empire, but it is a comparative, cross-cultural study that is very much about European scholarship and institutions, and even more, about their counterparts in the United States of America. Going beyond the institutional frames, I aim to unravel the complicated interactions between individuals — Westerners, Ottoman decision makers and officials, and local laborers. In fact, the labor landscape, perhaps the greatest gap in the existing scholarship, constitutes one of my main areas of research. Focusing on this issue led me at the same time to think about the meanings of antiquities for local people, triggered by Yannis Hamilakis's work on "indigenous archaeologies."[5] Methodologically, I jumped across so many disciplinary boundaries that I can no longer distinguish the fields into which I delved, sometimes nonchalantly. Nonetheless, my long-term scholarship in the history of architecture, cities, and visual cultures forms the backbone of *About Antiquities*. My chronological boundaries stretch from the 1880s to 1914, the beginning corresponding to the opening of the new building for the Imperial Museum in the Ottoman capital and the proliferation of popular Ottoman periodicals, and the end marked by World War I, which changed the political structure of the Middle East. Well aware of the risk of creating artificial ruptures, I did not remain strictly within these boundaries and treated them with flexibility.

The book follows in the footsteps of *Scramble for the Past: A Story of Archaeology in the Ottoman Empire, 1753–1914* (2011), which I edited with Zainab Bahrani and Edhem Eldem. Intending to explore the foreign and local archaeological enterprises in Ottoman lands, we initiated questions in that book on the meanings behind the competitive ownership of the ancient past, interlaced with concepts of civilization. Crisscrossing among the varied and fresh perspectives offered by fifteen scholars, we were able to put forward provocative arguments that, we hope, helped shift the enduring premises in the scholarship, still reiterating only one side, the Western side, of the story. While the chapters coalesced into a revisionist narrative, filling in some gaps came with the realization of many others. My effort in the current volume is a start toward addressing some of those areas — with many remaining.

About Antiquities picks up, at the same time, from where my last book, *Empire, Architecture, and the City: French-Ottoman Encounters, 1830–1914* (2008), ended. Engaging in a comparative study between the built forms of North Africa and the Arab provinces of the Ottoman Empire, I had attempted to shed some light on the parallels and intersections between the French colonial and Ottoman modernization policies in the age of the "connected world of empires." On the Ottoman front, the policies were initiated by the official turn to the neglected Eastern territories, which valorized them in accord with the pan-Islamist policies of Sultan Abdülhamid II (r. 1876–1909). The project to incorporate the region into the identity of the empire was accompanied by acknowledging the layers of history in these remote lands, manifested in the architectural character of the modern public structures, such as schools, hospitals, and government offices. Many eras of pre-Ottoman history, going back to ancient civilizations, gradually opened up, and archaeology entered the Ottoman discourse as a component of the intellectual and civilizational wealth of the empire. Other modernity projects, such as railroads and telegraphs lines, topics covered in *Empire, Architecture, and the City*, would also play instrumental roles in the Ottoman engagement in antiquities. Furthermore, the attitudes of Ottoman key figures toward the people of the Arab provinces were speckled by notions of superiority and even racial hierarchy, connected to their own concepts of "civilization." They would be shared by Ottomans involved in the antiquities of the Middle East in situ, face-to-face with the locals, and from the considerable distance of Istanbul.

My colleagues from *Scramble for the Past* and I are not unique in our concerns to triangulate and complicate the history of archaeology. I acknowledge the scholarship of authors who contributed to that volume with my gratitude, underlining the sustained publications of Zainab Bahrani, Edhem Eldem, and Wendy Shaw. Many other scholars have recently published revisionist studies, raising important questions and making invaluable contributions toward breaking the rigid templates of the field. Among those particularly insightful for my work, I highlight only several in two genres, general surveys and site-specific studies, which provoked me to ask questions about the political and ideological undertones of archaeology and to pay more attention to the topic on the level of individuals, from archaeologists to Bedouin women cooking for the workers.[6] Bruce Trigger's groundbreaking work on the development of archaeological thought opened up a new direction. Supporting the argument that "archaeology is strongly influenced by the positions that the countries and the regions in which it is practiced occupy within the modern world systems," Trigger analyzed three categories of "alternative archaeologies": nationalist, colonialist, and imperialist, in an article published in 1984.[7] The following decade saw a number of inquiries on the ideological implications of archaeology.[8] Two surveys, Margarita Diaz-Andreu's *A World History of Nineteenth-Century Archaeology* and an extensive catalogue accompanying an exhibition in the Ruhr Museum, *Das Grosse Spiel: Archäologie und Politik zur Zeit des Kolonial-usmus*, edited by Charlotte Trümpler, charted global pictures and framed them in their multiple political contexts and ideologies, touching upon the "other," especially the Ottoman, side. Research on colonial archaeology has also dealt with the ideologies framing the "scientific" work. Nabila Ouleb-sir's *Les usages du patrimoine: Monuments, musées et politique coloniale en Algérie (1830–1930)* (2004) and Clémentine Gutron's *L'archéologie en Tunisie (XIXe–XXe siècles): Jeux généalogiques sur l'Antiquité* (2010) should be mentioned as contributions to this area of study.

More focused studies provided closer treatment of the relationships between Western archaeologists and their counterparts in the East, especially in the Ottoman Empire. In *Down from Olympus: Archaeology and Philhellenism in Germany, 1750–1970* (1996), Suzanne Marchand examined the German passion for antiquities and its entanglements with Orientalism, with an emphasis on museums and scholarship. Maya Jasanoff's *Edges of Empire: Conquest and Collecting in the East, 1750–1850* (2006) scrutinized the political implications of collecting by tracing how antiquities would become a substitute for real power. Frederick N. Bohrer's theoretically ambitious analysis of the nineteenth-century representations of Assyria in Europe, *Orientalism and Visual Culture: Imagining Mesopotamia in Nineteenth-Century Europe* (2003), briefly brings Hormuzd Rassam, Austen Henry Layard's right-hand man in Mesopotamia and an archaeologist in his own right, into the field as "a distinctly hybrid cultural figure."[9]

Bruce Kuklick turned to American archaeologists who conducted work in Mesopotamia in *Puritans in Babylon: The Ancient Near East and American Intellectual Life, 1880–1930* (1996) and investigated their intellectual contributions to the discipline in light of their Protestant beliefs and Judeo-Christian heritage. Highlighting individual actors (among them, John Punnett Peters, John Henry Haynes, and Hermann Vollrat Hilprecht, all digging in Nippur) and the relationships between them, he argued that their blatant Orientalism enabled them, at the same time, to advance knowledge. Renata Holod and Robert Ousterhout's edited volume, *Osman Hamdi Bey and the Americans* (2011), examined some of the same American archaeologists in terms of their interactions with Osman Hamdi, the director of the Imperial Museum, who was in control of all archaeological research in the empire. Based on a wealth of textual and visual documents from both the American and Ottoman sides, the volume and the exhibition (held at the Pera Museum in Istanbul the same year) offered a comprehensive analysis of the "intersecting lives" of Osman Hamdi, John Henry Haynes, and Hermann Vollrat Hilprecht from a cross-cultural perspective. The trend to complicate the stories echoes in Mary Beard's semi-guidebook, semi-cultural study *The Parthenon* (2010), which includes the observations of Evliya Çelebi, a seventeenth-century Ottoman traveler who was among the early travelers to Athens.

Setting out to address archaeologists' "peculiar indifference" toward the cheap labor upon which the sites they excavated depended, and alluding to the field's continued "indifference to current labour and social relations," Stephen Quirke studied the archives of excavations carried out by Flinders Petrie in Egypt between 1880 and 1924 in his *Hidden Hands: Egyptian Workforces in Petrie Excavation Archives, 1880–1924* (2011), thereby introducing not only the main Egyptian players, the supervisors at the sites, but even more significantly, the full labor force.[10] Although Donald Malcolm Reid had already made a strong case about Egyptians who had played important roles in archaeology in *Whose Pharaohs? Archaeology, Museums, and Egyptian National Identity from Napoleon to World War I* (2002), workers had remained absent in literature until Quirke's book.[11]

About Antiquities starts with a comparative chapter on museums that was originally intended to offer a more inclusive picture situating the Imperial Museum in Istanbul in reference to the major museums of Europe and North America. However, my research led me to focus on the Imperial Museum and the Metropolitan Museum of Art in New York. These two institutions, both of which recorded a remarkably fast pace of growth during their early decades, made a curious pair, as they existed on the peripheries of the more established museums of Europe. Despite the strong support of the Ottoman government, the museum in Istanbul was limited in its resources, reflecting the economic difficulties of the late empire. Even so, it occupied a unique position among all museums for two reasons: it was in the capital of the vast Ottoman territory in the Middle East and Anatolia, arguably the richest agglomeration of ancient sites, and its administration had direct and ever-increasing control over all archaeological activity in the region. The Metropolitan was far from such a privileged location, but it was generously endowed by a wealthy private sector, driven in its devotion to antiquities and determined to create a top-notch museum. The Imperial Museum and the Metropolitan both became leading cultural institutions of the late nineteenth century, but their missions varied and sometimes contradicted each other's. In chapter 1, I investigate the specific agendas and the growing pains of the Imperial Museum and the Metropolitan in each other's mirror, placing them in their urban contexts as well. In doing the latter, I provide a broader comparison with the leading museums of Europe, reading several major world cities of the late nineteenth century through their most visible cultural institutions, and showing how the two ambitious museums at the margins inscribed themselves into their surrounding urban fabrics in comparable ways.

Osman Hamdi's goal to place the Imperial Museum on the map of international scholarship succeeded at a remarkable pace, following the inauguration of the new buildings and despite a wave of bitter reactions against the Ottoman claims to antiquities. After examining the European opposition to the Ottoman project, in chapter 2 I follow the increasing attention paid by the foreign scholarly press to the collections in the museum, centered on the spectacular sarcophagi Osman Hamdi had discovered in Sidon. Their painted reliefs supported the arguments on the uses of polychromy in Greek antiquity, a controversial topic at the time. If not with the same intensity as that devoted to the Sidon sarcophagi, archaeological journals also gave ample space to other objects in the collection, with some theoretization on the sumptuous characteristics of "Oriental" antiquities juxtaposed against their sterner Western counterparts.

Chapter 3 centers on the Imperial Museum and its public, measured against the Metropolitan. An analysis of a range of documents, including the museum's official publications, reveals that the Istanbul museum accommodated foreign visitors above all, with the priority given to scholars. There is no doubt that part of this lopsided picture depended on the personal penchant of Osman Hamdi, who single-handedly changed the Ottoman policies toward the preservation of antiquities in the empire by penning legislation and applying it. His collegial welcome of the community of European and American scholars must have been driven by his own commitment to making a respectable place for the museum as a site of international research. Ironically, it was some of these very same scholars whose archaeological activities were controlled under Osman Hamdi's eagle eyes. Once the museum opened its doors, local populations gradually started frequenting it, albeit in small numbers. School groups seem to be the most faithful visitors, with the numbers of students sometimes overpowering the staff. This chapter also looks at the place of antiquities in the broader cultural life by tracing how museums made their ways into novels.

Ottoman perceptions of antiquities in the late nineteenth century were among the topics *Scramble for the Past* opened up. Giving examples from a wide area of cultural productions, including paintings, novels, yearbooks on provinces (*salnames*), and periodicals, we traced the interest in the pre-Ottoman past.[12] In chapter 4, *About Antiquities* looks at the topic closer, relying on the leading periodicals published in Istanbul. Reports and articles on the antique sites in the imperial territories appeared often in their pages, accompanied by similar news from abroad. Earlier these had focused entirely on ancient civilizations, especially the Greco-Roman sites, but the first decade of the twentieth century witnessed a shift that brought the "Islamic" heritage to the foreground, provoked by the deteriorating conditions of the monuments. The chapter ends with a literary episode and considers two plays on the same topic, the fall of Sardanapalus, the last Assyrian king, one by Lord Byron and the other by the Ottoman writer Abdülhak Hamid. The comparative reading of the texts and their staging instructions reveals variations in the interpretations of the same legend and attests to yet another cross-cultural exchange, whose nuances say a great deal about the two contexts.

In chapter 5, the discussion moves to archaeological sites, and I explore the conditions under which the ambitiously displayed objects were extracted. The numbers of laborers, the organization of the workforce, and salaries are investigated on the basis of archaeological reports, which also provide insights into personal relationships between workers and archaeologists. The interactions between the three sets of actors — European archaeologists, Ottoman officers in charge of their supervision, and local laborers often belonging to different tribes or ethnic groups — display hierarchies but also shifting power relations. Even though Europeans came with money and conducted the work, they had to operate under the control of Ottoman officials. Workers, seemingly in the lowest echelon of the hierarchy, maintained their own power base and made their own decisions, often frustrating their patrons. They established their own schedules and refused to work if they had other priorities, among them planting and harvesting their fields when the weather changed. As data flow only one way, knowledge on the labor landscape depends uniquely on archaeologists' records, charged with an Orientalist baggage but also speckled with ethnographic observations.

Hoping to give some voice to the laborers themselves, I attempted to read between the lines of their reports.

The physical patterns of the residential fabrics that developed in the vicinity of the extraction sites are the topics of chapter 6. Not surprisingly, and reminiscent of the basic template for colonial cities, they exhibit a dual character, with distinct areas for Western archaeologists (and their Ottoman supervisors) and for laborers, each harboring different lifestyles. Archaeologists' headquarters get more elaborate with time, leading to architecturally ambitious dig houses, surrounded by "native" villages that developed spontaneously, adhering to vernacular forms and materials, thus inadvertently creating picturesque "authentic" sites conducive to ethnographic research. The chapter associates this duality constructed during the excavation process with a more "organic" one, that is, the earlier nestling of a "native village" into the ruins of Palmyra, a view described by many Western visitors speculating on the advanced civilization of antiquity in sharp contrast to the backwardness of contemporary peasants.

About Antiquities concludes with a broad-brush overview of the current debates on antiquities, their roots grounded in the earlier developments investigated in this book.

The nature of this project calls for reflecting on the research process and the many problems raised by it. The inevitable predicaments of a comparative study that is dependent on data from unequal archives, a difficulty I had encountered in *Empire, Architecture, and the City*, continued to haunt me in writing *About Antiquities*.[13] For example, documents on both the New York and Istanbul museums are abundant but still far more comprehensive and varied for the former and showing glaring gaps for the latter. Among the most blatant ones is the numbers of visitors—a statistic not recorded in Istanbul. I was also disappointed by not being able to locate any reports or journals by the Ottoman officials who supervised the operations of Western archaeologists. Their perspectives would have added an invaluable dimension to our understanding of the social dynamics on the sites.

As the history of archaeology is subjected to more inclusive and critical approaches, the role played by non-Western protagonists has been acknowledged, at least in passing. Nevertheless, the analysis is sparse and limited to a few names. In the case of the Ottoman scene, Osman Hamdi appears as the unique actor. His importance cannot be overstated, not only in archaeology and museum building but in all areas of late-Ottoman visual culture, from photography to architecture and, of course, to painting. Enjoying a unique power base, he was in a position to make key decisions single-handedly. Nevertheless, he was not isolated from his surrounding social context, which was undergoing a fast pace of change.[14] Osman Hamdi interacted and worked with others to materialize his visions. The singular concentration on this leading figure is understandable, as archival information on some of the other actors on the vast stage of archaeology in the empire is rare, often restricted to straightforward facts, such as appointment locations, salaries, or appreciations expressed in honorary medals. For example, the name of Bedri Bey, a "commissar" in the museum, comes across in numerous documents in the Ottoman Prime Minister's Archives pertaining to his salary and various additional payments, his appointments to Mesopotamian archaeological sites and to Pergamon as a supervisor to the research teams, and his responsibilities for transporting objects from these sites to the Imperial Museum. Bedri Bey also shows up in J. H. Haynes's site reports on Nippur and Hilprecht's accounts, but only in brief reference to his cohabitation with the American team in Nippur as the Ottoman inspector representing the Imperial Museum.[15] Confronted with documentary absences, I was not able to provide a conclusive narrative on Bedri Bey. His personal views cannot be constructed on the basis of such fragmented data, and the researcher is left only speculating on the value of a hypothetical journal kept by him, recording his observations on the Nippur expedition, for example.

Many other absences affected my research, especially in my drive to cast light on individuals—and not only the illiterate laborers. I searched in vain for accounts of local visitors to the Imperial Museum to bring in their personal thoughts and impressions. It is my hope that journals and family albums will surface in time and allow researchers to expand on the ways the people of Istanbul experienced this key institution, well knowing that their numbers were small. My curiosity about Ottoman women visitors and their impressions remained unanswered as well. I had expected to catch glimpses of at least upper-class women paying some attention to the museum, but there are no such records even for the ladies of Osman Hamdi's family. The only tidbit I stumbled upon was about the scheduling of trips by girls' schools. Unfortunately, I could only invent scenarios about these trips, imagining what it must have been like when Ottoman teenagers of both sexes in the early twentieth century encountered each other around the ancient objects. Interior photographs of the museum continued to disappoint me. While they are abundant in the archives and on the pages of the periodicals, giving valuable information on the halls and the displays, I was unable to find a single one that depicted visitors.

If information on a prominent person such as Bedri Bey is piecemeal, it is impossible to give voice to the army of workers on the sites. I am, of course, not the first or the last historian who acknowledges the "silence" of the subordinate people in the documents. Carlo Ginzburg and Natalie Zemon Davis, both working on the sixteenth century, problematized and addressed it elegantly and became inspirational models.[16] More recently, I was drawn to a term used by Dorothy Metzger Habel: "hearing voices."[17] Habel "listened" to the voices she "heard" on the architectural sites of Baroque Rome to write a history of rebuilding the city; I, too, heard them on the excavation sites and was compelled to include them in my stories. To meet the challenge, I experimented with unconventional methodologies. I took liberties in analyzing photographs and attempted to read archaeologists' accounts for hidden evidence, searching for meanings not intended by the authors. This approach calls for considering each site individually and situating it in its own political and ideological context, which was not made easier by the numerous conflicts between the multitudes of ethnic and religious groups that rocked the region at the time and by the Ottoman state's moves to gain control over them.

The diversity and dispersed nature of the Ottoman textual and visual primary sources, as well as the absences in the documentation, provoke the researcher to ask questions that can only be addressed by other questions. Nonetheless, set against the systematic and comprehensive archives on the Western (in this book, the American) side, their fragmented nature leads to an exciting process of synthesis, which remains open-ended.

CHAPTER ONE

BEGINNINGS:

THE NINETEENTH-CENTURY MUSEUM

*Two Museums at the Periphery: The Imperial Museum, Istanbul,
and the Metropolitan Museum of Art, New York*

A LETTER DATED November 7, 1912, and written by Howard Crosby
Butler to E. Robinson, made an urgent call for a representative of the Metro-
politan Museum of Art in New York to go to Constantinople "on the chance
of the Turks deciding to withdraw and wishing to part with heavy luggage."
The "heavy luggage" referred to the contents of the Imperial Museum in the
Ottoman capital, and the "withdrawal" alluded to Ottomans giving up their
claims to antiquities. A rumor about the sale of the museum had reached
Pierpont Morgan, as noted in a handwritten document dictated by the great
New York collector and the president of the Metropolitan Museum of Art
(1904–1913). Calling to dispatch Montague Parker from Paris to the Ottoman capital to check the situation, Morgan stated: "[It is] very important
to me to know the facts and possibilities to be in a position to act." Butler
believed the rumor to carry validity and wrote back: "If Turkey is obliged to
pay a heavy indemnity in order to hold the capital, she may be willing to part
with objects which interest less than 100 Turks all told." He highlighted the
emergency of the deal, as he was "sure that both Germany and Austria have
men on the spot waiting to make a good offer to the Government for the
sarcophagus of Alexander so called," the latter being the most valued and
cherished artifact in the museum (figure 1.1). A couple of weeks later, on
November 20, Morgan sent a cable to E. C. Grenfell in London, repeating

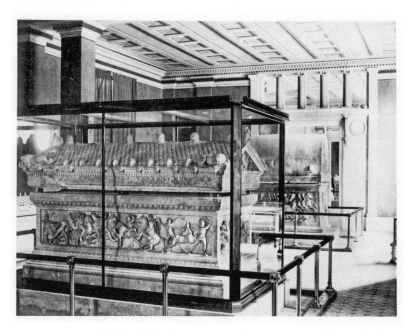

FIGURE 1.1 Interior of the Imperial Museum, with Sarcophagus of Alexander in the foreground. (İÜMK 90632-0015)

that he had "reason to believe Turkish Government would sell at reasonable price Museum at Constantinople with all its contents including the Sarcophagus of Alexander." He added, expressing his interest to purchase the collection wholesale: "It is quite important that we should accomplish this if possible. I apprehend both Germany and Austria would compete." The collection would be for the Metropolitan Museum of Art.[1]

The rumor proved to be false. The Ottoman state, the second constitutional government under the Young Turks (which had come to power in 1908), may have been totally bankrupt and engaged in disastrous wars in Libya and the Balkans at the time, but it did not entertain the idea of selling one of its celebrated public institutions. A brief look at the status of the museum and the sustained investments it benefited from reveals the unrealistic contention about such a transaction. In effect, the status of the museum had been raised by the 1906 Law of Antiquities (Asar-ı Atika Nizamnamesi), under the leadership of Osman Hamdi. Following practices in place since the 1860s, the 1906 law revised the 1884 law and gave the museum the responsibility to administer archaeological and preservation activities, while singling it out as the place for the collection and exhibition of all artifacts

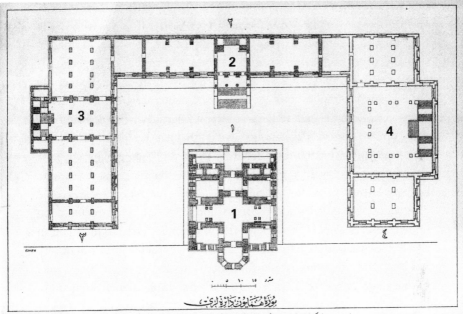

FIGURE 1.2 The Imperial Museum, plan showing the museum building with its extensions. The legend indicates the different parts as: 1. Çinili Köşk; 2. The old section; 3. The new section; and 4. The section that has been built most recently. (*Servet-i Fünun* [Year 13] 26, no. 676 [25 Mart 1320/April 7, 1904])

unearthed in these operations.[2] The physical growth of the museum, in accord with the ever-increasing numbers of objects, pointed to the significance of the institution. The original section, designed by Alexandre Vallaury in a neoclassical language derived from the museum's collections, was built in 1887–1889 but opened in 1891; the second extension to the north was completed in 1905; and the construction of the third extension to the south dated from 1908.[3] It was no secret that the construction of the new wings had necessitated endless struggles due to the scarcity of state finances, giving some rationale to the rumors that reached J. P. Morgan about the sale of the museum (figure 1.2; see also plates 1 and 2).

The later extensions were made possible after persistent and systematic pressure from the museum administration, which justified its demands by pointing to the "day-by-day" increase of the collection. Numerous documents underlined the inadequacy of the 1891 building and the Çinili Köşk (the Tiled Kiosk, 1472–1473), one of the earliest structures of the Palace of Topkapı that had served as the original museum. For example, museum administrators approached the Istanbul municipality for the assignment of engineers in 1893, and again in August 1897.[4] A letter from the Ministry of Education to the museum in 1899 reiterated the decision to build an addition to the "left" side (*cihet-i yesari*, north side) of Çinili Köşk, specifically for the display of the antiquities discovered in Marmaris, and summarized the budgetary complications. Another document (unsigned but possibly written by Osman Hamdi to the Ministry of Education) gave some further detail on the "very valuable antique works" that had been excavated in the "great temple" in Lakina and safely transported to the museum, but were unfortunately still waiting in crates for the new building. Yet they would certainly increase the "honor and fame" (*şan ve şöhret*) of the museum.[5] Another correspondence added that the buildings to be constructed upon imperial orders would acknowledge the "importance given to museums in all developed countries in this age of advancement"; at the service of history and education, museums would guide humanity to better horizons. While European efforts for centuries in this direction were mentioned respectfully, the Imperial Museum administration noted the remarkable progress registered by this "very young" institution. The expansions would make accessible thousands more artifacts then in storage, among them "very important and rare antiques works," as well as those from early Islamic civilizations. They would hence open a "new era of development."[6] Construction of the new annex started in 1899 with the traditional sacrificing of animals.[7] To maintain the efficiency of the process and to supervise and approve the expenses, a committee was established under the supervision of Halil Edhem, Osman Hamdi's brother. The other members consisted of the head accountant, Halil Edib; the director of interior affairs, Kadri Bey; and the director of the School of Fine Arts, Osgan Efendi. As the architect, Vallaury was also part of the team.[8]

Osman Hamdi died in 1910, but his legacy enjoyed a healthy life under the directorship of Halil Edhem (1861–1938, retired in 1931). In 1911, following Osman Hamdi's initiative to build up a collection of paintings by European artists, deemed essential for the education of students in the School of Fine Arts, the museum's budget was increased. By this date, the School of Fine Arts had been in existence for three decades. Inaugurated in 1882 and housed in special premises within the museum precinct, it was dedicated to art education, specifically painting, engraving, sculpture, and architecture. The two-year curriculum included mandatory courses on the history of antiquities, which, in all likelihood, used the museum collections.[9]

Based on the argument that the originals were not on the market and that even if they had been, the museum could not afford them, foreign artists, selected in consultation with the "most famous" galleries in cities such as Berlin, Paris, Munich, and Vienna, were commissioned to make copies of "triumphant works" of "elder masters." The thirty-five copies produced in one year were exhibited in one of the galleries of the Imperial Museum in 1912, with plans by the administration to construct a special gallery on top of the School of Fine Arts to accommodate the "European collection," which would continue to grow.[10] Regardless of the expansions, the Imperial Museum's other collections had expanded to the degree that the displays were extremely crowded and many objects continued to be stored in "miserable" conditions in cases in the basement and the garden.[11] When the School of Fine Arts was moved to another location in 1916, the museum administration appropriated the space it had occupied, and the "old Oriental collection," including Egyptian, Hittite, and Assyrian objects, opened in the spaces occupied until then by the school.[12]

It is not only the physical growth of the museum and the investments made in it that testify to its special status as a major Ottoman institution. Accounts from the time reveal the significance of the museum in the cultural consciousness. To cite one example, in a lecture to a group of students visiting the museum in 1914, İhsan Şerif qualified it as the "museum of the [Ottoman] future" and highlighted the Sarcophagus of Alexander alone as equal to "the total value of the world's most famous museum."[13] In 1918, while carving a place of prestige for the four-year-old Museum of Pious Foundations (Evkaf-ı Islamiye Müzesi) among the other museums of the capital, Ahmed Süreyya ranked the Imperial Museum as the "most colossal" museum of the empire.[14]

The rumors that had reached Pierpont Morgan hence had no basis. Nevertheless, Morgan's interest in the museum was understandable. The Metropolitan Museum of Art and the Imperial Museum were unlikely partners as newcomers to the world of museums dominated by the established European institutions. The Metropolitan was rich and hungry, and supported by private wealthy patrons who stood ready to acquire whatever was available at the market. A chronicler of its history pinned down its origins in one short sentence: "It had to be created out of nothing."[15] Another praised the "generosity" and "public-spirited" demeanor of the American collector.[16] In contrast, the Imperial Museum's existence was anchored in the Ottoman state. Relying entirely on funds from the state budget, it did not have comparable revenues to the Metropolitan's but was rich in its collections and, given the extent of the imperial territory and the legal measures to prevent the antiquities from leaving the country, looked ahead for continuous future growth. Nevertheless, the Ottoman side watched the American scene with envy, noting that private initiative and "millionaires who did not miss any opportunity to embellish their country or the place they were born and who did not refrain from spending part of their fortunes [for this cause]" had managed to build impressive museums.[17]

The Imperial Museum was not an unknown entity in late-nineteenth- to early-twentieth-century New York, and the excitement over the possibility of its wholesale acquisition makes sense. Aside from discussions of its collections in the scholarly press (see chapter 2), as American archaeologists increasingly engaged in scientific work in the Ottoman Empire, the Imperial Museum and the antiquities laws became diplomatic concerns, even common news pieces. Responding to an inquiry with respect to the archaeological explorations in western and southern Anatolia and Crete, Oscar Solomon Straus of the Legation of the United States in Constantinople had defined the difference between American researchers and their European counterparts. He defended the 1884 law by arguing that the permissions given by the imperial government to foreigners were so abused in the past that Ottomans were pushed to pass laws annulling the former privileges, and added that Osman Hamdi was inclined to show flexibility to "any American society whose objects are purely scientific."[18]

The debates surfaced in the pages of the New York Times. While repeated references were made to the restrictions imposed on archaeological work and the "endless need for diplomacy," the American position often appeared to contrast with European partisanship in its more sympathetic tone. One article summarized the common European reactions to the Ottoman claims to antiquity in overarching and sarcastic terms, distancing Americans from it: "The general idea was that the Turk had no rights, or the supposition was that he was indifferent to the despoiling of monuments." The same piece pointed to the "rancorous" situation created by archaeological jealousies between European powers: "In granting . . . a firman (imperial order) to France, Germany was sure to feel itself aggrieved, and England would give vent to its habitual growlings."[19]

Another article in the New York Times reiterated a similar perspective, linking it more directly to the Imperial Museum and its director, Osman Hamdi:

That the intelligent Mohammedan should want to preserve the relics of the past was, however, quite contrary to the wishes of those who represented foreign museums. What the Turks found in their territory was not to belong to them … It was considered very unfair that he [Hamdy Bey] should not at once have made over his sarcophagi [found in Sidon, and including the "sarcophagus of Alexander"] to the care of one of the great European museums. It was thought that the Turks had no right to keep these treasures of classical antiquity. Instead of being grateful that Turkey should have produced one real lover of ancient art, and that he should have gained the sympathy and generous protection of the Sultan, there were grumblings that Turkey should dare to call these treasures her own.

The article continued with the claim that the new museum in Constantinople, "thanks to the support of the present Sultan Abdul Hamid, and the perseverance of Hamdy Bey, … [was] one that any people could be proud of possessing." Indeed, there was no other collection of sarcophagi "in the world that could rival the collection in the new Imperial Museum at Constantinople."[20] The *New York Times* would periodically repeat the uniqueness and the "wonderful state of preservation" of the Sarcophagus of Alexander.[21] Other publications simply accepted the existence of the Imperial Museum.

Vincent Caillard, the director of Düyun-u Umumiye (the Public Debt Administration) in the Ottoman capital and a friend of Osman Hamdi, argued that as Constantinople had become more accessible, savants could now go there and "study antiquities coming from one origin, in their entirety, [rather] than to be compelled to piece them together … by journeying from one country to another."[22] Meanwhile, as gleaned from the annual report of the Archaeological Institute of America in the late 1880s, the Imperial Museum was recognized as a credible institution by the scholarly community — albeit with a begrudging tone:

> The maintenance of the Imperial Museum, of which Hamdi Bey, a Turkish archaeologist, is the capable director, proves the existence of a creditable solicitude for the monuments of the pagan past on the part of the Sublime Porte.[23]

Closer to the date of the sale rumors, and on the occasion of Osman Hamdi's death, the *New York Times* continued to praise "the wonderful collection" of the Imperial Museum, which aside from the chefs d'oeuvre (the sarcophagi of Alexander and of the Mourning Women),[24] included "many other marbles, which for artistry or archaeological uniqueness [were] without duplicate in the museums of Rome, Paris, Berlin and London." Nonetheless, the museum was applauded as the achievement of one man in a hostile environment, "alone in his desire to preserve ante-Moslem culture as expressed in sculpture and architecture." The news piece lamented that he had worked "in constant mortal fear that some enemy might denounce him as an unbeliever" and that he was not acknowledged duly even under the new constitutional government, which was deemed "too busy with politics to give any attention to arts." The duty of urging the government to recognize the work of Osman Hamdi now fell on the shoulders of the "foreign classical schools in Turkey."[25] This conclusion, eerily prepared the scene for the rumors that reached New York two years after the death of Osman Hamdi by pointing to the possible demise of the Ottoman investment in the Imperial Museum once its powerful and persistent director had perished.

The interest of the two museums in each other may not have been equal, but the Turks were not oblivious to the "New York Museum," as indicated, for example, by the photographs of objects from the Metropolitan reproduced in the six-volume *Büyük Tarih-i Umumi* (Great World History) of Ahmed Refik in 1910.[26] This record may give some indication of knowledge about the Metropolitan among a sector of the reading public in the Ottoman Empire, but the state's dealings with the museum went back to 1875–1877, to the excavation permits given to Luigi Palma di Cesnola, then its director, for work in Cyprus, followed by their cancellations and the rumors about Cesnola's illegal smuggling of antiquities to London.[27]

Regardless of the interchange between the two museums, their relatively marginal positions and their struggles to become part of the respectable world of European museums make them intriguing case studies to be viewed together. The unique measuring stick for both museums was Europe. Cesnola proudly stated in 1887 that museums in America already enjoyed worldwide influence and "an indelible place in the literature of England, France, Italy, Germany, and there contributed to uphold truth, grace, culture, and excellence."[28] The purchase of his collection by the Metropolitan was hailed later as "another example of the independent action of one generous man securing for America a prize that Europe would gladly have kept," and Cesnola was praised for turning down an attractive offer from London.[29] An article by John P. Peters pushed the American ambition to broader agendas by proposing archaeological expeditions. In an uncanny predecessor to Morgan's desire to buy the Imperial Museum's collections lock, stock, and barrel in 1912, Peters challenged "the patriotic American" to ask himself the following question in 1884:

> Why cannot we, like France and England, equip expeditions to explore those buried cities instead of contending ourselves with the purchase from dealers of antiquities which the Louvre or the British Museum did not chance to covet? Italy, Greece, Egypt have closed their doors to the exportation of treasures such as those with which the museums of the Old World had already enriched themselves, but the Turkish possessions in Asia still offer a field teeming with the previous metals of archaeology and art, out of which we might stock many museums.[30]

The tenth annual report of the Council of the Archaeological Institute of America (AIA) reported the growing role of American archaeologists despite European skepticism. The excavations in Assos were cited as an excellent response to "the distrustful eye of European criticism" that questioned the AIA as a serious institution.[31] Like the Turks, Americans were newcomers to the field. Often challenged by their European peers to prove their credentials, they learned to make the best of this position—as reflected in the support letters in response to J. R. Sitlington Sterrett's plea to "Americans of great wealth and the great American institutions" for archaeological research in Asia Minor and Syria in 1911. For example, writing from Illinois College, Clarence O. Harris explained the political advantage:

> The United States is in a peculiarly favorable position for this task, for it alone of the progressive nations of the world can go into Turkey free from the suspicion of desiring to impair the integrity of the Turkish Empire, and so their scholars will be allowed more freedom . . .[32]

A group of scholars from Tulane University endorsed the project by pointing to the fact that America had "led the way in the Levant with teachers, physicians, and missionaries" and that now "the times call[ed] for America to lead the way in that land in science, history, geography, and antiquities."[33]

European appreciation mattered to Ottomans, just as it did to Americans. The Imperial Museum's growing reputation among European institutions was widely celebrated in the Ottoman press. *Servet-i Fünun* maintained in 1892 that a recent issue of the *Gazette des Beaux-Arts* on the Sidon sarcophagi bore witness to the European admission that just like London, Rome, and Paris, Istanbul was now a center for treasures of antiquity.[34]

Within a short period of time, Osman Hamdi had succeeded in building a museum that matched the "richest museums in Europe" with antiquities that belonged to the highest civilizations; even its architecture was in the style of European museums.[35]

Comparing the Metropolitan Museum of Art in New York and the Imperial Museum in Istanbul frames some new questions about the role of a museum, its universality, and its sociocultural specificity in the late nineteenth to early twentieth centuries, with ramifications that continue to echo in today's debates.

Diverging and Intersecting Missions

The Metropolitan Museum of Art has its origins in the New York Historical Society, whose Executive Committee decided "to formulate a plan to establish a museum and art gallery for the public in Central Park" on August 4, 1860. The goal was to make the collections accessible to "all classes of the community."[36] The public, democratic, and practical nature of the new institution was reiterated in statement after statement. The charter enacted on April 13, 1870, defined a broad agenda, which consisted of "encouraging and developing the study of fine arts, and the application of arts to manufacture and practical life, ... advancing the general knowledge of kindred subjects, and, to that end, of furnishing popular instruction."[37] Four decades later, the mission continued to be "the education of the public and the cultivation of a high standard of artistic taste"; it made an appeal not to support "art for art's sake," but "art for humanity's sake."[38]

The Metropolitan Museum of Art was not the only American institution that strived to appeal to large masses. In fact, the democratic agenda seems to have turned into the motto of American museums. On March 30, 1880, the opening day of the new building in Central Park, Joseph H. Choate, a prominent New York lawyer and a founder of the museum, stated that art was no longer "the mere plaything of courts and palaces, ministering to the ride and luxury of the rich and the voluptuous." Quite to the contrary, "art belongs to the people and has become their best resource and most efficient educator."[39] Speaking in 1887 at the inauguration ceremony of the George West Museum of Art and Archaeology in Round Lake, New York, Cesnola described the goal of a museum as "a refiner, an elevator, a civilizer" that "refreshes and vivifies the whole population." He added that the American museums were "visited by every class, from the tired toilers in the kitchens and workshops, the shipyards and mines, to the merchant princes and the devotees of fashion."[40] George Brown Goode, the assistant secretary of the Smithsonian, wrote about museums as "agencies of the higher civilization" in the service of "public enlightenment" and advocated that "the museum of the future in this democratic land should be adapted to the needs of the mechanic, the factory operator, the day laborer, the salesman, and the clerk, as much as those of the professional man and the man of leisure."[41] The notion of the museum as a democratic institution was emphasized again in 1909 in a monograph on the Metropolitan. Insisting that a museum should not be "a mere plaything for a few," the author explained the broader program: "Belonging to the people, it may, and by rights should be, the best resource for their relaxation from strenuous labour, and also the most efficient educator to sharpen the taste and the artistic sense."[42]

The Metropolitan had a radically different administrative system than the European museums. It was a private institution, located on public land, and financed largely by the municipality. Its unique functionality was explained with pride on the opening day of the North Wing on November 5, 1895, by its president, Henry G. Marquand:

> The contents, though legally owned by the Corporation of the Museum and managed by the Trustees, are maintained by your use and appreciation. It was a fortunate moment for both landlord and tenant when the city began to erect these buildings, leaving the Trustees to fill them with proper objects of instruction.
>
> It seems to me that such a system is superior to that of most museums in Europe, where the Government provides buildings and money for the purchase of objects of art.... I do not believe that our people would care to have our Government pay $350,000, as the English Government has done, for a single painting, even though it may be a masterpiece by Raphael. A well-filled and arranged museum of art is an index of the general intelligence of the community, and if citizens are not capable of selecting and providing for such a collection, they have not reached the point of deserving it.[43]

The founding principles of the Imperial Museum displayed different concerns and targeted the Western interests in antiquities. Its "formal creation" in 1869 was directly linked to the first legislation on antiquities enacted in an effort to control the activities of archaeologists.[44] The rationale was explained in a few sentences: "Antiquities have historic importance. Therefore, they are particularly valuable for education. In every state, such antiquities are preserved in special museums. In contrast, antique works are everywhere in Ottoman lands, and one sometimes comes across some very rare and highly esteemed examples [in unexpected places]. They must be placed in the museum to be created in Istanbul."[45] The following laws, passed in 1874, 1884, and 1906, increasingly tightened the control over antiquities and restricted their exportation from degrees of *partage* to an absolute ban.

Echoing the developing awareness of the value of antiquities and the informed foreign interest in them, and acknowledging the lack of Ottoman experts, in the aftermath of the 1874 law, a government initiative stipulated the foundation of a school in 1875, designated to educate specialists of antiquity. According to its regulation, the School of the Imperial Museum (Müze-i Hümayun Mektebi), which would be temporarily housed in the Ministry of Education and moved to the museum building upon its completion, would accept twelve students on scholarship. During their two-year education, they were expected to master Turkish, French, Ancient Greek, and Latin and gain a solid base in history and geography. Their specialized courses included topics on "ancient works" (*asar-i atika*) and numismatics, as well as hands-on workshops where they would learn to make plaster copies, take photographs, and be introduced to different kinds of stones. The graduates would be appointed to positions in the museum and state-sponsored excavations.[46] The carefully developed regulation of this aborted institution testifies to another dimension of Ottoman concerns for owning antiquities. Its mission would be integrated a few years later into that of the School of Fine Arts.

The 1884 law defined "works of antiquity" as "all the vestiges of ancient peoples in lands that today form the Ottoman Empire" and stated that they all belonged to the state.[47] The official document echoed a few years later in a letter by Osman Hamdi, the author of the law, to Vincent Caillard:

> The Chaldeans, the Assyrians, the Hittites, the Aramaeans, the Phoenicians, the Nabatzaeans, the Himyarites, the Carians, the Phrygians, the Ionians—in a word, all of these peoples who formerly inhabited the territories which now form the Turkish Empire—have left traces of their civilization buried in the soil. Any stroke of a pickaxe may bring to light some precious object or inscription full of historic or artistic interest, every one of which will take the road of the Imperial Museum: already that road is beginning to be well worn and leveled. There each object

will find the place indicated for it by science or by art; and thus, within fifty years, the Museum of Constantinople will be the Great Treasury of the history of vanished peoples, the grand depository of the products of their genius.[48]

The definition of "objects of antiquity" along the lines established by the laws was reiterated by the popular press. An article on the discipline of archaeology, translated into Turkish as "the science of antique works" (*asar-ı atika fenni*), expanded the concept to include all kinds of objects that carried the memory of ancient times, extending from architectural works to medallions and conveying information on "historic events" and on the "spirit of civilization." Having acknowledged the importance of this science only recently, Ottomans had nevertheless paid great service to it by creating a great museum.[49] The linking of the Imperial Museum with the "necessities of civilization of a great nation" (*bir devlet-i muazzamanın ihtiyacat-ı medeniyesi*) became a repeated theme, and the museum was flaunted as "the envy of many civilized countries" because of its "perfection" and the value and importance of the antique works it housed.[50]

It was not only the Western press that attributed the creation of the Imperial Museum to one man, Osman Hamdi. Two years after his death, *Osmanlı Ressamlar Cemiyeti Gazetesi* (Journal of Ottoman Painters' Society) called attention to his invaluable services to the West and the East, to the former by depicting Oriental life (through his paintings) and to the latter by "bringing and applying the light of skill and civilization" from the West.[51] A couple of years later, he was applauded for his "love of duty ... [that] defeated every obstacle in the way" to building not only the "envelope" (*zarf*)—meaning the museum buildings—but also its "contents" (*mazrufe*) with immaculate attention.[52] Osman Hamdi's personal investment, commitment, and passion for the museum have an unprecedented place in the history of great public museums. His much-quoted words "Il n'y a pas de bassesse que je ne passe pour mon musée" crystallize his profound involvement in, as well as his strong sense of possession for this public institution.[53] The uniqueness of this position is accentuated by the fact that this was an imperial enterprise, a signature of Ottoman modernity that claimed all layers of the historic heritage in defining a new image.[54]

Carrying the idiosyncrasy of Ottoman modernity, the Imperial Museum during its early years seemed to cater to foreign scholars, among whom Osman Hamdi circulated comfortably. By 1885, the collection was labeled in Turkish and in French, and the admission fee of 15 piasters had been suppressed—a most welcome change to the old system that required a *fir-man* for seeing the collections.[55] The detailed discussions on the objects in the Imperial Museum in scholarly journals abroad attested to the fact that the institution was embraced by this closed milieu. Understandably, the international circle of men of "high culture" viewed the museum as Osman Hamdi's terrain and, furthermore, considered him justly as the only channel through which they could negotiate with the government for research permits. In brief, one high-ranking Ottoman intellectual played an unequaled role in the diplomacy of archaeology.

Museums and Cities

Nineteenth-century museums and their relationships to cities displayed similar characteristics. The impressive monumental buildings constituted anchors in the urban fabric and contributed to the changing nature of the urban image, which was beginning to be defined by public institutions. Surrounded by parks, considered the lungs of the city, they brought together public health and culture as essential features of modern life. Public transportation, another key development in city planning at the time, worked hand in hand with museums, expanding their accessibility to large groups of people.

All main European museums were prominently situated in city centers and surrounded by open spaces, be they squares or parks. The Louvre Museum, lodged in its enormous palace, was created as a result of the French Revolution. Opened in 1793 as the centralized art collection of the French nation, it was built of the royal art collections and those appropriated from the various palaces, churches, and monasteries after the revolution. Enriched further in subsequent years by artwork brought to Paris as war booty, it became known also as the "Musée Napoléon." The buildings of the Louvre dated from different periods; the location of the complex in the midst of the urban fabric could accommodate only restricted growth—to the west (figures 1.3 and 1.4). Nevertheless, immense and imposing in its academic architecture, it is one of the most outstanding monuments of Paris and a key feature of the urban image, due to its long façade visible from the River Seine and along the rue de Rivoli and as the vista of the Tuileries Garden. The Place du Louvre to the east, the Place du Palais Royal to the north, the embankment along the Seine (formerly the Quai du Louvre, now the

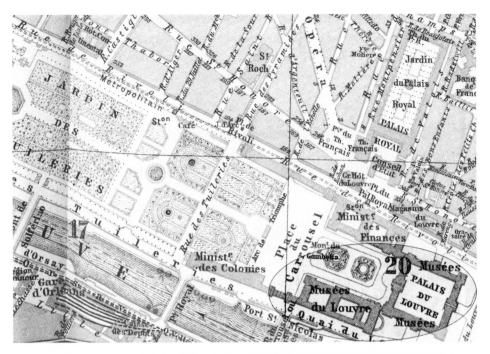

FIGURE 1.3 The Louvre, site plan showing the urban context. Occupying a central location in Paris, the Louvre enjoys high visibility from all sides. The Tuileries Garden to the west establishes a convenient relationship between a major cultural public institution and a public park. (Baedeker, *Paris et ses environs*, 1900)

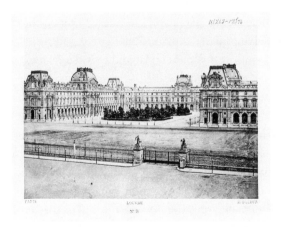

FIGURE 1.4 The Louvre, general view, 1851; photograph by Édouard Baltus. (Library of Congress, Prints and Photographs)

Quai François Mitterand), and the Tuileries Garden to the west ease the museum from the urban fabric, providing different kinds of public spaces around it. Served by public transportation (trams, omnibuses, and the subway system), it was also easily accessible from different parts of the city—made possible by the urban transformation projects of Napoléon III and Baron Haussmann, with their origins going back to the time of Napoléon I and thus to the opening of the museum as a public institution.

The British Museum, also situated in a tight urban fabric, did not enjoy the visibility of the Louvre and made its contribution to the urban image through its scale and architectural ambition that stood in contrast to the surrounding buildings. Founded on the collection of Sir Hans Sloane in 1753, and standing as a keystone in the development of museums from a private collection to a public one, it opened in the Montagu House on Great Russell Street. The acquisition of the Elgin Marbles in 1816 marked a turning point for the museum, and the debates on the purchase raised ethical questions about the transportation of antiquities on the one hand, and on the other, about the "benefit of the public" and "the honor of the nation," as well as the role they would play in the "elevation of our national character, ... our opulence,... our substantial greatness."[56] By the 1820s, the Montagu House could not accommodate the collection, and in 1823 a new building was commissioned, to be designed by the architect Robert Smirke, whose classical revivalist style was also pursued by his brother, Sydney Smirke, who completed the building in 1852. Other nineteenth-century additions were the Reading Room (1857) and the White Wing on the southeast side (1879). Two public squares, Russell Square on the northeast and Bedford Square on the southwest, accommodated the visitors, the latter allowing for an unobstructed view of one façade of the museum. The impressive public transportation (with over two hundred lines of omnibuses that crossed the city in every direction in 1894) made it easily accessible, and again as in Paris, it could be reached on foot from a wide radius within the city[57] (figure 1.5; see also plate 3).

Berlin's experiment in creating its central museums followed a different path than those of Paris and London. A complex of museums was constructed incrementally from the 1820s to the end of the century, and each museum was dedicated to a different theme, giving the city a highly visible "cultural center." As an urban planning practice, this center added a new element to the nineteenth-century modernization process and even introduced the concept of institutional zoning (figure 1.6). The Museum Island

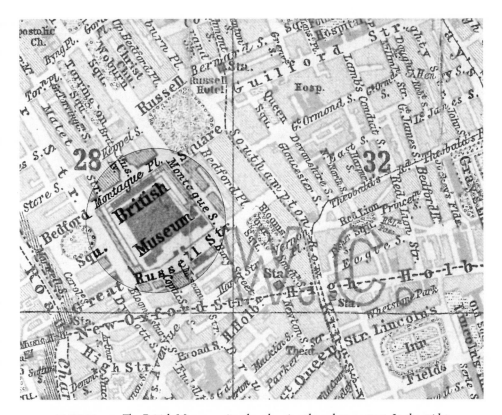

FIGURE 1.5 The British Museum, site plan showing the urban context. In the midst of a dense fabric, the British Museum benefits from the presence of Bedford Square and Russell Square, two open public spaces in its immediate vicinity. (Baedeker, *London and Its Environs*, 1911)

was developed on a piece of land between the two branches of the Spree River, with open spaces between the various buildings. Karl Schinkel's much-celebrated Altes Museum (1823–1830), organized around a round courtyard covered by a dome and with a long colonnaded façade in the manner of a Greek stoa overlooking the park, created an innovative relation between the inside and the outside by means of an open stairway behind the colonnade; its collections consisted of the art of the Greco-Roman period (see plate 4). The neo-Renaissance Neues Museum (1843–1855), designed by Friedrich August Stüler, was built to the north of the Altes Museum and connected to it by a bridge that crossed the Bodestrasse. It had three main sets of objects: Greek casts; Egyptian artifacts; and a rich collection of engravings, woodcuts, lithographs, and pre-1800 drawings and books. Again

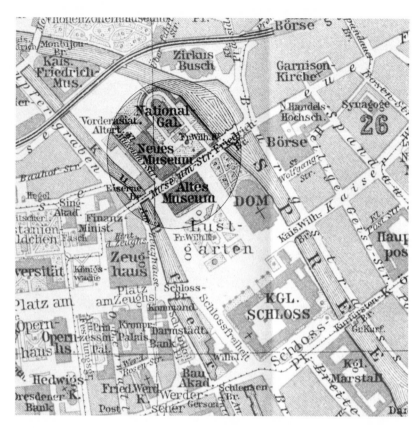

FIGURE 1.6 The Berlin Museums, site plan showing the Museum Island and the urban context. The main museums in Berlin occupy an "island" zoned exclusively as a cultural enclave. They contribute to the overall image of the city as an ensemble, with open public spaces between them. (Baedeker, *Berlin and Its Environs*, 1908)

by Stüler, this time in the shape of a "Corinthean temple," the National Gallery (1866–7186) to the east of the New Museum was home to the work of nineteenth- and early-twentieth-century German artists. Next came, in "an unpretending edifice," the Pergamon Museum (1897–1901) by Fritz Wolff, which housed fragments from excavations undertaken by the Royal Museums in the western Anatolian Hellenistic towns of Pergamon (1878–1886), Magnesia (1891–1893), and Priene (1895–1899). The museum was named after the first site, from which the Altar of Zeus, complete with its "Great Frieze," was carried to Berlin; Wolff's structure was demolished in 1908 to be replaced by a more ornate neoclassical Pergamon Museum, designed by Alfred Messel. Finally, the Kaiser Friedrich Museum (1898–1904), designed by Ernst Eberhard von Ihne on the triangular site where the two arms of the

Spree River met, was dedicated to the sculptures of the Christian period and objects from the early Christian, Byzantine, Coptic, Romanesque, and "Persian-Mohammedan" eras.[58] The association of certain collections with specific buildings gave a new classification to museum organization, one that differed significantly from that of the Louvre and the British Museum, where all objects belonging to all periods and civilizations coexisted under one roof. Nevertheless, the proximity of the Royal Museums to each other continued to underline their interrelationships.

The history of the Metropolitan Museum of Art, which was to be created from scratch, is intertwined with that of Central Park. The initiative for a public park in Manhattan dates back to the 1850s, to the reformist ideas of the landscape architect Andrew Jackson Downing, who believed that a vast five-hundred-acre park would enable the classes to intermingle and elevate "the working men to the same level of enjoyment with the men of leisure," while serving as the "lungs of the city."[59] After years of negotiations and contestations between various power groups, including landowners, merchants, unionists, and reformers, an agreement was reached to apply legislation on eminent domain in order to create a park, and a design competition was launched in 1857. Eminent domain would allow for the appropriation of low-income "villages" inhabited by about 1,600 Irish, German, and black residents, scattered in the area between 59th and 106th Streets and Fifth Avenue and Central Park West (the park was extended to 110th Street in 1863). Construction started the same year, based on the groundbreaking design of the team of landscape architect Fredrick Law Olmsted and architect Calvert Vaux, the winners of the competition, both working in the reformist tradition of Downing; the first section (the southern part) was opened to the public in 1858, and the entire park was completed in 1875.[60]

With a keen eye on the new park, the museum's board of trustees could not settle for a better site than a large area within it. Following complicated negotiations with the municipality, the privately owned Metropolitan Museum of Art succeeded in securing its place in Central Park. On April 5, 1871, the legislature passed "an act in relation to the powers and duties of the Board of Commissioners of the Department of Public Parks" of the city of New York, by which the museum was "authorized to construct, erect, and maintain upon that portion of the Central Park formerly known as Manhattan Square, or any other park, square, or place." Its permanent location was fixed a year later as the area between 79th Street and 84th Street (figure 1.7).[61]

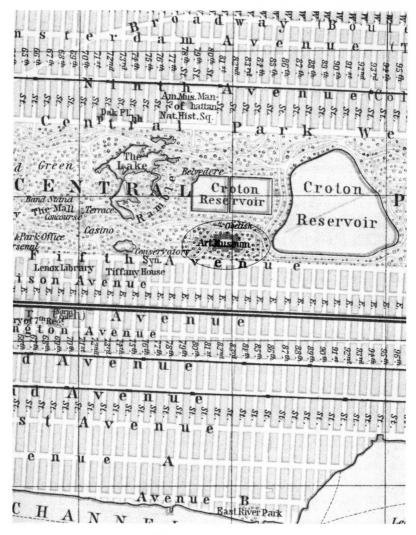

FIGURE 1.7 The Metropolitan Museum of Art, site plan showing the urban context. With its main façade on Fifth Avenue, the Metropolitan occupies a unique location in the city. (Baedeker, *The United States*, 1904)

The groundbreaking for the new building happened in 1874, the construction was completed in 1879, and the permanent Metropolitan Museum opened its doors to the public in March 1880. The museum was housed in two temporary locations prior to this date. The first temporary quarters, leased in 1871, were in the Dodworth Building, 681 Fifth Avenue (between 53rd and 54th Streets). It was with the acquisition of the Cesnola Collection of Cypriot antiquities that the Dodworth Building could no longer accommodate the growing collection and in 1873 had to be moved farther down the grid to the Douglas Mansion at 128 West 14th Street. The collection was transported to its permanent home upon the completion of the building in the park by the architects Calvert Vaux, Olmstead's partner in the design of Central Park, and Jacob Wrey Mould in a redbrick High Victorian Gothic style (see plate 5).[62] The *New York Times* described the building as "unpretentious … and … constructed to give full admittance to light [rather] than with much idea of symmetrical proportion." The interiors were "sombre." In summary, it was "an honest, good building, quite appropriate for what is required of it, and answers perfectly all the purposes of a museum."[63]

The growth of the Metropolitan Museum of Art in the next three decades was phenomenal. Theodore Weston designed the first addition to the south as a wing that was one and a half times larger than the original building; it was inaugurated on December 18, 1888. Several months prior to the opening, on June 15, 1888, the legislature had already authorized the appropriation by the city of funds for further extension of the building. In October 1894, the third addition, the North Wing, by Arthur L. Tuckerman, was completed, sandwiching the original structure from both sides. The core building and the two wings were entirely concealed on the east by a sweeping addition in 1902 by Richard Morris Hunt: the ornate Beaux-Arts façade on Fifth Avenue gave Manhattan one of its most prominent urban landmarks (figure 1.8).[64]

The Imperial Museum's location in Istanbul paralleled the trend to pair public open spaces with great museums, and its history and growth showed comparable aspects to other museums. Nevertheless, its evolution followed a different pattern, and the resulting relationship of the museum to the city diverged from that of its counterparts. The museum had started in 1846 as a collection of weapons and antiquities housed in the former church of Hagia Eirene within the walls of the Palace of Topkapı. In 1869, the year of the first antiquities legislation, the Collection of Antiquities was renamed the Imperial Museum (Müze-i Hümayun), and the Grand Vizier Ali Pasha

FIGURE 1.8 The Metropolitan Museum of Art, view from Fifth Avenue, ca. 1900–1910. (Library of Congress, Prints and Photographs)

appointed Edward Goold, a teacher at the Imperial High School (Galatasaray), as its first director. The collection grew significantly under Philipp Anton Déthier, its German second director, especially around eighty-eight cases of antiquities from Cyprus, provoked by Cesnola's acquisitions, which had ended up at the Metropolitan Museum of Art. As Hagia Eirene could no longer accommodate the much larger scope of the collection, it remained as the "military museum," and in 1875 the antique works were moved to the nearby Çinili Köşk, also in the gardens of Topkapı Palace. Çinili Köşk was restored to suit the requirements of a museum, acquiring, most notably, a columned entrance porch, and opened its doors to the public in 1880 (see plate 6).[65] The beginnings of a museum complex may have been based on convenience and availability of unused historic structures on imperial land; indeed, convenience and availability became the determining factors in the final location of one of the most important modern Ottoman institutions. The new museum buildings were situated in relationship to the historic buildings where antiquities were exhibited, especially to the Çinili Köşk, and carved more land from the outer gardens of the Topkapı Palace. Under the persuasive and persistent leadership of Osman Hamdi, the museum administration dealt directly with the sultan, who would issue the needed edicts, thus eliminating the thorny problems of appropriating private property and demolition.

A survey of the Imperial Museum's construction history, published in 1927 (four years after the declaration of the Turkish Republic), reminded readers along the way that the institution had reached its respectable status among the greatest museums of the world during a period of "tyranny" (*zulum*) and "despotism" (*istibdat*), the last decades of the now defunct Ottoman Empire. It described the buildings and the setting with pride that overrode their original political setting. The 64-meter-long new structure across from the Çinili Köşk owed its existence to the discovery of the Sidon sarcophagi in 1887, which could not fit into the historic building. The construction was completed in 1889, but the interior organization took another two years, pushing the inauguration to 1891.[66] A foreign observer reported at the time that the ground floor was large enough to hold all the sarcophagi excavated in Sidon, that the latter were arranged "in their proper order," and that ample room was left around them so that the visitor and the student could examine every side of each one.[67] The comments were repeated in the Turkish press: "The halls are large and full of light. Every monument, every sculpture, every piece is given the space it deserves." Furthermore, "in each hall a crowning work is displayed in a manner to emphasize its value." The important objects were thus in full sight, whereas the less important ones were gathered around the former in groups according to their formal or chronological relationships.[68]

As spacious as the museum was, the acquisition of the impressive "friezes" found during an excavation in the Manisa region necessitated a significant extension, which added 32 meters to the north of the earlier building before turning to the west to create a wing of 64 meters. Started in 1894, it was finished nine years later after numerous delays (figure 1.9). The decision to build the next extension was secured while "the painting on the walls [of the second one] was still wet"—thanks to Osman Hamdi's amazing political move of dealing directly with the sultan. The resulting 1908 addition consisted of an 81-meter-long appendix to the south of the original one, culminated by a 49-meter-long wing toward the west. In two stories, the total area covered 8,000 square meters. In 1918, the museum took over the spaces formerly occupied by the Imperial School of Fine Arts to house its "ancient Oriental" works, including Egyptian, Hittite, and Assyrian works.[69]

FIGURE 1.9 The Imperial Museum, construction of the northern wing. The Topkapı Palace is in the background. (İAMA, R509-8)

Like all great museums, the Imperial Museum was endowed with a library in its southern wing. Sheltering a collection of over twenty thousand books organized neatly on shelves and vitrines, this "perfect library" was open to visitors who wanted to broaden their knowledge of antiquities (figure 1.10). Here, with the windows facing "the most beautiful view in the world," visitors could work in peace and solitude.[70]

In its final configuration, the "long and beautiful" façade of the new museum "seemed to take the Çinili Köşk in its arms and protect it with respect and affection." Its "Greek and Roman" style, which fit the historic context of the artifacts housed, expressed a "correspondence between the envelope and its contents" (*zarfın mezrufa mutabeketi*), while adhering to the general principle of the architectural style of museums ("classical" or "Renais-

مُوزهٔ همايونه كتبخانه‌سى

FIGURE 1.10 The Imperial Museum's newly built library. Books are being placed on the shelves. (İÜMK 90518-0008)

sance") in all "civilized cities." As such, it did not attract attention to itself, but valorized the "stylistic elegance, the colored tiles and the marbles" of the fifteenth-century pavilion, just like a frame that enhances the beauty of a painting (figure 1.11).[71]

The complex may have joined the collective architectural vocabulary of late-nineteenth-century museums, but its location in the city differed from that of its counterparts (figure 1.12). Secluded in the palace gardens, it did not announce its presence to the public and did not draw random passersby unaware of its existence and, unlike many other nineteenth-century institutional buildings, did not make a contribution to the urban image. Writing in 1910 in *Servet-i Fünun*, Mehmed Vahid noted that its exceptionally quiet and isolated surroundings were not common to museums. He saw this as a positive trait. Although the museum occupied the "most exciting, liveliest, and most pleasant place in the capital of the Ottoman state," it was "free" from the chaos of the streets, peaceful under the dark green of the trees.[72]

The Imperial Museum's accessibility took a new turn in 1913, with the opening of Gülhane (Sarayburnu) Park "for the benefit of the residents of

مُوزَهِ هُمَايُونَدَارِهِ جَدِيدَهِ وَسَطَلَةِ رَسْمِي

FIGURE 1.11 The Imperial Museum, view of the North Wing, with Çinili Köşk to the left. (İÜMK 90518-0002)

Istanbul" to the west and south of the museum complex, in the outer gardens of Topkapı Palace. Within a year, the entrepreneurial mayor of Istanbul, Cemil Pasha (Dr. Cemil Topuzlu) decided to build a wooded park that would extend to the waterfront (figure 1.13).[73] To this end, he bought "from Europe" twenty thousand rare trees, including some fine pine trees, endowing the capital with its largest public park.[74] Located to the south of the Golden Horn, in the historic peninsula, the park targeted a population different from that attracted by Taksim and Tepebaşı Parks in Pera, the first public parks in the city, dating from the 1860s. If Cemil Pasha's critics accused him of spending the city's resources on fancy projects, his supporters defended him by emphasizing his concern for public health and commending his efforts to "transform Istanbul into a [real] city and the people of Istanbul into a civilized society."[75] The new park was indeed part of the larger urban planning activities undertaken by the mayor, which included the widening of streets, improvements of infrastructure, and demolishing the built fabric between the Hagia Sophia Square and the Sultan Ahmed Mosque to create another public park there. These interventions, under the

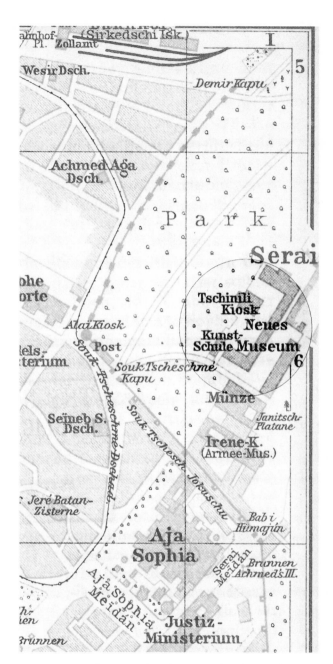

FIGURE 1.12 The Imperial Museum, site plan showing the urban context. The museum is separated from the urban fabric around it by the outer walls of the Topkapı Palace. The black line indicates the tram route. (Baedeker, *Konstantinopel, Balkanstaaten, Kleinasien Archipel, Cypern*, 1915)

سراى برونئك استانبوليله كادى : كلخانه يارق ساحلنده شرك خربه‌لك مجدداً انشا ابتديريدكى اسكله

Le nouveau débarcadère du Parc de Kulhane

FIGURE 1.13 The new ferry stop at Gülhane Park. (*Servet-i Fünun* 47, no. 1208 [17 Temmuz 1330/July 30, 1914])

supervision of the director of road construction services (*directeur des services de la voirie*) André Joseph Auric, who had served as the chief engineer of the city of Lyon, followed in the footsteps of the first large-scale modernization projects of the late 1860s under the leadership of the İslahat-i Turuk Komisyonu (Commission for Road Improvement).[76] Electric trams replaced the horse-drawn ones in 1912, also during this active period under Cemil Pasha.

The main tram line that connected the Galata Bridge to the heart of the historic peninsula had a stop at the entrance to Gülhane Park before reaching Hagia Sophia Square. From this stop to the Imperial Museum was a short walk up the hill, on a narrow, leafy street. The museum was hence easily accessible by the main mass transportation line, as well as being within walking distance from several busy centers of the city—among them, the Galata Bridge; the Eminönü ferry stop and quays; the central markets; Hagia Sophia Square and its new extension, Sultan Ahmed Park; and Divanyolu, the historic main avenue of the old city. According to a guidebook, the common approach by tourists was through the Soğuk Çeşme Gate on the outer walls of the Topkapı Palace, then following the road to the right. The road on the left led to Seraglio Point, which commanded beautiful views.[77]

Despite the museum's central location and easy accessibility, nothing announced its presence to passersby. "Following the cool, hilly path sheltered by plane trees," according to one description of the journey, visitors reached the square in front of the museum buildings, itself "in a silence that was interrupted only by the chirping of the birds and the voices that echoed from long distances."[78] It was from here that the impressive complex could be seen. Yet this was not an imposing frontal view, as the buildings formed an introverted unit around another quiet garden, dotted with antique fragments. Compared to the main museums in the European capitals, the Imperial Museum in Istanbul sits in an unusual setting, and unlike them, does not make a visible contribution to the urban image. It thus seems to display an ambiguous relationship to the "public" and stands out more as an isolated elite institution, evoking a serene and scholarly atmosphere not entirely out of accord with Osman Hamdi's original intentions.

CHAPTER TWO

SCHOLARSHIP AND

THE IMPERIAL MUSEUM

The Discontents

FOREIGN SCHOLARS viewed the Imperial Museum with conflicting sentiments. On the one hand, as seen in chapter 1, it was highly praised; on the other, it was greatly resented; and an ambivalent third position in between acknowledged its presence but did not approve of its mission. While the Western scholarly and archaeological community eventually had to come to grips with the fact that the Imperial Museum was there to stay, the news of its expansion into a major museum of antiquities in Istanbul was not welcome. With a persistent argument that classical antiquities did not belong to the culture and history of the Ottoman Empire but were the foundation stones of European civilization, campaigns were launched in the hope of halting the project. These arguments jumped from the pages of professional publications to newspapers and popular periodicals, pressuring foreign diplomatic offices in the empire to negotiate with Ottoman authorities. The debate started in Europe and became particularly heated after the passing of the 1884 law, soon spreading to the United States as American archaeologists engaged more and more in expeditions in Ottoman lands.

As pointed out earlier, the opposition to the foundation of a major museum was fueled by the Ottoman law of 1884. However, the reactions went back to earlier measures, with the 1874 law marking a turning point from the 1869 legislation. George Smith, on a mission from the British Museum and working with permission to excavate in Nimrud and Nineveh, encountered the new law during his expedition. Informed by local authorities that he was now under the obligation to give half of his findings to the Imperial Museum, he protested, stating he "could not part with half of his collection without spoiling it." He challenged the governor of Mosul: "What would be the use, if they had one part of an inscription in Constantinople, while we had the other half in London?" The persistence of the response frustrated Smith further and sharpened his sarcasm toward the relevance of the Ottoman claim to local culture.[1]

In an essay dating from 1883, and on the eve of Osman Hamdi's planned changes to the 1874 law, Salomon Reinach voiced a strong opinion on the shifting Ottoman positions toward antiquities, in effect echoing a view commonly shared by Western scholars. Published in the widely circulated *Revue des deux mondes* under the catchy title of "Le vandalisme moderne en Orient," the article's central argument emphasized that "the antiquities of the Greco-Roman Orient were of no interest to their new masters [the Turks]" and that "Europe, the heir to the civilization of [the] Greeks, had to impose the responsibility and the honor of taking back the monuments from them." According to Reinach, the Ottoman laws were not fair to European researchers; the Ottoman state did not have the means to afford the preservation and maintenance of the antiquities, besides not having any interest in them; and the "Turkish race" had its own "national art," which had nothing to do with the Greco-Roman past. He supported his claim by stating that Turks visited the museum in Çinili Köşk only very rarely and that they revealed "a legitimate enough displeasure that money was spent on maintaining the statues." Reinach went as far as recommending the diversion of Ottoman funds from antiquities to Islamic monuments, abandoned in ruinous state but with the potential to represent "the honor of the Turkish race in the face of history." His advice to Ottomans was to free the art trade and permit exportations instead of passing laws of "illusionary preemption." They would be wise, he insisted, to organize sales of antiquities in their possession every two or three years in official venues, attended by representatives of all European museums. They could then invest the money secured to restore their own monuments and to buy back from Europeans artifacts of "old Turkish art," such as arms and Kütahya and Bursa tiles, which had been taken out of the country. Çinili Köşk could be turned into the most "unique museum of Ottoman art in the world."[2] Reinach was also adamant about the incompetence of the museum staff in handling the delicate antique objects. He complained about the "brutal" cleaning and scraping of a marble statue attributed to Artemis that had led to the disappearance of the patina. This practice, "too often followed by the Turkish Museum," he added, was typical of "the reckless stupidity of officials, who treat[ed] marble statues as they would a dirty stone wall."³

A year later, the *Revue archéologique* published the 1884 law, with a short introduction by Salomon Reinach. Reminding the readers of his article on "vandalism" and stating that his earlier struggles to involve the learned European community in the defense of their patrimony had proved futile, and that Osman Hamdi's laws did not raise the slightest protest in the diplomatic world and in the scholarly press, Reinach nevertheless felt it was his responsibility to expose the entirety of the document in the journal dedicated to discoveries of the past. He emphasized that the "restrictive and prohibitive" law derived from its fifty-year-old Greek precedent undoubtedly would work against the interests of archaeology and art.⁴ The same year, he also sent a letter to the editor of *The Nation*, the left-wing American journal, addressing the numerous attacks against his *Revue des deux mondes* article for angering the Ottoman authorities and inducing them to enforce the laws severely in order to "retaliate upon the civilized world" and to "exclude Western scholarship from Oriental archaeology." He clarified that the laws were already developed at the time of his publication and noted that only one archaeological journal, *Revue archéologique*, had protested against the barbarity of the regulations. He used the opportunity to disseminate the "nature and extent of the injury" to the "liberal-minded readers" of *The Nation*, and projected the consequences of these "absurd prohibitions" as an increase in the prices of antiquities in Europe and the likelihood of having the pieces broken up for easier smuggling, without any significant impact on their secret exportation.⁵ Within a couple of years, Reinach felt obligated to call attention to Greek and Turkish laws prohibiting the exportation of antiquities in a set of recommendations to "archeologist travelers." While he admitted he would only congratulate a traveler who stumbled upon "a Venus of Milo" and who courageously and cleverly managed to transport it to a "secure place," Reinach chose not to facilitate or encourage contraband activities.⁶

Salomon Reinach's sentiments were shared by some Americans—and with great passion. An article published in Boston five years after Reinach's "Vandalisme," and penned by archaeologist James Theodore Bent, started with praise for the extraordinary qualities of Osman Hamdi and concluded with his much-resented obstinacy about keeping the antiquities at home.

He was described as "the greatest anomaly of all" (among the many late-nineteenth-century Ottoman anomalies), "for one would as soon expect an artist and an archaeologist from amongst the Kaffirs or the Hottentots as from amongst the Turks." The author quoted Osman Hamdi on how "things [were] now altered," and now that he was the director of the museum, "as long as [he] live[d], nothing more [would] be exported." Likening him to a "dog with many bones, [who] refuses to share what he cannot eat with the hungry archaeologists who are gathered around," Bent attributed the following words to Osman Hamdi: "You rich English, French, Americans may excavate, but it shall be for the embellishment of my museum." Yet, the author claimed, there was no guaranty that the museum would survive at the end of Osman Hamdi's career, and, he concluded, "Constantinople is certainly not the place for a museum under present *régime*; better far that the earth should retain her treasures until others rule in this land and a happier race of archaeologists can enjoy in peace the results of their labors."[7] The negative impact of the 1884 law on archaeological science continued to be repeated in the American professional press, often with a nostalgic recollection of the "reasonable law" of 1874.[8]

Not everybody agreed. In an article on the newly discovered Sidon sarcophagi, T. Hayter Lewis of the Athenaeum Club offered another perspective by framing the debate around keeping the monuments in their original location or transporting them to the museum in Istanbul. He did not quarrel with the idea of a museum in the Ottoman capital under the guidance of Osman Hamdi, even though the better alternative would have been to leave the antiquities in their original sites — a position that went back to the debates at the time of the moving of the Elgin Marbles. Yet, he continued, "My experience in the East makes me confident that such a course [leaving the antiquities in situ] would have resulted in the eventual destruction of these splendid monuments by Moslem fanatics and Arab dealers."[9] He thus made a distinction between the "civilized" Ottomans in Istanbul and the primitive populations in the eastern provinces of the empire in a manner that would most likely have agreed with Osman Hamdi's own sentiments.

There were other supporters of the Ottoman right to keep the antiquities found in the imperial territories to be displayed in local museums; their acceptance can be understood as a realistic acknowledgment of the facts on the ground, especially after the construction of the new museum. F. Max Müller was one. Pointing to the wealth of the treasure in the "Turkish soil," so far "very imperfectly explored," Müller argued in the *New Review* in 1894 that if Ottomans undertook more systematic work, like that begun in such a promising way by Osman Hamdi, their museums would rival the best European museums. He mocked the European mentality that complained of the "very unfair" claims of Turks to the "treasures of classical antiquity," notably the sarcophagi discovered in Sidon, and resented the tendency to break the Ottoman laws at every possible occasion. He went as far as calling the acts of Europeans who "carried off . . . whatever ancient works of art can be recovered [from] the Turkish soil" stealing. He reminded readers of the existence of the same law in many countries, but remarked that "in Turkey alone it [was] thought fair to decry it, nay, to defy it, in the interest, it is said, of archaeological science."[10] The position was picked up by others, as expressed in the pages of the *Literary News*: referring to Müller's paper, a news piece voiced appreciation for the efforts of Osman Hamdi and the "treasures he has collected," in a criticism of "the European archaeologist [who] perceives something grotesque in the destination of these important finds, and thinks their natural resting-place would be the British Museum or the Louvre."[11]

An Ottoman evaluation of the radical changes made to the 1874 law and their importance for the Imperial Museum eerily precedes the current debates in defense of the Western "encyclopedic" and "humanistic" museums' claims to antiquities by a century, but framed from the "other" side.[12] The goal behind the shift from the three-way *partage* of the antiquities found on a site (between the owner of the property, the excavator, and the Imperial Museum, as specified by the 1874 law) to the absolute ownership of all discoveries by the museum was stated, above all, so as not to harm the historic heritage. The author, a reporter for the Düyun-u Umumiye (Public Debt Administration), noted the "understandable" criticisms from Europeans — "understandable" from the foreign excavators' perspective, as they could no longer take the antiquities to European museums. They refused to accept that the change would serve scholarship well. Instead of "running from one country to another" in pursuit of pieces from one place, researchers could travel to Istanbul, now easily accessible, to study them in their original integral groups. The 1874 law caused the random scattering of the pieces, and if it had been left intact, it would have created further dispersal, not only to collections in Europe but also to those in America and even Australia. The new museum in Istanbul resolved the problem in a manner that was "appropriate to the honor of the great state of Ottomans."[13]

Regardless of the heated arguments against the idea of a museum of antiquities in the Ottoman capital, once the Imperial Museum opened its doors in its new buildings, with the Sidon sarcophagi as its centerpiece, the international academic community was forced to welcome its contribution to scholarship. The Imperial Museum turned into a well-respected institution on an international scale. Abigail G. Radcliffe closed her survey of sculpture with the Museum of Constantinople in a chapter on European museums. In her elegant words:

> Each museum serves as a revelation of the treasures scattered through many lands, enabling them [the visitors] to begin at the beginnings of history, to feel themselves citizens of the most foreign climes, and kindred of the artists of all ages who have left them inheritors of their thoughts and of their works.

Together with the leading museums, among them the British Museum, the Louvre, the Museums of Berlin, the Glyptothek of Munich, the Vatican, and the museums of Athens, the new museum on "Europe's remotest verge ... well indicate[d] the spirit of the nineteenth century." Its collection, crowned by the Sarcophagus of Alexander with its "spirited polychromatic reliefs," included "some of the best phases of both Oriental and classic art."[14]

Others accepted the Imperial Museum with varying degrees of resentment. Repeating the prevailing sentiments among scholars, one noted how the museum, "established among a people who hate antiquities," as it was "in the nature of Islamism to despise relics of bygone people," was welcomed by an "outcry of astonishment for all the learned world at the splendor of the great sarcophagus it now contains."[15] An article in the *New York Times* recognized that "there is no collection of sarcophagi ... in the world that can rival the collection in the new Imperial Museum at Constantinople, and there is every prospect of a large increase of the present collection."[16] An obituary for Osman Hamdi (spelled as Hamid throughout the essay) acknowledged that his tireless work had made the museum home for "... marbles, which for artistry or archaeological uniqueness are without duplicate in the museums of Rome, Paris, Berlin, and London," and that its impact could be traced in "European art periodicals [that] began to contain articles on the Ottoman Museum and the wonderful collection to be found there."[17]

The Sidon sarcophagi began to occupy a central place in the discussions on the characteristics of Greek art, in the aftermath of Osman Hamdi's report in the *Revue archéologique*, which gave a day-by-day account of the expedition, describing the findings in a matter-of-fact manner and providing sketches of the graves.[18] The article was republished the very same year to a different audience in *Revue d'ethnographie*.[19] A brief and selective survey of the literature roughly covering the couple of decades that follow the discovery attests to the impact of the sarcophagi. The year of Osman Hamdi's publication, 1887, witnessed a flurry of reports, commentaries, and speculations. As summed up by Théodore Reinach, "The discovery of the sarcophagi marked a date in the scholarship of antique art."[20] At the center of the discourse was the topic of polychromy—a groundbreaking if not always well-received debate that arose in the nineteenth century as excavations began to reveal traces of color, first surfacing in the 1811 discovery of the pediment sculptures on the Aphaia Temple in Aegina by Charles Robert Cockerell and Carl Haller von Hallerstein.[21] A few years later, the art and architectural theorist Antoine-Chrysostome Quatremère de Quincy argued for the use of color on the Panathenaic procession on the exterior colonnade of the Parthenon, especially apparent on the costumes.[22] Furthermore, he presented several reconstructions in color—most famously, the "Jupiter à Olympie" (see plate 7).

The scholarly community was soon divided into parties with strong opinions: some (notably, Gottfried Semper) favored "total polychromy" and argued that not only the sculptures but entire buildings were painted, others rejected it completely, and yet a third group opted for a restrained or partial coloring. Although ancient texts referred to the painting of sculptures, their meanings had become distorted in translations, and defenders of polychromy, among them Quatremère de Quincy, had to turn to philology, to classical texts, in order to make their case. Quatremère de Quincy expressed his astonishment that even though the topic of polychromy appeared frequently in many classical texts, it had been ignored in "modern analysis," and consequently in architectural practice.[23] The architect Jacques-Ignace Hittorff was one of the most committed advocates of polychromy. In an attempt to develop a theory on the general system of polychrome architecture during the Hellenic era, Hittorff had relied on "reasoning and induction," piecing together the arguments of others but also presenting an in-depth analysis of one building, a small temple on the acropolis of Selinunte in Sicily. He rationalized his choice for Sicily by the presence of many monuments (maybe even more than Greece) from all the different periods of Hellenic civilization in the region. He explained the merits of concentrating on one building as a means to reveal the combined application and interdependence of architecture, sculpture, and painting to prove the "system of polychromy" in a concrete and focused manner.[24] Although Hittorff's inquiry was geared toward the "modern practice" of architecture by showing the merits and limitations of the system for nineteenth-century buildings, his theoretical impact on the archaeological discourse was enormous — as reflected decades later in the discussions of the Sidon sarcophagi. By the time the Sidon discoveries had come to the scrutiny of the scholarly community, polychromy had already found a following, leading to often speculative reconstitution drawings, among them Ludvig Peter Fenger's depictions of the Aegina Temple and the Parthenon, collected in a large portfolio (see plate 8).[25]

The Sidon findings, initially accessible to only a selected few, opened a new platform for the debates on polychromy. A wide range of journals from different contexts joined the discussion. Citing a colleague, one of the first to have actually seen the sarcophagi in Sidon, a writer for *The British Architect* reported in 1887 that the sculptures reflected the Greek commitment to "truth" in the representation of nature not only in their forms but also in their vivid colors. If they were "wanting simplicity in the composition and shirking details" and hence were inferior to the Parthenon frieze, the pieces were "most valuable … as specimens of Greek polychromy."[26] Hayter Lewis, to whom Osman Hamdi had shown photographs of the sarcophagi, did not have any quarrels with the stylistic complexity of the sarcophagi and disagreed with the article in *The British Architect* by arguing that these "purely Greek" monuments were "splendidly sculptured," especially the largest, whose sides were "filled with sculptures of marvelously fine execution." For him, the architectural details of all the sarcophagi were "of the Greek type of the best period, without a trace of Roman influence," and the sculptures "appeared to be of the highest class," resembling "the beautifully delicate carving of the Parthenon frieze" and so different from the examples found in Pergamon. Nevertheless, it was the "most careful and artistic … coloring" in "different reds, purples, violets, etc. being put on in various tints and gradations with great delicacy" and the sparingly applied gold that placed the sarcophagi among "the finest in Greek sculpture." He added that this colored decoration confirmed Hittorff's theories.[27]

The Reverend W. K. Eddy of the American Presbyterian Mission in Sidon, who proudly claimed he was the only Westerner to have personally seen the tombs discovered by workmen quarrying for stones, described the sarcophagi extensively in the *American Journal of Archaeology*. He added that having heard of the news, the authorities had "fastened and sealed" the chambers and put them under guard, waiting for instructions from Istanbul. Praising the "beautiful workmanship and finish" of the Mourning Women, he pointed to the paint on the eyeballs of the figures and on the robes of the smaller figures — unfortunately almost completely washed off by moisture. However, the "chief sarcophagus," which Reverend Eddy was allowed "only a hurried view of," shone in its "fullness and variety of scenes, in the graphic expression of the various passions, in minuteness of detail, and in the fine preservation of the colors of the painted versions." Not theorizing on the meaning of polychromy in Greek art, he documented in a straightforward manner the use of color, for example, the blue eyes of the warriors, their scarlet cloaks, their blue tunics, and the brightly colored saddle clothes.[28]

It is tempting to suggest that Osman Hamdi's "jealousy" over the Sidon sarcophagi was part of a clever plan. Knowing well he had in his protection a unique collection of antiquities that would enhance the current discussions on Greek art, he must have carefully devised a spectacular venue to exhibit them for the first time to the scholarly community. As he waited for the completion of the new museum building, he leaked bits and pieces of information to raise curiosity in a dramatic atmosphere, tinted with rumor and suspense. From his article in the *Revue archéologique* to showing photographs of the objects to Hayter Lewis, he seems to have cunningly designed steps for the grand opening, which, he must have been confident, would put the Imperial Museum on the world map. A news piece in the *American Architect and Building News* conveyed the flavor of the wait. The reporter, writing from Istanbul, mentioned Osman Hamdi's article in the French journal on the four Phoenician sarcophagi and brought up the fact that he had "saved" seven more for a forthcoming book he wrote. Meanwhile, all eleven were waiting in boxes to be exhibited. The rumors about one of the Greek sarcophagi hinted at its "huge proportions, magnificence of sculpture, and coloring." The colors were reported to be so unusual that the tomb was first thought to be that of an Assyrian king.[29] The anticipation of *Une nécropole royale à Sidon* appeared in the pages of *The Athenaeum* as well, with a statement that "Hamdi Bey's forthcoming publication on these remarkable objects will mark an era in archaeological research." Explaining the difficulty of producing a book of this kind, the author listed the tasks the museum director had already completed: photographs of all sides of the sarcophagi, plans showing the places where the objects were found, and several chapters of description and analysis. He added that "facsimiles of the painted coffins will be given in full colours and no pains are being spared in producing what will undoubtedly be a great history of a great discovery."[30]

After all the waiting, the archaeologist John Punnett Peters announced in December 1891 that the sarcophagi "were just being thrown open to the public in the new museum built to receive them." He recalled the mystery created by Osman Hamdi, who refused to publish all of his spectacular discoveries and who did not allow anybody else to see or study the artifacts. The process had reached its climax as "the building [was] now about completed, the sarcophagi on exhibition, and Hamdy Bey's work [*Une nécropole royale à Sidon*] on the same making its appearance." Even before the opening, the collegiality between the two archaeologists had resulted in Osman Hamdi's invitation to Peters in September and October of 1891 to view the sarcophagi, which were stored in the basement of the museum still under construction. Especially at the sight of the "sarcophagus of Alexander the Great," Peters was "amazed and utterly carried away," as he was "not prepared to find such wonderful art treasures," despite the rumors that they were "in the very front rank of the art treasures of the world, and that it [was] worth a long pilgrimage to see and study them" (see plate 9).[31]

With the Imperial Museum open and attracting foreign visitors, Théodore Reinach repeated the same words in 1892 about the "seduction" of the Sarcophagus of Alexander as the "capital piece that by itself was worth a trip to Constantinople."[32] In two subsequent articles, he made a case for its Greek character, adding that so far no sarcophagus from the "plus belle époque" of Greek art had been discovered. Describing the reliefs, he declared them contemporaries of those on the Parthenon, even though of a lower quality.[33] Its size, decorative features, and especially the polychrome reliefs made the Sarcophagus of Alexander unique among the Hellenic sarcophagi. Undoubtedly belonging to this category because of its general elongated form and Ionic elements, it offered at the same time certain modifications to the prototype, developed freely. The many colors were still sufficiently lively to excite artists and provoke the curiosity of archaeologists.

Arguing that thanks to this discovery, the issue of polychromy in antique reliefs could be considered resolved, Reinach delved into a detailed, four-page description of the colors.[34] The same year, Reinach's thesis was integrated into a general discussion on color in Greek sculpture in a more popular journal, *Revue de deux mondes*, where Maxime Collignon emphasized that the famous sarcophagus not only proved the use of color but offered a rich palette of bold colors, hence forming a contrast to the three or four tones used in the sixth-century examples already known.[35]

Percy Gardner, a professor of classical archaeology and art at the University of Oxford, who concluded his learned survey of the tombs of Hellas with a discussion of the Sidon sarcophagi, reiterated the claim that they belonged to the "pure Greek style." He noted that this made sense during a time when the rule of Greek art in the Levant had become more pronounced. Gardner mentioned the use of polychromy only in passing, but concentrated on the "pure Greek" stylistic qualities of the adornment on the flat surfaces, which demonstrated the dissemination of Greek art in the East. Nevertheless, he pointed out that the subjects often diverged from Greek themes. The sarcophagus of Satrap, for example, stood between the classical Greek and the Assyrian in its subject matter:

> Our sarcophagus lies half-way between the reliefs of Assyria, recording the great deeds of the kings, in an exaggerated and ideal historical record, and the sculpture of purely Greek monuments, ... where the battles of Greeks and Amazons ... take the place of the contests of ordinary men.

Gardner drew parallels between the stylistic characteristics of the Sidon sarcophagi and classical sculpture. The Sarcophagus of the Mourning Women, "an artistic lament, written in many verses and composed in different keys," reminded him of the works of the second Attic school of ca. 370 BC, especially in the poses of the mourners that expressed pensiveness and sorrow as observed in the Attic family groups. However, Gardner felt unable to situate the Sarcophagus of Alexander, which he described as "one of world's masterpieces," demonstrating "a style of wonderful vigor of grouping and skill in execution." He admitted being confronted with something new here, "in some ways, a more masterly work of the Greek chisel than we had before possessed." The artist had mixed the clear stylistic division of the Greek relief into high, half, and bas relief, in a "masterful boldness," leaving the scholar unable to decipher the artistic genealogy.[36]

It was not only scholarly publications that discussed the Sidon sarcophagi, but college textbooks and general surveys on ancient art, addressed to a wider readership, also included the Sidon sarcophagi in their repertoire, providing a description of the reliefs. A survey on Greek civilization distinguished them as belonging to "the purest Greek style" and maintained that the tomb where they were found did not belong to Alexander, but dated from his era, and argued that they were brought to Sidon to be buried there. They proved "that Hellenic art, and so Hellenic culture, was in the generation when Alexander spread it over a large part of Asia."[37] A manual intended for students who expected to pursue the study of Greek archaeology seriously described the sarcophagi, signaling yet again the special place occupied by the Alexander sarcophagus, "because its coloring is more completely preserved than that of any other ancient work of sculpture." Nevertheless, reflecting Gardner's questioning of its "purity," the book cautioned its readers that while the sarcophagus "still breathe[d] the spirit of Attic idealism," it showed "the beginnings of other things" and "belong[ed] already to the time when Greek art found its chief mission in the glorification, not of Hellenic gods or Hellenic athletes, but of the rulers of Asia, Egypt, and Italy."[38] To exhibit copies of the sarcophagi was a major affair. The Museum of Fine Arts in Boston publicized its recent acquisition of "a cast of one of the marble sarcophagi found in Sidon," admired for its "beauty of proportion" and the "refinement and sobriety of [its] decoration."[39] Displayed in the corridor dedicated to Greek sculptures, the cast saluted at the same time the Imperial Museum in Istanbul.

The Sidon sarcophagi featured in the Ottoman press, especially after the opening of the museum, in short news pieces. *Servet-i Fünun* was the most systematic in its coverage. For example, celebrating the opening of the new building, the journal called attention to the fact that its two exhibition halls on each side of the main entrance were designed according to the principles of their European counterparts; their contents, the sarcophagi, were of an importance seldom found in the richest of European museums.[40] It reported on the arrival of the important sarcophagi, such as that known as the "Plürüz" (Les Pleureuses, the Mourning Women).[41] In three subsequent issues from 1904 that gave detailed descriptions of the entire contents of the museum, the Sidon sarcophagi constituted the centerpieces. Among them, the Sarcophagus of Alexander, still associated with the name of the great king despite the well-known fact that this was not true, would alone be worthy of the most famous museums of the world. Its beautiful reliefs, delicately carved and painted, made it one of the wonders of the art of

FIGURE 2.1 Sarcophagus of the Mourning Women, south and north façades. (O. Hamdy Bey and Théodore Reinach, *Une nécropole royale à Sidon*, Planche IX)

sculpture. The other most amazing work of the ancient Greek art was the Sarcophagus of the Mourning Women. Although the cover displayed "some heavy and inelegant" features, which disqualified it from belonging to the school of Attica, its reliefs and adornments were executed with perfect skill, making it a great work of art (figure 2.1).[42]

The following issue of the journal was dedicated to the description of the contents of Çinili Köşk, now sheltering works of Islamic, Egyptian, and Assyrian art.[43] *Servet-i Fünun* also printed a plan of the museum, indicating the additions according to their chronology (see figure 1.2). A summary of the excavations within the imperial boundaries was provided as a background to the collections in the museum. Predictably, the Sidon excavation was singled out for its findings, "unequalled among the objects found in many excavations since the beginning of the history of the science of antique works all over the world." The Sarcophagus of Alexander, spectacular for its delicately carved and polychromic reliefs, had already attracted many American and European experts.[44]

Aside from such informational articles in repetitious language that described the contents of the museum, the Ottoman press covered the Sidon sarcophagi in a more scholarly way during the same years as its Western counterparts. For example, in 1892, *Servet-i Fünun* published an abridged ver-

خط اسكندر كبير

Sarcophage d'Alexand.e

FIGURE 2.2 Sarcophagus of Alexander as the centerpiece of the most cherished treasures of antiquity. (*Malumat* 1, no. 5 [1311/1895])

sion of Théodore Reinach's article published in the *Gazette des Beaux-Arts*; following an introductory text that defined the discipline of archaeology and its importance for civilization, the journal noted that it was finally included among Ottoman sciences and observed that the Ottoman contribution was acknowledged by Europeans.[45] In 1895, *Malumat* presented the Sarcophagus of Alexander in a unique manner in photomontage, placing it in the center of the most cherished works of antiquity, which formed a frame around the larger image of the sarcophagus (figure 2.2). The text started out by qualifying the monument as "one of the most important" of Greek antiquity, dated it as fourth century BC, specified the dimensions, and described the reliefs in detail, noting that the colors had "paled" a little. It then moved on to list the surrounding works and gave basic information on each. Most of the objects — those defining the two sides of the frame — were identified in terms of the places they were found and where they were now, hence, for example, a marble head that came from the pediment of the Temple of Theseus was now in the Central Museum in Athens, a piece from the metope of the Temple of Zeus from Olympia was in the Louvre, the Aphrodite of Epidaure (found in Epidaure) was in the National Archeological Museum in Athens, the sculptural piece from Pergamon was in Berlin, the Venus of Tralles was in the Belvedere in Vienna, the Venus of Milo (found on the island of Milo) was in the Louvre, the statue of Heracles and that of a horse's head from the Parthenon's eastern pediments now belonged to the British Museum. On the top of the frame, two general scenes from Athens depicted the Hellenic sites par excellence: the acropolis of Athens and a distant view of the Temple of Theseus overlooking the agora, with Mount Aegaleo in the background. Two Dionysian scenes from the reliefs of a sarcophagus found in Rome were situated at the bottom, separated by a rather curious addition of the monogram of Comte Philippe Vitali (1830–1914), an engineer who was affiliated with the Ottoman Bank and was involved in railroad construction in the Ottoman Empire. A bust of Alexander—discovered in Tivoli, given to Bonaparte, and now in the Louvre—crowned the collage and, as the "only authentic portrait" of Alexander, made a link to the Sidon sarcophagus. A row of coins from Alexander's time connected the sarcophagus to the bust of the king above.[46]

The composition displays conflicts while offering glimpses of Ottoman perceptions of antiquities and their use for political goals. The most obvious dilemma is about the identification of the sarcophagus. By titling the article the "So-called Sarcophagus of 'Alexander,'" the anonymous author agreed with the opinion of the international scholarly community. Yet the collage made several strong references to Alexander in an attempt to maintain the original misinformation, likely based on the speculation that the sarcophagus gained spectacular importance by association with the emperor. Another curious question is the language of the article, which is French. *Malumat* was a Turkish-language periodical, which employed French selectively, limited to the captions (in addition to Turkish). The selection of French for this article blurs its targeted audience.

Contextualization of the sarcophagus by well-known works of Hellenic art and architecture, ranging from groups of buildings to building details, sculptures, and reliefs from other sarcophagi, identified it as belonging to this era. Associating it with the most valued period of classical antiquity endorsed its historic prominence and helped put the monument on the high pedestal of art treasures. The power injected into the monument extended to the institutional level. The collage, made up of photographs of artifacts from the major museums of the world, reduced these to the secondary level by relegating them to the frame and, in partisan competition, lifted the Imperial Museum in Istanbul to the highest rank as the centerpiece of the composition. The overloaded image thereby functioned as a multilayered empowerment device, in accord with Osman Hamdi's own relentless endeavors.

Nevertheless, it took three more decades for a comprehensive analysis of the sarcophagi to appear in Turkish. Published in two subsequent issues of a scholarly journal of Istanbul University and written by the art historian Mehmed Vahid, the article referred to the literature on the Sidon sarcophagi, sometimes agreeing with the European authors and sometimes opposing their theses. Echoing the previous writings on the sarcophagi, and especially the Sarcophagus of Alexander, Mehmed Vahid celebrated the importance of the unusual beauty of these works of "classical Greek art" and repeated that they made it mandatory for scholars to add Istanbul to their itinerary, which commonly included Athens, Olympus, Rome, and London. He then gave the long history of the research in Sidon and the many assaults on the site by treasure seekers and antique dealers, which had caused serious damage to antiquities. He argued that the French discovery of the sarcophagus of Eshmunazar II in 1855 and its transportation to the Louvre was a turning point in bringing Sidon to the foreground of serious scholarship on Phoenician culture. It was following this discovery that the French government sent Ernest Renan to Sidon, where he found a series of sarcophagi in the shape of human figures. According to Mehmed Vahid, these *anthropoïdes* (the term was coined by Renan and translated into Turkish as *şeb-i insan* — "looking like human beings") did not carry much artistic value but allowed for a better understanding of the impact of Greek art on the Orient.[47]

Mehmed Vahid shifted to the Ottoman appropriation of the site with the memorable event of workers coming across a well when working on the field of Mehmed Şerif Efendi. Drawing an analogy to the legendary discovery of Venus de Milo by a peasant, he marked the initiatives of the local authorities in 1887, which four months later led to Osman Hamdi's excavations. He gave a description of the graveyard and the setting of each sarcophagus following the dates the different artifacts were found and keyed the data to plans and sections (taken from various sources, including Osman Hamdi and Théodore Reinach's *Nécropole royale à Sidon*; see plate 10). In a chart, he summarized and reorganized the information in five phases according to the chronology of the objects, starting with the early fifth century BC and ending with the late fourth century BC. The conclusion to the first part of the article debated and speculated on the results of research. Mehmed Vahid's main question focused on whether the sarcophagi were bought secondhand, acquired after military campaigns, or commissioned specially. Challenging the widespread arguments that favored the former position, and given the status of the objects that showed no wear and tear, he deduced that they were special artistic commissions. He defended his claim by stating that the sarcophagi artistically formed four neat groups, which could not have been a coincidence: the "Egyptian," the *anthropoïde*, the *theca* (boxlike, with cover), and those similar to the *theca*, but with no personal depictions (notably, the Sarcophagus of Alexander). He expanded his thesis further with concrete evidence: the "Egyptian" sarcophagi were unfinished, hence recycling was out of the question, and delicate sculptural details of the Sarcophagus of Alexander would not have survived the rough transportation procedures.[48]

The rest of the article, published in the next issue of the journal, focused entirely on the Sarcophagus of Alexander. Examining it façade by façade and pediment by pediment using photographs to clarify his points, Mehmed Vahid gave the scenes titles such as "war between Greeks and Iranians" and "lion and deer hunting"; he described the actions, the details of the costumes, and the faces. The big issue for him was the identity of the extraordinarily skillful artist. Was he from Athens, or from Ionia but working under the influence of Athenian masters? Did he belong to the school of the "second Attica"? Dating the sarcophagus to the last era of classical Greek art, he distinguished it as possibly the most delicate, the most refined artistic production among its counterparts in the entire world. The colors, though narrow in range, were used selectively to punctuate their value and create unusual effects. In brief, the beauty and perfection of the reliefs were so attractive that they led to an instinctual desire to gently caress them.[49]

Mehmed Vahid's article was a groundbreaking evaluation of the scholarship on the Sidon sarcophagi in Turkish. He kept the celebratory tone low and pursued the common stylistic conventions of art history writing at the time, dominated by long and dry descriptions. He credited the scholars who preceded him, synthesized their research and arguments, and expressed his agreements and disagreements with them. He punctuated his narrative with his personal, self-confident voice, based on his intimate knowledge of the objects and the discourse on them. Placed in its own historical context and in light of the author's teaching career at Istanbul University and the School of Fine Arts, the article also points to the introduction of art history as an academic topic in the repertoire of fine arts and humanities curricula during a critical transition from the Ottoman to the Turkish Republican era.

Middle Eastern Antiquity Orientalized

European scholars who recognized the importance of the Sidon sarcophagi argued, at the same time, that they displayed an ornate quality, which separated them from the pure and authentic examples of Greek art. Within the hierarchy of the antique works of art, they therefore did not deserve a high enough rank, not coming close to the serene beauty of the Parthenon sculptures. Appreciation for the "great freedom" of their compositions was balanced with reservations about their "confused" nature, equated with "decadence."[50] Théodore Reinach summarized the reservations expressed by art and architectural historians on the Sarcophagus of Alexander by saying that its "sumptuous décor ... announced the seeds and symptoms of future decadence."[51]

"Decadence" was a popular and primarily aesthetic term in the late nineteenth century, used in relationship to "history," or rather, to the "grand narrative" of historical change. Like its counterpart, "decline," this historicizing concept identified a society's temporal context in reference to other periods.[52] Relying on philological and historical readings, nineteenth-century European scholars regarded Periclean Athens (fifth century BC) as the ultimate locus of Greek genius and the highest stage of Greek creativity, a yardstick by which all other periods were evaluated. Furthermore, aiming to address the political concerns of their time, they linked this line of thinking to the impact of social and climatic conditions in the delineation of national boundaries in terms of the development of art.[53] Although the trend started to change toward the end of the century with art historians turning toward examining works of late antiquity, especially in the Middle East, the term "decadent" endured in the discourse.

A significant shift in art historical thinking occurred with the publication of *Orient oder Rom: Beiträge zur Geschichte der spätantiken und frühchristlichen Kunst* (Orient or Rome: Contributions to the History of Late Antique and Early Christian Art) by Josef Strzygowski in 1901. Strzygowski challenged art history's biased exclusion of late antiquity from Greco-Roman traditions and, arguing for the interpretation of art by concentrating on the works alone, directed his attention to the impact of the "Orient" in the foundations of early Christian and medieval European art. Strzygowski's hypothesis made a major impact on art historical discourse, bringing the sites in the "East" to the foreground. Baalbek, Palmyra, and "cities east of the Jordan," seen as an ensemble, were identified by their "many peculiarities" and their "profuse barock [sic] decoration." The art and architecture of these places raised a new and important question because of their relationship to the art of Rome, deemed "undoubtedly one of the most far-reaching in the history of art": Was it "the ancient artistic force of the Orient … stirring here?"[54] A review essay in *Revue de deux mondes* confirmed Strzygowski's position that the "return to Orientalism" was already evident in the monuments of Baalbek and Palmyra, founded by "Hellenized Arab dynasties."[55] As ultimate representatives of the "decadence of Oriental classical architecture," these monuments stood in their "strange enormity," linked to the "aspirations of the Oriental spirit."[56] The debate was thus endowed with racial undertones and colonial hierarchical thinking, accompanied by their indispensable partner, Orientalism.

A Connected World of Museums

Sidon discoveries had put the Imperial Museum on the international map of scholarship, and the series of laws on antiquities had enhanced the attention the museum received. The late-nineteenth-century journals included many short articles and news pieces on the Istanbul museum, introducing certain objects briefly, describing others in detail. A short discussion of this literature gives a broad idea of the connected nature of geographically dispersed institutions—a system that was now compelled to include the Imperial Museum. Regardless of claims of ownership and cultural hierarchies, these museums functioned together to create a network of scholarship that crossed national boundaries. Political entanglements remained rooted in the history of archaeology and cultural heritage, but knowledge about the past expanded without boundaries through discovery and its dissemination through publications.

The Imperial Museum began to appear in the pages of the European journals before the construction of the new buildings. The renowned British Assyriologist and linguist Archibald Henry Sayce reported in 1879 on his visit to the museum, thanks to the courtesy of Henry Layard and Philipp Déthier, the director at the time. Newly transferred to Çinili Köşk and still in crates, the artifacts Archibald Sayce was allowed to examine included a Babylonian inscription that described the construction of the great court in the Temple of Bel, a large collection from Cyprus, and another from Hisar-lık. In his opinion, the latter, Heinrich Schliemann's discoveries, were superior to the ornaments in the South Kensington Museum. However, stating that the most intriguing objects were a series of sculptures from Darfur, in "a style of art once peculiar and barbaric" and reminiscent of Mexico, he described the scenes represented on them.[57]

Salomon Reinach was a frequent reporter on the objects in the Çinili Köşk. His articles illustrate well the bridges constructed by scholars between different museums over the discussion of single objects. He wrote in the *American Journal of Archaeology* in 1885 that "the charming figure," which was found on the island of Lesbos and which could be "safely pronounced to represent Artemis," called for comparison with a copy of a statue of the goddess, deemed to have been modeled after the "Artemis-statues of Praxiteles" in the Louvre. The stylistic analogy between the "Paris Artemis" and that of the statue in the Istanbul museum was remarkable. In the absence of the fabled originals, when added to the scholarship on the Paris statue, the Çinili Köşk Artemis could convey "a true, if not adequate idea of some master-piece of the fourth century which has long ago been converted into lime."[58] Reinach's other piece on the two marble Medusa sculptures from the Çinili Köşk appeared in the same journal in 1886. The first Medusa, a medallion, allowed Reinach to trace the evolution of "the type of Medusa" from "an emblem of horror and dismay" (as in the "Ludovisi Medusa in Rome") to the disappearance of its "grotesque ugliness" (as in the "Rondanini Medusa in Munich"). Like its Munich counterpart, the Medusa in Istanbul did not "petrify her opponents," but was "petrified herself into the dull stiffness of ornament." Another "Medusa of Constantinople," a bust, bore a striking resemblance to the bust from the Farnese collection in the museum at Naples.[59] To support the theory that Archaistic reliefs did not all belong to the time of Augustus and Hadrian (first century BC–second century AD) and that the "mannerism" that showed stylistic affinities to Archaic Greek art (ca. 700–480 BC) originated at a much earlier time, the British archaeologist Paul Perdrizet relied on three reliefs from the Imperial Museum, found in Tralles (Aydın).[60]

The officers of the University of Pennsylvania's museum presented their "cordial relationship" with the Imperial Museum as a product of mutual respect and collaborative scholarship, initiating a liaison between the two institutions. Hermann Hilprecht's knowledge of cuneiform came in handy. The museum's *Bulletin* stated that Hilprecht had spent many months between 1893 and 1896 preparing a catalogue of the Babylonian and Hittite collections in the Imperial Museum, and in acknowledgment the sultan had given the university's museum "a very large number of valuable antiquities excavated in Nippur," as well as the permission to cast copies of various objects in the Istanbul museum. The museum of the University of Pennsylvania had thus acquired a core collection of Babylonian objects, and was now taking advantage of Osman Hamdi's "praiseworthy efforts" to expand his museum's collections of Hittite and Phoenician works, as Hilprecht's casts would be invaluable for educational services back in Philadelphia. Two large Hittite sphinxes were to flank the entrance to the Biblical Room, to be opened in the near future. Meanwhile, more "tablets, bricks, pottery, and objects of art of the earliest period of Babylonian civilization and over 30 large, well-preserved sarcophagi," excavated in 1895 and 1896 in Nippur by John Henry Haynes, were on their way to the Ottoman capital. Hilprecht was to examine and catalogue them. In exchange for his services, the university hoped to renew its excavation permit in Nippur.[61] When one historian of Mesopotamia referred to the gifts of the sultan to the university museum, he reasoned that the "gracious" act was in direct response to the work Hilprecht had conducted on behalf of the Imperial Museum, but also to "the dignified and generous course pursued by the authorities of the University of Pennsylvania," who had "honestly handed over the antiquities to the Constantinople authorities."[62] The implications for the common practice of European dealings with the Ottomans could be read between the lines.

American operations did not always follow the "honest" route. A shadier practice was begun earlier by William Hayes Ward, who led the Wolfe Expedition to Babylonia in 1884–1886. Ward, maintaining that he strictly obeyed the directions of the Ottoman government against digging, admitted nevertheless that he "put himself in communication with every man I could hear of who dealt in antiquities, Christian, Jew, or Moslem." He thus relied on the contraband trade that centered in Hillah and Baghdad to start "an excellent collection of small engraved and inscribed objects in gold, chalcedony, lapis lazuli, and clay," which would be placed at the Metropolitan Museum of Art. Indeed, he argued, "a fine collection of Assyrian and Babylonian antiquities can be made without waiting for a *firman* to excavate," following the example of the British Museum. It was not too late for Americans to compete with Europeans in acquiring such collections for the encouragement and development of scholarship in their country.[63] The museum of the University of Pennsylvania followed Ward's advice and purchased, for example, three large collections in 1888 and 1889 from Joseph Shemtob, an "Arab Jew" well known for dealing in tablets, thereby benefiting from the continuing excavations of "native Arabs" who did not "acknowledge the rule of the Turkish government."[64] The cylinder and the tablets, "these small and inconspicuous written monuments," had already been singled out by Ward as fundamental documents for scholarship, preferred over the "large and showy slabs and bulls."[65]

The University of Pennsylvania consistently framed its relationship with the Ottoman authorities around the concept of knowledge. Corresponding to the beginning of the first expedition to Nippur, an album of photographs by Eadweard James Muybridge, depicting humans and animals in motion, was presented to Abdülhamid II as a gift from the university (where the photographs were produced in the 1880s, using students and animals from the Philadelphia Zoo). This was a thoughtful present for the sultan, who had a profound interest in photography. The letter that accompanied the album introduced it as a token of gratitude in exchange for the "debt the West owed to the East." Because, the document continued, "the University of Pennsylvania never forgets that the Well-Protected Lands bear the origins of and hold the scholarship and science created by the world."[66] In turn, Ottoman officials shared the language that capitalized on the contribution to scholarship in their dealings with the University of Pennsylvania. The explanation for the renewal of the permission for digging in Nippur in 1898 stated that the goal was "to serve scholarship and science" and "to conduct research on antiquities." It was also noted that the work would be carried out by a "committee of scholars and scientists," reminding at the same time that all of the antiquities found at the site "belonged to the Imperial Museum in any case."[67] The same year, a request from the Ministry of Education to the authorities in Baghdad, asking them to allow Haynes's equipment through customs, declared that the "usefulness of this dig belonged to the Imperial Museum."[68] Another renewal several years later again rationalized the decree by the fact that "the Imperial Museum benefited from the numerous excavations."[69] To conclude, the production of knowledge on antiquities was a collaborative enterprise that served all museums.

CHAPTER THREE

THE IMPERIAL MUSEUM

AND ITS VISITORS

Museums in Novels

A COMPARATIVE LOOK at three museums in three cities as they feature in three canonical novels allows for a tentative introduction to the places they occupied as public spaces in the cultural life of their respective cities, the scope of their acceptance by individuals, and the kind of visitors they appealed to. The Louvre, the Metropolitan, and the Imperial Museum have their memorable places in literature, and each reveals something about its own character. All written from the safe distance of time, the three novels, which take place in Paris, New York, and Istanbul, offer meaningful and rare glimpses into the museums' publics through their unique lenses.

Émile Zola dedicated several pages to the Louvre in *L'assommoir* (1877). Following the spontaneous working-class procession, which ended up in the museum to fill in the hours of boredom after the wedding lunch of the laundress Gervaise and the hard-drinking Coupeau, Zola's description of the visit is a relentlessly satiric account. The wedding party finds the Assyrian galleries so chilly that they think of wine cellars; they sneer at the "monstrous beasts half cat and half woman with faces like death masks" and the "innumerable fragments of broken pottery and battered busts of ugly figures" of Greco-Roman collections; the gold of the picture frames catches their attention in the French gallery, as does the "gleaming parquet floor, as clear as a mirror" of the Apollo gallery; *Mona Lisa* in the Salon Carré reminds Coupeau of one of his aunts; and the paintings of the Italian and

Flemish schools, with their "confusion of people and things" and "commotion of glaring colors," begin to give them a "frightful headache." As "centuries of art passed before their bewildered ignorance," Zola comments, this uncultured and loud group itself becomes a spectacle for the sophisticated visitors, who watch them "with astonishment."[1]

In Edith Wharton's *Age of Innocence* (1920), Ellen Olenska and Newland Archer, impossibly in love and locked into the prison of New York society in the 1870s, go to the "Art Museum—in the Park" in order to be alone. There, "avoiding the popular 'Wolfe collection,' whose anecdotic canvasses filled the main galleries of the queer wilderness of cast-iron and encaustic tiles known as the Metropolitan Museum," they move to "the room where the 'Cesnola antiquities' mouldered in unvisited loneliness." In this "melancholy retreat to themselves," they stare at the glass cabinets, and Archer comments: "Some day, I suppose, it will be a great Museum." In the final chapter, Archer is back in the Metropolitan to attend "a big official reception for the new galleries." In a trip to the past, he compares "the meagerly-fitted vistas of the old Museum" with the "spectacle of [the] great spaces crowded with the spoils of the ages, where the throng of fashion circulated through a series of scientifically catalogued treasures."[2]

The protagonist of the Turkish novelist Kemal Tahir's *Esir Şehrin İnsanları (People of the Captive City)*, Kamil Bey, is a man of knowledge immersed in European culture. After years of living in European capitals, he returns to an Istanbul under foreign occupation following World War I and becomes involved in a newspaper affiliated with the Kemalist struggle. At a difficult moment of political and personal crisis, he takes refuge in the Imperial Museum. Indeed, he remembers that whenever confronted with a problem, he would repair to the same refuge in Europe. Museums restored his depressed state of mind:

> He gazed at the statues he knew well and [had] considered his close friends for a long time. He forgot his helplessness to some degree. When he left the Museum, his heart was cleansed, stronger ... Constantly thinking of the marble people in the Museum, he walked away, surprised at how they would easily cure [his mental state] without saying anything, without moving.[3]

In these works, the two new museums, the Metropolitan and the Imperial Museum, do not seem to draw crowds as large as the older Louvre does: they serve rather as safe shelters for characters with profound knowledge of European art and culture. Yet, as acknowledged in Wharton's novel, the Metropolitan had a popular section, where the Wolfe collection was located. Archer's first comments on the future of the museum, through Wharton's half century of hindsight, make a significant statement on the public's confidence in the institution; his predictions are affirmed at the end of the novel. Kamil Bey's passage through the Imperial Museum depicts an aura of loneliness in which the protagonist interacts with the sculptures without any intrusion. Kamil Bey's fictional persona is the kind of late-Ottoman intellectual who would feel completely at ease among the international community of scholars and intellectuals that surrounded Osman Hamdi thirty years before his time. It is thus not surprising to find him searching for solace among the antiquities. Yet the spaces he wanders in come across as static and melancholic. In contrast to Wharton's and Kemal Tahir's scenes at the Metropolitan and the Imperial Museum, Zola's rowdy crowd in the Louvre portrays the vibrant presence of the institution in the city, including its back streets. Furthermore, the author situates his wedding party in galleries full of people who know and appreciate art, and who stare at the uninformed reactions of Gervaise and Coupeau's unruly entourage.

These passages make relevant predictions about the future of the three museums. The Louvre continues to grow and change; the Metropolitan turned into a great museum from its modest beginnings; and the Imperial Museum remains relatively unchanged since its conception, with the original core collection still marking its main attraction. The Louvre and the Metropolitan are at the top of Paris and New York attractions, but the Istanbul Archaeological Museum (as the Imperial Museum is now called) does not rank among the most-visited museums in Istanbul today—neither by foreign tourists nor by locals.

Western Visitors: Travel Accounts, Guidebooks, and Catalogues

A set of two photography albums, dating from 1906 and assembled by an American couple who had spent their honeymoon traveling in the Middle East, covered the conventional touristic itinerary of the monuments of Egyptian antiquity; a voyage on the Nile; views of Cairo, Istanbul, and İzmir, as well as streets, docks, landmark historical and contemporary buildings, people, and even the infamous stray dogs of the Ottoman capital. Taken by the well-known photographers Antonio Beato and Félix Bonfils, they presented familiar images, which now included five photographs from the Imperial Museum in Istanbul: a photograph of the Sarcophagus of the Mourning Women and four of that of Alexander.[4] Their inclusion is just one indication that the Imperial Museum, and especially the Sidon sarcophagi, had begun to figure in the trajectory of travelers. It also gave a hint of visits by foreign women.

Paralleling the growing scholarly attention that centered on the Imperial Museum, it would be reasonable to expect the well-versed foreigners to at least be curious about the famous sarcophagi. Nevertheless, they were still relatively few in number, despite the rising popularity of Istanbul as a destination on the grand tour. The various spaces of the city were crowded by all kinds of tourists, forming curious sights for locals. An observer in front of an antique shop in Istanbul described a small group of women as "obvious female tourists, evident from their behavior and costumes, and especially from the presence of the translators accompanying them."[5] A satirical poem listed the places visited by tourists, which included the markets, squares, quays, bridges, cafés, "old walls inhabited by lizards," "all the holes and all the bazaars," the obelisks, the Hippodrome — in brief, all the antique monuments, the vestiges of history, and the popular sights, among them "our porters wearing beautiful vests," "our glorious firemen," the street dogs, and the beggars. Coming from places as far as New York and Bremen, and "often perhaps from Mars," they were:

> Like sheep that are gathered
> By the guide, with a sign of his hand
> Counted at each step
> To see if any were lost on the road.[6]

In French, the poem seems to have targeted among its readers tourists themselves and the French-speaking local public.

Théodore Reinach started his scholarly presentation of the Sidon sarcophagi in the Imperial Museum with a word of advice to the common tourists to Constantinople, who tended to search for exotic sites. He suggested that they visit the museum. Çinili Köşk was an architectural jewel in itself, where "a little bit of everything could be found" (*on y trouve on peu tous*), but, he added, the real treasures were the sarcophagi from Sidon in the new building.[7]

In her travel accounts dating from 1894, published three years later under the title of *Letters from Constantinople by Mrs. Max Müller*, Georgina Adelaide Müller dedicated an entire chapter to "The Museum and the Sidon Sarcophagi." Visiting her son, the secretary of the British Embassy in Istanbul, Mrs. Müller was taken to the Imperial Museum by a learned Ottoman guide, Sadık Bey. Among its contents, which had "lately become accessible to the public at large," she marveled at the collection of the unrivaled sarcophagi. She commented that the few other visitors she met there were "serious students who have come from many parts of Europe" and speculated that with time, the sarcophagi would prove "a powerful attraction to many intelligent travelers, just as the Parthenon marbles draw people to the British Museum, or as the Venus of Milo collects hundreds of worshippers around her in the Louvre."[8] In a separate publication, her son, Max Müller, regretted similarly that many foreign visitors left the city "without having heard" of the new "Museum of Antiquities" and that even the guidebooks said, "as yet," very little about its "treasures."[9] Of the twelve photographs printed in Mrs. Müller's book, two were from the museum: not surprisingly, they showed the sarcophagi of Alexander and the Mourning Women. In fact, the praise for these two objects ran throughout the travel literature, in a vocabulary reduced from scholarship to a popular tone, and amounting to repetitious and predictable passages.

The Imperial Museum may not have attracted as many tourists as the whirling dervishes and the stray dogs of Istanbul, but it appeared increasingly in travel accounts. A French traveler wrote his impressions before the new building was constructed. Çinili Köşk was a "charming Moorish kiosk" in the middle of a vast garden, planted with cypress and plane trees. The museum, the initiative of "Muslim Hamdy, enlightened and erudite amateur, with an intelligent patriotism and a real artistic taste," sheltered important antique sculptures, statues, sarcophagi, and tombstones; its most impressive collection consisted of the objects found by Schliemann. Yet, he added, foreigners were the only visitors, as artistic education lacked in the Ottoman Empire and "indigenous" visitors were rare. He concluded that the museum "could not have the pretension or even a distant hope of equaling those in other capitals."[10]

According to William Holden Hutton, although "one of the finest in the world" and a meeting place of civilizations, the Imperial Museum was not duly recognized:

The museum, with its treasures scattered about the rooms and in the gardens, as yet hardly half known and studied as they deserve, may not unfitly serve to represent the endless interests of the great city, its associations with every phase of the historic life of East and West ...

He argued that although the entire collection was noteworthy, the "splendid" group of sarcophagi ranked "superior to any in the world." The three terra-cotta examples from Clazomene, near İzmir, were "the only complete monuments of the archaic period" other than the two in the Louvre. The "beautiful Mourners, an exquisite series of weeping women," and the "glorious 'sarcophagus of Alexander' ... [alone were] worth a visit to Constantinople."[11]

Having taught at Robert College of Istanbul, Edwin Augustus Grosvenor was not a casual traveler to the Ottoman capital. His two-volume monograph on the city starts with a lament on the disadvantages of the "Western eye," covered with "a veil of mystery and separation," due to the city's physical remoteness and the complexity of its historic levels, as well as its "variety of races, languages, customs, and creeds." He admitted that "it is difficult for the foreign resident to know it well, and for the passing stranger or tourist, utterly impossible" and that he had been privileged to learn its story and enter into "the life of the kaleidoscopic city." Loaded with this "precious" privilege, Grosvenor chose to write "not ... for any one narrow range of readers, but a book for all."[12] The book concludes with a chapter on the Imperial Museum, richly illustrated with full-page photographs of an exterior view of the new building, two of the Sarcophagus of the Mourning Women and four of the Sarcophagus of Alexander. A disclaimer about the inadequate powers of photography and verbal description to convey a real sense of the monuments alerted the readers that the visual and textual depictions "shadow faintly the varied and divine beauty of the original." He isolated these two sarcophagi emotionally as "two on which one hangs rapt and breathless" and added that they "repay a pilgrimage of the art student, of the lover of art, of whoever would drink in their ideal perfection." Grosvenor gave the history of the museum and noted that it had "marvelously expanded during recent years." He listed the seven main departments as Assyrian and Egyptian, Greek and Greco-Roman sculptures, Cypriote, Byzantine and medieval, bronze and jewels, faience with terra-cotta and glass, and inscriptions. He also remarked that although the Byzantine and medieval objects were "scanty and possess[ed] little artistic value," the Cypriote collection rivaled the one in New York and surpassed all others. In terms of the sculptural bas-reliefs, "perhaps in no other museum [was] there an equal number." The sarcophagi from Sidon eclipsed everything else in the museum, their discovery marking "an epoch in the history of ancient art."[13]

One visitor, who placed the Imperial Museum on the same level as the most important collections of art in the world, argued that it had opened a "new period for the arts" in the Ottoman capital, as Osman Hamdi had not only rendered a great service to scholarship, but by encouraging the "indigenous" to study painting and sculpture in the School of Fine Arts had also begun to change an "Islamic" artistic attitude, that is, the centuries-old convention of not representing living creatures. Foreign visitors to this city of contrasts found it a "delicious pleasure to walk around the galleries where old and authentic Aryan works of art" were displayed in a "distinctly European" establishment, one that was "so opposed in spirit to that of Islam." They offered a "repose" from the "monotony of mosques, which, despite their magnificence, left [the tourists] weary." The author described the objects in the museum in a personable, seductive vocabulary: the torso of Apollo was "larger than nature"; the Phoenician statue of Cybele "caressed" a lion; in the rich, yet delicate sculptures of the famous Sarcophagus of Alexander, "personages seemed to jump out of the marble" so that one felt the "emotions of their soul" and the "passions that motivated them."[14] The book, published in the Villes d'Art Célèbres series, included eight photographs from the museum: four of the Sarcophagus of Alexander, three of the Mourning Women, and one of the statue of Hercules in the gallery of the Çinili Köşk.

In several accounts, the mention of the Imperial Museum was brief and anecdotal. The "reminiscences" of Lord Ronald Sutherland Gower did not list any other site besides the museum during his visit to Istanbul. Claiming he "lost no time in visiting the Museum" upon his arrival, he acknowledged the courteous welcome he received from Osman Hamdi, who showed him the "wonderful archaeological 'finds' from Sidon, placed in the newly-built Museum," but only for a few minutes in fear of exposing them to light. Lord Gower admired the vivid colors and observed that four of the "famous sarcophagi" were "probably the finest in existence," and the hunting and fighting scene on one reminded him of Leonardo da Vinci's *Battle for the Standard*.[15] Nevertheless, many well-circulated books on Istanbul did not mention the museum at all, notably Paul Eudel's travel journals; Frances Elliot's *Diary of an Idle Woman in Constantinople*; John Stoddard's *Lectures*, which identified Çinili Köşk as "The Treasury" and printed a photograph;

Harry Griswold Dwight's *Constantinople, Old and New*; and, most surprisingly, Robert College professor Alexander Van Millingen's *Constantinople*, an illustrated survey of the city's history, with an emphasis on the pre-Ottoman period.[16]

In her letters, Mrs. Müller had resented the fact that even the guidebooks did not say much about the museum's "marvelous treasures."[17] Her observation pertained especially to those published before the opening of the new buildings. Organizing a touristic route over twelve days, one such guidebook scheduled the Çinili Köşk Museum for the second day, praised its architecture, and stated simply that the articles had "for the most part a very high artistic and archaeological value"; it mentioned a few, referring the visitor to the catalogue of the museum, which listed more than six hundred artifacts.[18]

Upon the construction of the new buildings, guidebooks began to include the Imperial Museum among the main tourist attractions in Istanbul. In the scarcity of data on foreigners visiting the museum, these publications serve as indirect sources to identify some aspects of this elusive group. For example, the prioritization of certain objects over others; the manner in which they are described; their formal, aesthetic, and historic relationship to artworks in other museums, as well as the sequence in which the visitors were taken through the collections allow for assumptions and give clues about their expectations, backgrounds, educational levels, sensitivities, and even emotional tendencies. Guidebooks are hence examined as another set of fragmented documents that help paint parts of the larger picture.

One of the first comprehensive guidebooks to the Ottoman capital, published in 1892 (an earlier edition dated from 1886), concentrated on the new building, labeling it the *galerie* and calling it "the most interesting part" of the Imperial Museum and glossing over Çinili Köşk simply by giving straightforward lists of the artifacts it sheltered. The monuments displayed in the *galerie*, namely the Sidon sarcophagi, were subjects of "envy by the richest galleries of Europe." Citing the French archaeologist Georges Perrot, the guidebook explained the sarcophagi to visitors in two groups: the anthropoid, which displayed an Egyptian characteristic, and those made from Paros marble, which had Hellenistic features. The language in which they were described often appealed to emotions. For example, the Mourning Women sarcophagus represented "a novelty in the evolution of Greek statuary [because it was] so expressive, so profoundly sad." The statue of Hercules from Cyprus, which shone above the principal works in the museum and had no equal in any European collection, bore "an almost repelling ugliness."[19] The 1912 edition of the same guidebook offered more even and systematic information. Describing the Imperial Museum as two distinct buildings, the Çinili Köşk and the museum proper, the book gave plans of the two stories of the "museum," a massive U-shaped building after the completion of the additional wings, together with a list of the collections in the lower and upper levels, then proceeded to explanatory notes of the objects on a room-by-room basis. The language had a calm, neutral tone, as illustrated, for example, in the description of the Mourning Women: the sculptures adhered to "the well-known motif of Greek funerary sculpture of the draped woman with a melancholic expression."[20]

Demetrius Coufopoulos's *Guide to Constantinople* (1895), intended for the "ordinary sight-seer" and not for the "specialized student," pointed to the growth in the importance of the Imperial Museum during the previous decade, gave a brief history of the museum since the 1850s, and described in detail, without any commentary, the objects in each room, including the Çinili Köşk collection.[21] As expected, Coufopoulos highlighted "the matchless collection of ancient monuments unearthed in Phoenicia." Naming Osman Hamdi's two expeditions to Sidon, he listed the finds from the two contiguous tumuli and explained their stylistic characters: the anthropoid sarcophagi were of "Phoenician and Egyptian origin," "that said to be Alexander's and the three similar smaller ones came out of an Attic studio," another was typical of "Lycian art," Satrap's sarcophagus belonged to the Isthmian school, and that of the Mourning Women was likely by an Athenian artist. On the basis of the multiple influences and the resulting range of formal differences between Phoenician objects in the museum, he deduced that a "Phoenician national style of art" did not exist.[22]

The guidebook as a genre in the European publishing world became firmly established with two houses, which organized journeys in a rational manner: Murray's in England (beginning in the 1830s and hence corresponding to the earliest rail travels in Europe) and Baedeker in Germany (beginning in the 1850s). *Murray's Handbooks for Travellers*, lovingly called by their readers *Red Handbooks* because of their covers, gained great popularity, as they served as a reliable "guide, philosopher, and friend." Murray's first decade focused on Europe ("the Continent"), as well as Greece, Turkey, and Egypt to the degree that in 1855 one traveler associated its expansion with conquest: "Murray's Guidebooks now cover nearly the whole of the Continent and constitute one of the great powers of Europe. Since Napoleon no man's empire had been so wide."[23] Baedeker followed Murray's leadership, openly admitting his debt.[24] Unlike Murray's, however, Baedeker's first two decades included only European countries. It turned to Greece, Palestine, and Syria from the 1870s on, issuing one volume on Constantinople in 1905, with a second edition following in 1914. It is with these books that the Ottoman capital firmly entered the respectable and widely popular guidebook series. The Imperial Museum appeared as an essential stop in both.

The 1900 edition of Murray's *Handbook*, which gave a substantial space to Istanbul in addition to Bursa and the Troad, began its coverage of the Imperial Museum with a brief history and described the architecture of the Çinili Köşk, celebrating its place among "the oldest Turkish buildings in Constantinople" and hence turning the building itself into a sightseeing object. A plan helped visitors locate the collections and gave very brief explanations on the artifacts. The new museum, which housed "one of the most interesting collections in the world," namely the Sidon sarcophagi, was surveyed in the set format developed for museums, moving from gallery to gallery. The ground floor of the two-story structure consisted of two rooms separated by a vestibule; an upper story had three rooms. Plans of the ground-floor halls accompanied the text, showing the artifacts numbered to correspond to the descriptions in the text, which referred to a selected set of objects that would appeal the most to tourists. Among them, Satrap's sarcophagus and that of the Mourning Women in the first hall were given the most detail, down to the state of the remaining color on their surfaces and the feeling of "profound sorrow" and "heart-rending grief" transferred to stone by the sculptor in the latter. The crowning piece of the second room was, of course, the Sarcophagus of Alexander, "remarkable for the perfect harmony of all its parts, for its fine colouring, for the creative power of the artist who displays the highest qualities of architect, painter, and sculptor, for the freedom and spirit with which he has treated every part of a complex design, and for his complete mastery of every detail." Among the second-floor objects, those in the third room held special interest for foreigners, as they included "interesting specimens of Oriental and Osmanli art," in the form of well-designed but worn carpets, a Kuran box with mother-of-pearl that belonged to Sultan Ahmed III (1703–1730), a mihrab from the mosque of Sultan Alaeddin in Konya, inlaid woodwork, lamps from mosques, embroidered girdles, gold plates, and even a model of Yeni Cami, a seventeenth-century mosque.[25] Their display here in a scholarly format affirmed their value as historic artifacts that merited being next to works of classical antiquity, but their marginal location assigned them a secondary place in the collection—a subdued acknowledgment by the museum, which must have perpetuated the feelings of cultural superiority common to Western visitors.

The Baedeker guide treated the Imperial Museum in a manner similar to that for all museums in the Baedeker and Murray's guides. With plans for the lower and upper stories of the first building and its northern wing, and the Çinili Köşk, the book listed the objects sequentially following the halls. Unlike in the other guidebooks, Baedeker included all artifacts, even down to those in the glass cases. Explanations were brief, to the point, and in a neutral language, only in rare instances mentioning the "beautiful friezes"—of the sarcophagi of the Mourning Women and the Satrap, for example. Predictably, the Sarcophagus of Alexander occupied the largest space; the condensed description included a few words about some of the war scenes in the reliefs.[26] The history of the Çinili Köşk's architecture was narrated, and its tiles were mentioned in passing, but no attention was paid to the architecture of the imposing new building—an omission that echoed Murray's *Handbook*. This is in contrast to Baedeker's detailed history of the British Museum, the description of the principal façade in architectural terms, and the sizes and decorative programs of its main halls.[27] The Baedeker guide to the United States cited the size of the Metropolitan Museum of Art, its history, and the extensions to the building, singling out the Cesnola Collection of Cypriote Antiquities as "the largest and most valuable collection of Pheonicia and archaic Greece in the world." Taking a unique position among other Baedeker handbooks, this one also mentioned the value of its holdings, presumably as a sign of its unique and spectacular growth: in 1879, the collections of the Metropolitan were worth $400,000; in 1899, the sum was $9,000,000.[28]

The turn-of-the-century template shaped the 1908 Macmillan guide by and large, albeit with some curious diversions. It described at the outset the architecture and history of the Çinili Köşk and, offering some new information, added that it would be devoted entirely to the accommodation of Ottoman antiquities—deeming it an appropriate decision that suited the architecture of the building; the objects in it would be transported to the new wing of the "annex," the grand neoclassical building on which the name of the museum was engraved. A plan of the "annex," indicating the places of the objects, was accompanied by short descriptions. While the majority of the descriptions were limited to a few words ("Statue of Marcus Aurelius: Beyrout," "Scutcheons of Knights of Rhodes," "Hercules," "Funeral water jars," etc.), a few inscriptions were isolated, presumably because of their importance. Among them was the Siloam Inscription, in a "pre-exilic alphabet" and "one of the oldest Hebrew inscriptions," cut on a block of limestone and found in Jerusalem in 1880; a translation of the entire text was given, accompanied by some commentary. The Greek inscription of "The Jerusalem Stele," found in 1871, was reproduced in Greek, followed by an English translation. In some cases, brief and vague didactic statements accompanied the labels, such as "Objects from Dr. Schliemann's diggings at Hisarlik, Troy, belonging some to a historic civilisation, others to the Mycenian civilisation."[29]

If not considered architecturally as glamorous as the Çinili Köşk, the collections "the annex" held were treated much more thoroughly, and ranked above those in the fifteenth-century building. Again, a detailed plan (only of the first floor) helped orient the visitors, accompanied by explanatory texts for all the objects, systematically moving from room to room. Even the shortest entries outlined basic factual data and compared favorably with the descriptions of the objects in the Çinili Köşk: "Fragment of white marble sarcophagus of Roman period: battle with the Amazons," "Funeral stele: from Pella, Macedonia: Greek work of 4th cent. B.C.," and "Votive tablet from the Acropolis of Pergamon: end of 4th or beginning of 3rd cent. B.C."—all on the first floor. Only very rarely was an object identified simply as "funeral stele." Long texts explained the showpieces, namely the sarcophagi of Satrap, Tabnith, the Mourning Women, and Alexander, the last with the most elaborate narrative on its reliefs. In a "Note on the Sarcophagi of Sidon," the stylistic shift from the Egyptian to the Greek was mentioned, and the history of the excavations under Osman Hamdi was brought to the attention of tourists. The plan included the artifacts lining the stairs and the landings, which were introduced briefly. The "right" room of the second floor was identified by the Mesopotamian excavations carried out by American and French researchers and had cuneiform tablets from Nippur and Tello. The "left" room had the Ottoman collections, with "two large vases, ... manufactured at Constantinople or Kutayah during the reign of Sultan Suleyman the Magnificent" and "very valuable." Concluding the tour of the museum, the author called attention to the "new annex," the second extension recently completed and destined to receive the "archaeological treasures" from various parts of the empire, and alluded to the fact that "the Museum authorities have now the legal right to claim all such discoveries."[30] Unlike the others, the Macmillan guide integrated information on archaeological research and reminded visitors that the museum would continue to amass riches thanks to Ottoman laws.

Published in Istanbul, a French-language guide from 1909, considerably leaner than Murray's, Baedeker, and Macmillan guides, did not mention the contents of the Çinili Köşk at all, but described the spaces and the tiles ("magnificent blue and green Persian tiles"), making an analogy to the fifteenth-century buildings in Bursa. The raison d'être of the new museum and its extensions was associated with the discoveries in Sidon and a collection of Greek and Roman funeral monuments that was "unique in the world." The perseverance and talent of Osman Hamdi and his service to science by the creation of the Museum of Antiquities concluded this section.[31]

Developing hand in hand with the boom in guidebook publishing in the late nineteenth–early twentieth centuries was the postcard industry—another indispensable component of tourism at the time. Istanbul's general views, historic monuments, colorful streets, and people dominated the images reproduced. If not on the same scale as the most visible sights, the Imperial Museum entered the collection as an indication that it was a stop on travelers' itineraries. Following the depiction pattern of major museums in other parts of the world, the majestic façade of the new building appeared on postcards, its architecture belonging to similar revivalist languages (see plates 1 and 2). Postcards of the Çinili Köşk were also common, but the views excluded the late-nineteenth–early-twentieth-century structures that surrounded it and presented the building as an isolated and exotic curiosity. In an early version, the Çinili Köşk was not identified as a component of the Imperial Museum, but labeled simply as "Palais des Faïences," despite the glaring presence of antique fragments scattered around it (see plate 6). Interiors and objects from the collections were not commonly shown on postcards, with very rare exceptions, as in the case of one focusing on the famous sarcophagi (see plate 11).

The expansion of the museum was duly recorded on postcards over the relatively short time between the late 1890s and the turn of the century, reflecting the same phenomenon in the case of the Metropolitan Museum of Art (see plate 12). Nevertheless, an unusual description on the back of the postcard of the Metropolitan revealed its unique position. After giving the basic facts and dates concerning the expansion to the first building (1880) in 1889 and 1894, the cost of the "East wing" in 1901 was noted as $2,000,000. The text then added that the museum in its entirety "was designed to cover

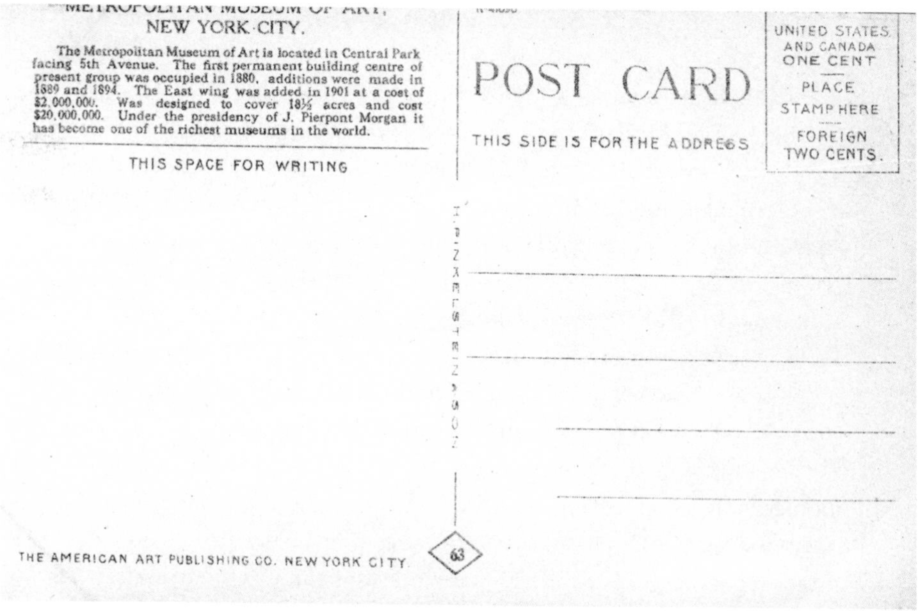

FIGURE 3.1 The Metropolitan Museum of Art; the unusual text printed on the reverse of the postcard mentions construction costs. (Postcard, author's collection)

18.5 acres and cost $20,000,000. Under the presidency of J. Pierpont Morgan it ha[d] become one of the richest museums in the world" (figure 3.1). This unusual attention to the amounts spent on the Metropolitan recalled the entry in the Baedeker guide and applauded American wealth and what it could buy.

A museum's outreach to the world depended to a significant degree on the publications that disseminated its contents in a scholarly manner. Museums issued catalogues that concentrated on certain collections and followed standard formats, recording basic information on the objects and giving detailed descriptions of their prize artifacts. The publications sometimes included special volumes on related activities, mainly archaeological research. Like the guidebooks, catalogues convey piecemeal information about the visitors. They address an assumed public when they single out certain collections and objects and when they insert social and cultural remarks here and there. Speculation on the nature of this group can only remain tentative, although it is fair to suggest that the museum publications reflected some familiarity with the visitors, stemming from the experience of the administrators. Once again, reading between the lines of this special-

FIGURE 3.2 A plate from Goold's catalogue. (*Catalogue explicatif, historique et scientifique...*, 1871)

ized literature allows for some triangulation of the open-ended conclusions reached earlier on the Western visitors to the Imperial Museum.

The Imperial Museum's increasing ambition to become a world player was reflected in the development of its publication program, which consists of three types of catalogues: general catalogues, catalogues on special collections, and books on Ottoman archaeological expeditions. The early catalogues fall into the first category.[32] They begin not with an independent volume but an article, penned by Albert Dumont on the Greek, Greco-Roman, and Byzantine artifacts exhibited in Hagia Eirene, in the *Revue archéologique* in 1868. Dumont brought to the attention of the archaeological community the value and the promise of the collection, even though it was not open to the public and could be visited only by special permission. The lack of order and classification made his work difficult, he admitted, but he attempted a conceptual organization of the collection by pursuing a chronological order: Greek, Greco-Roman, early Christian, and Byzantine; he provided elaborate descriptions, without being able to give precise dates.[33] A catalogue proper from 1871 by Edward Goold, a history teacher at the Lycée de Galatasaray who was appointed in 1869 as the director of the Imperial Museum, did not include all the objects in the museum, only 147 of them (figure 3.2). Goold described each in detail and indicated the donors, who happened to be governors or high officers in the provinces.[34] He thus presented the collection as an official Ottoman enterprise. In 1882, a year after the transportation of the collection from Hagia Eirene to the Çinili Köşk, Salomon Reinach's "summary catalogue to temporarily serve as the guide to visitors" introduced the museum to the "grand public" with selected examples and without the "scientific discussions on the issues that the collection raised." Almost apologetically, the preparation of a more complete and scholarly catalogue for those visitors who wanted to penetrate deeper into the scholarly aspects was left for a later date.[35]

A decade later and paralleling the construction of the new building, the catalogues of the Imperial Museum started focusing on singular collections. André Joubin's *Monuments funéraires* (1893) covered only the funerary monuments, in accord with the decision to dedicate three halls of the "new museum" exclusively to funerary monuments. Launched by Osman Hamdi as a concept "unique in the world," the galleries "present[ed] to the public the complete development of funerary sculpture in antiquity." Before going into the descriptions of the artifacts, in an introductory essay Joubin stated that the funerary objects formed an uninterrupted series from the Ionian to the Byzantine periods, hence revealing a range of styles and allowing for a comparative study.[36] Osman Hamdi proudly announced later that due to the popularity of the catalogue among visitors, it soon had to be reissued in 1898 (and went out of print in 1904), and then again in 1909 (only to sell out in one year). The second edition allowed Joubin to undertake certain revisions to his introductory essay and add a section on the ensemble of the Sidon sarcophagi, along the way making the visitors aware of Osman Hamdi's important excavations, as well as punctuating the historic and archaeological value of the sarcophagi and the interpretations provoked by them among the learned community. Joubin's essay synthesized the scholarship on the stylistic qualities and dating of the monuments, while listing a set of questions that remained as "hypotheses, fantasies, imaginations, and controversies," on the artists who created them and the patrons for whom they were created.[37] The same year, Joubin prepared another thematic catalogue, this time on the sculpture collection exhibited in the Çinili Köşk.[38] Volumes on other specialized collections were published in the ensuing years, among them catalogues on the Himyarite and Palmyrian antiquities, on Egyptian antiquities, and on bronzes and jewels.[39] Joubin clarified the idea behind them: to simply locate the objects, which were "very" briefly described; for further information on the particular pieces, they were referred to other publications. He also used the opportunity to boast about the popularity of the museum's catalogues: for example, referring to the "bronzes and jewels" volume, he wrote that "if this catalogue will be sold out as rapidly as those that preceded it, we can hope that a re-print will be necessary in two or three years."[40]

Catalogues from the first decade of the twentieth century began making ample use of photographs, sometimes collecting them at the end of the volume, sometimes inserting them into the texts. Gustave Mendel prepared the publication on the Greek terra-cotta figurines, following their move in 1903 from the Çinili Köşk to the new wing across the garden, where they were given a special hall so that "their variety and value could be appreciated" (figure 3.3). Osman Hamdi clarified that in their present state, the holdings offered a "sufficiently exact image of Anatolian coroplasts," but the situation was soon to change and be completed by new research. Architectonic terracotta examples from Larissa, as well as Mesopotamian and Phoenician figurines, and those found in Cyprus would form the subject of a forthcoming catalogue to be prepared by Georges Nicole, a former member of the École Française in Athens and a professor at the University of Geneva. Osman Hamdi also remarked on the recent discoveries of Théodore Macridy Bey in Samsun, coming too late to be included in the current volume. Proudly announcing the ongoing and future projects of the museum, he reminded visitors that the institution enjoyed a "happy privilege," being "in this kind of perpetual growth."[41]

Expanding considerably Joubin's catalogue of 1893 and replacing it, Mendel also wrote the three-volume catalogue on Greco-Roman and Byzantine sculptures, published before World War I. Covering the entire building complex, including the Çinili Köşk, he provided long descriptions of the objects, relying on recent scholarship and illustrating them with drawings. A plan in the first volume, on which all objects were numbered, oriented the visitors to the collections. Concluding with an impressive bibliography, *Catalogue des sculptures grecques, romaines et byzantines* served both as a guidebook and a scholarly work.[42]

Given Osman Hamdi's penchant toward pre-Islamic antiquity, it is not surprising that the "Islamic" objects listed in the guidebooks did not get much attention and no special catalogues were dedicated to them, with the exception of seals and numismatics. It was İsmail Galib, Osman Hamdi's younger brother and the first Ottoman expert on numismatics, who produced several catalogues on the coins in the museum. Dating from the late

Pl. VIII

H. DEMOULIN, SC.

FIGURE 3.3 A plate from Mendel's catalogue. (*Catalogue des sculptures grecques, romaines et byzantines,* 1914)

PLATE 1

The Imperial Museum, Istanbul, the original building.

(POSTCARD, AUTHOR'S COLLECTION)

PLATE 2

The Imperial Museum, Istanbul, view showing the additions.

(POSTCARD, AUTHOR'S COLLECTION)

PLATE 3

The British Museum, London, ca. 1903.

(LIBRARY OF CONGRESS, PRINTS AND PHOTOGRAPHS)

PLATE 4

The Altes Museum, Berlin, ca. 1890–1900.

(LIBRARY OF CONGRESS, PRINTS AND PHOTOGRAPHS)

PLATE 5

The Metropolitan Museum of Art, New York, original building.

PLATE 6

The Imperial Museum, Çinili Köşk.

PLATE 7

Quatremère de Quincy's reconstruction of Jupiter in Olympia.

(QUATREMÈRE DE QUINCY, *LE JUPITER OLYMPIEN*,
1814, FRONTISPIECE)

NORDWESTECKE DES GEBÄLKS DES PARTHENON

PLATE 8

Fenger's reconstruction of details from the Parthenon.

(FENGER, *DORISCHE POLYCHROMIE*, 1886)

GRAND SARCOPHAGE

Face Nord

a,b,c,d,   Fragments de l'angle droit du tympan

PLATE 9

"The Great Sarcophagus," details of the north tympanum, drawing.

(O. HAMDY BEY AND THÉODORE REINACH,

UNE NÉCROPOLE ROYALE À SIDON, PLANCHE XXXVI)

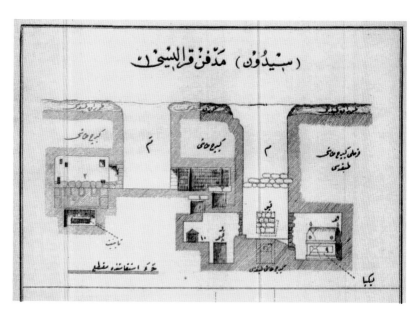

PLATE 10

Tombs, Sidon excavation, section drawing.

(*DARÜLFÜNUN EDEBIYAT FAKÜLTESI MECMUASI* 1, NO. 2 [1925])

Sarcophagi of Alexandre the Great and others at Constantinople found in Sidon.

Sarrafian Bros., Beirut (Syria).

PLATE 11

Various sarcophagi at the Imperial Museum, Istanbul.

(POSTCARD, AUTHOR'S COLLECTION)

The Metropolitan Museum of Art, New York City.

PLATE 12

The Metropolitan Museum of Art, New York,
Fifth Avenue façade after the expansion.

(POSTCARD, AUTHOR'S COLLECTION)

1880s and early 1890s, these catalogues were in Turkish, with the exception of the one on Turcoman coins published in both Turkish and French.[43] İsmail Galib thus added "Islamic" holdings to the systematic documentation of the museum collections, heralding a future orientation, which would be taken on by Halil Edhem, yet another younger brother of Osman Hamdi, who published a catalogue in Turkish on Arab, Arabo-Byzantine, and Ottoman lead seals in 1904. After clarifying that the majority of the some two thousand seals in the museum were from the Byzantine era, and only a relatively small number from the Arab and Ottoman periods, the author isolated the extreme rarity of those with Arabic writing on one side and Greek on the other. He argued that the museum's fourteen such seals should therefore be considered one of the most important collections in the world. He added that the Arab seals were also rare and could not be found in Istanbul; the examples in the museum had been brought from Syria and Iraq.[44] During the tenure of Halil Edhem, who became the director of the museum after the death of Osman Hamdi in 1910, much more attention would be paid to Islamic collections, ultimately leading to the creation of a Museum of Pious Works, or the Evkaf Müzesi, in 1914.[45]

To this library of catalogues from the Imperial Museum, two important books on archaeological expeditions (that are discussed in other contexts) need to be appended. They supplemented the fragmented information that speckled the miscellaneous guidebooks on Ottoman expeditions and emphasized their importance for scholarship. Osman Hamdi and Théodore Reinach's *Une nécropole royale à Sidon: Fouilles de Hamdy Bey* (in two volumes, the first containing the text and the second, the illustrations), although published in Paris, functioned as a flagship of the museum because it documented the monuments that made the museum what it was on the world stage. Osman Hamdi's collaboration with Yervant Osgan, more commonly known as Osgan Efendi, *Le tumulus de Nemroud-Dagh*, was not about artifacts in the museum, but rather a proud record of a major expedition carried out by the museum that brought to light a remarkable collection of monuments in southeastern Anatolia; their location and sizes necessitated their preservation in situ.[46]

The publication record of the Imperial Museum was impressive and displayed the ambition to create a world-famous institution. Matching the traditions of its counterparts, a significant effort was made through the scores of volumes on the collections to put the museum on the touristic and cultural map of the capital, in addition to drawing the attention of scholars, some of whom came especially to see the famous artifacts. Furthermore, when acquired by major libraries abroad, these publications contributed to the dissemination of knowledge on the museum among foreign scholars who did not visit the city. The publication list, heavily in French, revealed clearly the priorities of the museum administration: foreign visitors were targeted over local ones, in addition to a small section of the upper stratum of the Ottoman society.

Certain characteristics about the kind of foreign visitors who came to the Imperial Museum can be glimpsed from the nature of the guidebooks and the museum catalogues discussed above: relatively well educated, acquainted with other museums and archaeological sites, confident in their cultural superiority, and perhaps resentful of the holdings in the museum and the Ottoman antiquities laws—the latter implicitly provoked by recurrent hints on the growth of the collection and its brilliant future thanks to Ottoman initiatives in the museum publications. Their interest in Islamic objects, the exotica, may have been underplayed in the collection, but the emphasis in the guidebooks on the architecture of the Çinili Köşk and on its colorful tiles affirmed it. In contrast, their indifference to the architecture of the neoclassical new buildings points to a common Western attitude of the time, that is, overlooking Ottoman modernity.

The scale and the quality of the work achieved by Osman Hamdi in the Imperial Museum should be contextualized in terms of the financial restrictions caused by the larger problems of the Ottoman Empire at the time. A quick comparison with the publishing activities of the Metropolitan Museum of Art, a famously rich institution, may not be fair, but explains something about the Imperial Museum's scale of operations from a broader perspective. The Metropolitan's Annual Reports of the Trustees, issued regularly from 1872 on, clearly mark its main difference from the Imperial Museum, at the same time highlighting the role and power of the board of trustees, a body of influential and wealthy individuals and a truly American phenomenon. The annual reports summarized all the activities carried out during a particular year, including the state of the holdings, the new acquisitions, and donations from private parties. They outlined management and financial issues, the decisions taken on the extensions and transformations to the building, and the often thorny negotiations with the city administration. Education as a public service constituted a main concern, and the yearly achievements in that area were summarized, with due emphasis on the industrial art schools. The state of the museum library was also addressed systematically.[47]

The Metropolitan's catalogues show an ever-increasing level of activity from the late 1880s to 1914, culminating in more than 110 publications. They bear witness to the variety and galloping growth of its holdings. Some were on idiosyncratic objects, such as the rudimentary and typed *Catalogue of Original War Medals awarded to the British, French, and American Soldiers* (1888), and others were on temporary exhibitions on American topics, such as *Catalogue of an Exhibition of Colonial Portraits* (1911) and *Catalogue of an Exhibition of Silver Used in New York, New Jersey, and the South* (1911). Others recorded the donations by patrons, among them *Catalogue of the Cosby Brown Collection of Musical Instruments of All Nations* (1903) and *Catalogue of the Morgan Collection of Chinese Porcelains* (1907 and 1913). The wealth of European objects in the museum was attested, for example, by *Catalogue of European Arms and Armor* (1905) and *Catalogue of Romanesque, Gothic, and Renaissance Sculpture* (1913). Nevertheless, antiquities were given special attention with several catalogues on Egypt dating back to 1896 that described the rich collection in different rooms and culminated in a concise, illustrated, and accessible volume, *A Handbook of Egyptian Rooms* (1911); *A Handbook* went through the Egyptian halls and described the artifacts in their historic context. Two catalogues, *The Terra-cottas and Pottery of the Cesnola Collection of Cypriote Antiquities* (1895 — in two volumes, one recording those in Halls 5 and 3, the other in Halls 4 and 15) and *Catalogue of Casts from Cypriote Statues of the Cesnola Collection* (1902), celebrated the prize collections, consisting of the Cypriote artifacts excavated and brought to New York by Cesnola, which competed with those in the Imperial Museum in Istanbul. Curiously, the Metropolitan gave Oriental rugs, a topic that had not merited a publication by the Imperial Museum, a catalogue on the occasion of a temporary exhibition. Titled *Catalogue of a Loan Exhibition of Early Oriental Rugs* (1910) and prepared by Wilhelm M. R. Valentier, the curator of Decorative Arts, it included sixty-two plates and offered information on the dates, regions, and patterns of the rugs, some of which were owned by the museum, while others were on loan. The goal of the catalogue was to teach the uninformed public some essential facts about rugs, an especially meaningful mission, given that "in no other city is the market for modern Oriental rugs so extensive as in New York; only those of Constantinople and Paris are comparable to it."[48]

The relationship of the Imperial Museum with Istanbul residents was unique in comparison to museums in Europe and North America and its impact on local populations followed unpredictable venues. It was a stop for visiting foreign dignitaries—for example, the Bulgarian prince Ferdinand (Karl Leopold Maria) went to the museum on the second day of his one-week voyage to Istanbul[49]—but it had also turned into a center of attention for foreigners living in Istanbul. Foreigners' views on the museum would sometimes find their way into the Ottoman press. To cite one incident reported in *Servet-i Fünun*, shortly after the inauguration of the new building, Canon C. G. Curtis, the first chaplain of the Crimean Memorial Church in Istanbul, lectured in Pera to an English audience on the Sidon sarcophagi, presenting a view counter to the common interpretation of the images on the Sarcophagus of the Mourning Women as portraying several different figures. In Curtis's opinion, these showed aspects of grief of one woman who had lost her beloved.[50] It would be exceptional to find public lectures of this nature delivered to Ottoman audiences during this early period (I have not come across any), and it would be a challenging exercise to even imagine Osman Hamdi taking on such a task. Nevertheless, the reporting of the event in a popular Ottoman periodical indicates how ideas could reach a relatively large local readership, possibly leading to visits to the museum, endorsed by a European measuring stick.

If the Imperial Museum started out as an exclusivist institution that addressed foreign scholars and visitors first, its mission broadened in the following decades to encompass a local audience, with a concentration on the educational mission. In 1883, Salomon Reinach could claim that "Turks rarely entered" the museum, using his observation to deduce that they were not happy to spend money for the maintenance of antiquities.[51] Behind these words Reinach had a particular agenda on the question of the real owners of antiquities (see chapter 2), but his statement on the numbers of Turks visiting the museum reflected the reality. Still, signs of change began surfacing gradually. In 1895, a long article in *Servet-i Fünun*, titled "Benefits of Museums," made a strong case for the "extraordinary service rendered to the development of education" by museums in Europe and America and the importance of "always appealing to the temperament of the people" in making them relevant. To support his argument, the author, a certain Kemal, capitalized on the "important opinions Mister (Gud), the director of a Washington Museum," had expressed. As discussed in chapter 1, "Mister Gud" (George Browne Goode of the Smithsonian) was a proponent of the museum as a democratic institution. His position offered a fresh detour from the more traditional references to European ideas in the Ottoman press. To draw visitors to museums, he advocated, the displays should be designed so as not to bore them and not to demand their constant effort. It was essential to change the manner in which objects were exhibited every now and then so that the same people could view the same objects from different perspectives. Museums hence should persistently search for ways to raise the curiosity of the people, or at least, show the familiar objects in new ways and according to new fashions. In an implicit criticism of Osman Hamdi, Kemal Bey argued that museum directors had a great deal to learn from the directors of public entertainment establishments such as casinos and theaters, who changed their repertoires frequently, and he proposed a dynamic display strategy for museums, one that often reorganized its exhibitions. He concluded: "To secure spiritual benefits, some minor entertainments must be used to draw the people to the museum."[52]

The Imperial Museum held on to its academic and static displays, but judging from the long hours it was open to the public, the numbers of local visitors must have grown significantly.[53] The proper functioning of the museum, including holding its officers fully responsible for their duties, emphasized the importance of keeping the schedule of the museum — as revealed by documents issued from the Directorate. Upon receiving reports that members of the staff abandoned their duties to engage in "activities other than their official work," the administration passed stipulations that all officers, custodians, and guards were to be present at their assigned sites during the hours the museum was open to the public. If they diverted from their assignments, they would be forcefully punished.[54]

According to reports, student groups constituted the largest number of local users. Random records asking for free admission for students and faculty indicate the range of educational excursions: from Kızanlık (Bulgaria) and from the girls' high school in İhsaniye (Üsküdar) in 1907; from a Greek religious school in Bulgaria in 1910; and from the Teachers' College in Bursa in 1914.[55] In effect, by 1914 the museum administration could not easily handle student crowds. Complaints were voiced that sometimes several schools overlapped in their visits, with the disastrous consequence of failure from the educational point of view, in addition to creating enormous difficulties for keeping discipline and order. To resolve the problem, principals were asked to apply with an official letter a week before the visit so that they could be given a specific time slot.[56] The transcription of a lecture for the students of a teachers' college on-site casts some light on the nature and sequence of school visits. Delivered in the garden between the Çinili Köşk and the new building before the students entered the galleries, the lecture focused on the status of the museum before and after the efforts of Osman Hamdi, emphasizing the remarkable development due to the "love of duty," hard work, and persistence of the director and his discoveries in Sidon. As future teachers, the students were invited to derive inspiration from this immense project in their commitment to serve "their schools, their nation, and their country." This was followed by an analysis of the etymology of the word *müze*, after which the students entered the museum to be given specific information on the displays.[57]

The publication of catalogues in Turkish gives some indication of the museum's educational mission. Preparing for school excursions, teachers must have consulted them to introduce the students to the collection. It is reasonable to imagine that they would rely on the guidance of these publications to organize their group's movements through the galleries, depending on them for information on the objects, perhaps even reading the relevant passages aloud. The catalogues must also have helped increase the visibility of the museum for the Ottoman public, even if not with the intensity of the coverage on the museum in popular periodicals. Nevertheless, appealing to locals emerges as a secondary concern, supported by the fact that the catalogues were not written for the Turkish-speaking audiences but were translated from the French originals.

The fast pace of the publication schedule reflects some intention on behalf of the museum administration to include the broader public. The first catalogues to appear in Turkish were on specialized collections. Joubin's catalogues on sculptures and funerary monuments appeared in Turkish in 1894, only one year after the original.[58] They were followed by the translation of the Egyptian catalogue in 1899, again a year after the French original.[59] The reprint of *Luhud ve Mekabir-i Atike Kataloğu* (on the funerary monuments) in 1900 attests to the sustained, and presumably growing, numbers of Turks coming to see this particular collection. Osman Hamdi's introduction to the volume presented the museum as "worthy of pride" (*iftihara şayan*), in a "perfect state" (*hal-i mükemmeliyat*), and "abundant and growing to a degree comparable to [that] of European museums" (*Avrupa müzeleri derecesinde fiyuzat ve itilaya mezkur*)—all achieved due to discovery of the antique works excavated throughout the empire and transported to the capital, but especially to the Sidon sarcophagi and the special building erected to house them.[60] The cover was illustrated with a drawing depicting the side view of the Sarcophagus of Alexander, and the volume included a plan with the objects marked on it.[61]

The first comprehensive guidebook in Turkish, published in 1903, went through the artifacts room by room, also giving short entries for those in the garden; a glossary at the end introduced the visitors to a basic archaeological vocabulary. The three following editions provided the same level of information for the new wings. The "warning" (ihtar-ı mahsus) page preceding the text summarized the protocol for the visitors in its most essential elements: walking sticks, umbrellas, bags, and cameras had to be left at the entrance; it was forbidden to smoke in the halls, to touch the displays, and to write on them. Following these cautions, which seemed to target people unfamiliar with museums, more sophisticated audiences were addressed: if visitors desired to make drawings of the objects, they should obtain the permission of the museum director and obey the conditions dictated by the administration. The visitors were also reminded that they could buy the catalogues and photographs of certain objects at the entrance.[62] Despite such initiatives, local visitors to the museum continued to be small in number. Writing in 1913 from Paris, Nazmi Ziya reflected back on it as "a small museum." He added that as its contents were uniquely works of antiquity, its appeal was not to "us"; the collection appealed to foreigners. Even among the "enlightened" sector of Istanbul's people, many remained distant from the museum.[63]

The educational role of the museum extended to the provinces in indirect ways. Salomon Reinach, in his rant about the restrictions of the 1874 law regarding transporting antiquities to foreign museums, had reported in 1883 (tellingly, just on the eve of the passage of the more severe law of 1884) that as there were no provincial museums, the objects found in different parts of the empire were transported to the nearest government palace to be stored temporarily (and carelessly) on their way to Istanbul.[64] Read from the "other" side, this phenomenon surely reveals the valorization of the land's heritage, associating it with the new state institutions of Ottoman modernity—both the museum in the capital and the government palaces, which represented imperial authority and the centralization of its administration. It would be fair to assume that a considerable number of people must have developed some interest in the antiquities showcased in the government palaces, ranging from those who were responsible for guarding them to others who worked in the offices or came in and out for various businesses, to people who simply watched the objects being carried in. At least in one case, that of Beirut, the courtyard of the government palace (built in 1884) was proudly transformed into a temporary open-air museum for antiquities on their way to Istanbul.[65]

A later account, by the *kaymakam* (district head official) of Sungurlu and written following the excavations of the Hittite site of Boğazkale, opens up another perspective on the procedures used for the preservation of the artifacts, in this case, for the "historically important inscriptions on bricks." Macridy Bey, the commissar sent from the Imperial Museum to conduct the expedition, had personally supervised the fabrication of special crates, constructed with "great care and expertise." Furthermore, in order to provide a safe storage space that would, at the same time, serve as a resting place for foreigners who visited the site to examine the objects and for the security forces at night, a "solid" structure was built by the Imperial Museum. The fact that this building would shelter antique artifacts "permanently" (*suret-i daime*) and "continuously" (*mütemadiye*) points to its possible use as a local museum of sorts.[66]

High school buildings were also used to store antiquities, in some cases permanently. As reported in 1897, newly found artifacts would be transported to nearby high schools, where they would be photographed. The "most important" would then be sent to the Imperial Museum, while the rest would be exhibited in the courtyards of these schools.[67] It may not be possible to verify the impact of such displays, but it would not be far-fetched to imagine references to them in classes and the curiosity they must have raised among the teachers and the students.

In some situations, authorities in Istanbul requested that all civil servants, high school principals, education commissioners, and teachers be alert to the theft of antiquities — as in the response to the transportation of four sculptures from Nimrud by a German archaeologist in 1898.[68] It is significant that local authorities, for example in Mosul, acknowledged the need for "individuals familiar with the science of excavation," since the sites in certain regions of the province would undoubtedly reveal "many invaluable antique works."[69] Osman Hamdi brought the key role played by the Ottoman officers to the attention of the Ministry of Interior in a request to increase the salary of Bedri Bey so that he could fulfill his great responsibility to fully "supervise the excavations in the region [in Mosul Province] by foreigners," that is, the "valuable" antiquities dating back to the Assyrian times.[70] The surveillance of excavations reached unprecedented levels, even encompassing railroad construction. In concessions given to foreign companies to build railroads, the regulations stipulated that if antiquities were found during the operations, the museum should be notified and the relevant law applied.[71] This meant that even the construction workers would keep an eye on the operations. Coined by one American observer as "a network of espionage," Ottoman public servants at all ranks, urged to keep a close eye on foreign archaeologists, created a much-dreaded force, a new inconvenience for archaeologists.[72] The relegation of the policing of antiquities to a wide group of officials, the laws themselves that prohibited theft and smuggling, and the awards given to those who discovered artifacts must have all played some role in the growing consciousness of their value among ordinary people.

Public appreciation of antiquities through education (in direct and labyrinthine ways) became integrated into the mission of the Imperial Museum, even though it may not have been the primary concern in the foundation of the institution. The administration's response to the increased visits by schools was not written in its charters and by-laws, but was improvised according to the new demands. The scene at the Metropolitan Museum of Art was different: public education was a priority from the outset (as stated in the charter enacted on April 13, 1870, and quoted above). Its constitution and by-laws were developed to encourage visits from all income groups of the society by opening the museum to visitors without an entrance fee four days a week, in addition to all legal holidays—with the exception of Sundays.[73] Admission to the museum on Sunday, the only day when working-class people could visit the museum, was a contested issue, objected to by the board of trustees and a number of religious organizations—among them the American Sabbath Union, the Presbytery of New York, the Ladies' Christian Union, and the New York East Conference of the Methodist Episcopalian Church. Nevertheless, due to increasing pressure from 1881 on, a groundbreaking petition in 1882 sent to the Department of Parks and signed by over 100,000 people, and support from newspapers and organizations such as the Central Labor Union and the American Secular Union, the museum administration opened its doors to the public on Sunday with great success: on the first such Sunday, May 31, 1891, 14,624 visitors crowded the halls.[74] To refer to one specific year, in 1894, of 511,881 people who had visited the museum, 176,589 had come on Sundays.[75] Such responses speak clearly to the public's embrace of the Metropolitan in New York City.

Educators were given extensive privileges: "All professors and teachers of the public schools of the City of New York, or other institutions of learning in the said City in which instruction is given free of charge, shall be admitted to all the advantages," including the museum's library.[76] In March 1905, a resolution by the trustees notified the Board of Education that upon application, a teacher, alone or accompanied by up to six students, would be admitted free. The results revealed the success of the motion: between May 1 and November 1, 1905, 320 teachers had brought their students to the museum.[77] In 1906, the number of students who came with their teachers was 2,224, whereas in 1907, it had jumped to 5,527.[78] The museum reported proudly in 1908 that while its doors were open to teachers and schoolchildren "at all times when it is open to the public, . . . Mondays and Fridays were reserved especially for them." On these days, the public had to pay. An agreement was made with the Metropolitan Street Railway System to ease the transportation of children to and from the museum so that the teachers could make arrangements by stating the numbers of students, the destination, and the time.[79]

The museum was directly involved in the use of its collections in school curricula. Working together, the staffs of the Public Library, the Metropolitan, and the American Museum of Natural History had selected certain objects in the museum for study and identified relevant reading material in the branch libraries. Placards with this information were posted in all classrooms of five grades of public elementary schools in Manhattan, the Bronx, and Staten Island. During the 1905–1906 school year, forty-five thousand calls were recorded in the various branches of the New York Public Library for materials listed on the placards.[80] For the museum staff to be able to accommodate instruction on-site, teachers were advised to indicate ahead of time the objects around which they would give their classes. They could also reserve classrooms, equipped with stereopticon lanterns, so that introductory lectures could be given before visiting the galleries. Books and photographs could be brought from the library to the classrooms for study purposes.[81] While the museum staff was not available to give lectures to teachers or students, if notified several days ahead of time, they would be available to help teachers prepare their talks on the collections.[82]

The Metropolitan Museum of Art had also initiated a number of "industrial art schools" for the public from 1880 to 1887, first offered tuition-free, then at "moderate cost." They taught a large number of subjects, including woodwork; metalwork; ornamental painting; design; modeling; freehand, architectural, and mechanical drawing; tile making; and weaving. Not situated inside the museum, but scattered throughout Manhattan, from Union Square to First Avenue in the upper 60s and to East 34th Street, these well-attended "museum schools" played an important role in integrating the Metropolitan into the ordinary fabric of the city during the early period of the institution's history.[83]

The incompatibility of the historical records makes it impossible to engage in a point-by-point comparison of the two museums. Nevertheless, the available data point to two trends: the Metropolitan started out as a public institution dedicated to the education of the masses and remained so in addition to its commitment to scholarship, whereas the Imperial Museum evolved slowly from its exclusively academic beginnings into a more inclusive educational institution, albeit never achieving the level of public outreach and reception that the Metropolitan enjoyed.

CHAPTER FOUR

THE OTTOMAN READING PUBLIC
AND ANTIQUITIES

A NETWORK of formal and informal channels nourished the public interest in antiquities. Museums opened their doors to large groups of visitors, public transportation made access easier to them, textbooks expanded their coverage on ancient civilizations, classics were integrated into curricula, contemporary literature increasingly used classic references, travelogues gave personalized accounts, guidebooks provided matter-of-fact information, popular books with historical topics appeared on the market, and periodicals reported regularly on museum collections and archaeological finds. If European capitals were in the forefront of the dissemination of information on the culture and artifacts of antiquity, American cities caught up fast with their new institutions that were growing by leaps and bounds. The Ottomans, with Istanbul in the lead, took part in this connected world, casting an awareness and acceptance of antiquities as part of the package of modernity. While it is beyond the scope of this book to present the extent of the Ottoman scene, a broad-brush review of the Istanbul periodicals sheds light on the nature of the coverage and the arguments put forward, as well as the shifting ideological positions behind them. The use of antiquity in literature, illustrated with the analysis of a play by Abdülhak Hamid that is set in Nineveh, read against Lord Byron's *Sardanapalus*, complements the scene from another perspective.

A scholarly interest in antiquities may have remained restricted to a small group within the Ottoman elite, but by the late nineteenth century the culture of antiquity had begun to penetrate wider sectors of the society through publications. Historical surveys and textbooks played instrumental roles, integrating antiquities into the main narratives of general history and school curricula. Paralleling these, and propelled by the foundation and expansion of the Imperial Museum and the tightened legal measures designed to supervise archaeological research and prevent the looting of antiquities, the Ottoman periodicals began publishing editorials and news pieces on museums and excavations at home and abroad, introductory texts to specific sites, and general essays on the value of understanding the distant past and the importance of preserving the historic heritage. A wide spectrum of popular journals, a significant number of which were illustrated, took part in the discussion, even though one, *Servet-i Fünun,* was at the forefront in its coverage. As the longest-running periodical in print (1891–1944, bridging the Ottoman and early Turkish Republican eras), the journal devoted many pages to the topic, dealing with its different aspects in articles that varied in depth, length, and format.

A 1902 article on the "science of antique works" attempted to popularize the developments in the scholarship, based on the argument that archaeology was among the newest sciences. Tracing the uses of the past to Greeks and Romans, the author explained that early engagements with antiquities were limited to their status as "booty" (*ganimet*); even the obelisks transported from Egypt remained as "signs of victory" (*nişane-i zafer*) and were not understood in terms of their historical value, and the few Roman thinkers who described famous Greek works did not develop a systematic methodology for studying them. During the Renaissance era, it was the artists, and not the scholars, who examined and interpreted Greco-Roman antiquities, and in the seventeenth and eighteenth centuries, travelers started examining the Greek works on-site. However, the real "science of antiquities," which determined specific "methods and rules" (*usul ve kevaid*) for analyzing old works and devising classification systems, was a nineteenth-century phenomenon, evolving hand in hand with the establishment of museums. To make sense of history, it was essential to understand its physical manifestations, which included architecture, sculpture, paintings, medallions, everyday utensils, jewelry, and weapons, in conjunction with the literature of the old civilizations; archaeology and the "science of languages and philology" had to depend on each other to provide a healthy perspective.[1]

Contributions from the new science of antiquity were highlighted in several articles dedicated to specific sites within the imperial boundaries. A piece of copper, unearthed between the Tigris and Euphrates Rivers (the journal did not identify the location) and under examination by a "famous French chemical scientist," was presented as possible evidence for a groundbreaking discovery regarding early civilizations by raising the question of the existence of a "copper era" prior to the "bronze" era.[2] The "serious" excavations that had begun in the 1870s in Aydın Province and were carried out following "scientific methods" had revealed extremely valuable artifacts, which had enriched museums.[3] Hoping to gain better insights about the ruins found during the excavations in Babylon, the archaeologists had started to work with historians and philologists.[4] The Sardis site, dug only in sections at the time, was entrusted in 1910 to the American archaeologist Howard Crosby Butler, well known for his "scientific" expertise proven through his work in Syria. The result of his ongoing work could already be observed in the "perfect state" in which he had unearthed the temple of Artemis during a "massive excavation."[5] Archaeology's collaboration with other disciplines served as a corrective to the history of civilizations, filled the museums with objects, and brought ancient monuments back to life.

News from sites abroad touched on the same theme. The revealing of Egyptian antiquities, which belonged to a civilization several thousand years old and which were buried under sand, would provide reliable information on what was considered the first phase of the history of humanity. However, as monuments and objects alone could not fulfill this mission, European scholars had developed an independent science called "Egyptology." The work done on Egyptian civilization was in the forefront of the science of antiquity and had turned the museums in Egypt into some of the most important in the world.[6] Archaeologists excavating the Roman city of Timgad (Algeria) were faced with the difficult task of collecting the dispersed fragments and resituating them in their original places—an endeavor that required a great deal of expertise and hard work. For example, when the work started in 1892, only two columns of the Temple of Jupiter were found; the clearing of the entirety of the ruins took two years. The triumphal arch, completely buried, had been reconstituted to its original state by 1898.[7]

The popular press frequently reported on the wealth of antiquities in the empire. The news pieces and longer essays offered straightforward descriptions but were interlaced with comments guided by the authors' particular interests. The accompanying illustrations complemented the texts and told visual stories. From this rather comprehensive coverage, selected examples illustrate the foci of arguments, as well as the range of topics and genres of writing.

The pieces incorporated sketchy notes on the histories of the civilizations that created the cities discussed; though not referenced, these seem to have been collated from random and at times admittedly unreliable sources. By acknowledging their questionable reliability, the authors warned their readers about the shortcomings of a still-developing discipline they admired. In some cases, for example for Babylon, the knowledge was rather tentative: it was accepted that the city went back to 2600 BC and was founded by Nimrod, had prospered under the Assyrians, and had endured until AD 500.[8] However, some years later, disagreement surfaced among scholars on the history of Babylon, raising doubts on the hypothesis that it had originated with Nimrod. Semiramis's involvement in its development and Alexander the Great's unfinished projects may have carried some truth, but all of this information depended on the rather sparse writings of Greek historians.[9] According to some history books, Palmyra's history went back to King Solomon. Due to its location between Damascus, Aleppo, and Homs, Palmyra had served as a trade center on the Iraq-Syria route and had become a famous and rich city. It had prospered during Roman times, enjoying its own rulers, one of whom had even gained the title of "Augustus" because of his support of the Romans against the Persians. However, when his wife Zenobia resisted the Romans, they invaded and destroyed Palmyra in AD 272, capturing the queen. Even though the Byzantine emperor Justinian repaired much of the city, it never reached its former glory, and was destroyed again during the Umayyad occupation.[10] Baalbek's origins also went back to the era of King Solomon, as this settlement was built during the same time as Palmyra and had grown especially after the Roman invasion of Syria. Romans had named the city Heliopolis, recognizing its original name, Baalbek, which meant "the city of Sun" in the Suryani (Syriac) language.[11]

The information on Gerasa (Jordan), qualified as comparable to Palmyra and Baalbek in its impressive scale and its artistic works, was first disseminated by early European travelers. *Servet-i Fünun* cited them as reliable authorities in dating the foundation of this "remarkable" city to the time of the ancient Greeks. Specifically, the 1806 expedition of the German Orientalist Ulrich Jasper Seetzen and the 1810 and 1812 expeditions of the Swiss traveler John Lewis (or Jean Louis) Burckhardt, whose *Travels in Syria and the Holy Land* was published in 1822, were key for the discovery. Subsequent and more detailed accounts sustained the validity of their claim: George Adam Smith's *Historical Geography of the Holy Land* (1894) and *The Jordan Valley and Petra*, published in 1905 by the American travelers William Libbey and Franklin Evans Hoskins, who had visited the region. The Americans were credited for the meticulous facts and details they provided on both Gerasa and Petra.[12] A few years later, another article added that the development of Gerasa to the level of "a mature status" happened under the Romans in the first century AD, showing their power and domination in the area.[13]

In his essay on Sardis in *Şehbal*, Gustave Mendel, a commissary at the Imperial Museum and the author of several catalogues (see chapter 3), stated that the ruins belonged to one of "the most renown among antique settlements" and were subjected to a great deal of scholarly research, still ongoing. Yet his references to the research were restricted to naming "Mösyö Butler" as the authority in charge and did not get into further detail. As historical information, he gave a series of notes: Sardis had been the capital of the Lydian kingdom and the place of residency of Croesus, the "richest" and "happiest" man on earth; Alexander the Great had visited it; it had been damaged during the occupation by the Syrian king Antiochus, but rebuilt by the Romans; it had a vibrant Christian population; and it was destroyed completely and terminally by Tamerlane (Timur) in the fourteenth century.[14] As to Troy, its history, published in the same periodical earlier the same year, was reduced to the episode of the Trojan Horse.[15]

The brevity and randomness of the history of the empire's main archaeological sites as observed in these examples indicate the nature of the late-Ottoman approach to archaeological discourse, as well as the general state of the discourse itself. The piecemeal quality of the reporting should also be understood within the format of the popular press and balanced with the more comprehensive and systematic treatment of it in history books and scholarly journals in order to grasp the full picture. The periodicals conveyed basic information and familiarized the readers with the sites in a concise and accessible manner. Along the way, they exhibited the complexity of the history of the land, the multilayered civilizations it harbored, and their

بر غمجه جوامده کی آثار عنیقه‌نك برموزع قولنجه مبلاددده ادع عصر اولكی حالی

FIGURE 4.1 Pergamon, ca. third century BC, reconstruction drawing. (*Servet-i Fünun* 4, no. 66 [4 Haziran 1308/June 16, 1892])

vestiges in a valiant attempt to raise a new consciousness about and pride in the past. The endorsement of the value of this historic wealth by Western experts undoubtedly played a large part in the endeavor to engrave it in the Ottoman mind-set as another aspect of intellectual progress and modernity.

In comparison to the brevity and sketchy nature of the historical background information, descriptions of the sites in the very same articles were more elaborate and involved, reflecting the authors' personal experiences and impressions. Illustrations, increasing with time in number and with explanatory captions, complemented the descriptions and in some cases even told their own stories. All descriptions began by locating the particular site within its broader geographical region, in terms of its proximity to other landmarks, such as rivers, valleys, and mountains; the nearest inhabited settlements; and the main cities from which it could be accessed. If they happened to be on major new transportation routes, this was underlined. For example, the village of Sard near Sardis was on the İzmir-Afyon railroad line, and the Hijaz railroad passed close to Baalbek.[16]

In interpreting archaeological data, European researchers had produced hypothetical reconstructions—as in the case of the agora in Pergamon, printed on the cover of *Servet-i Fünun* in 1892 (figure 4.1). The accompanying text explained that the view showed the settlement in 233 BC and cautioned readers that the periodical could not attest to its accuracy (literally, "health" or *sıhhat*), despite the fact that it was founded on ideas derived from the antiquities unearthed in the area.[17] A few months later, another piece on Pergamon referred to the same drawing, now indicating that it was done by a member of the German archaeological team that had begun excavation work in 1879 and had revealed many valuable ancient works. The image expressed a splendor difficult to capture from the state of the existing ruins as conveyed in photographs. Yet the prominent exposure of the drawing must have etched the antique site memorably in the minds of the readers. The text described the buildings with "holes in their domes" (*kubbelerinin örtüsü delik bulunan*), the remains from the vast library, and the impressive ruins of the castle on the acropolis, but the "advanced position of Pergamon among early civilizations" was not traceable in them, only in the dazzling rendering.[18]

Even more than Pergamon, the remains of Babylon left a great deal to the imagination, as the present state of the land on which this old city was constructed had only "some ruins, small hills, water scales, and trenches."[19] The reconstruction drawing of the city's "famous walls of gardens," reproduced in *Hamiyet* in 1886, brought a visual dimension to legends about Babylon, even though it may have only belonged to the dream world of the artist (figure 4.2). The extensive use of brick in all buildings was evident on the site, but the strong fortifications with their one hundred bronze gates and 250 castles, surrounded by a moat; the wide arches that carried the vast gardens; and the tall trees grown over the infill land were accessible only through written accounts by various authors.[20] Repeating some of the same information on Babylon in a longer article, *Servet-i Fünun* credited Herodotus, who maintained that the height of the fortifications was 92.5 meters (303.5 ft.) and their width 23 meters (75.5 ft.); between the two rows of fortifications there was enough space for carriages to make U-turns. If Herodotus's words seemed exaggerated, the author insisted that they represented the truth and supported his claim with another ancient philosopher, Philo, who had argued that six carriages could travel side by side on the fortifications. Philo had also written that the interior organization of Babylon was highly orderly and that the streets intersected each other at right angles. Based on textual material, the article in *Servet-i Fünun* continued to report that the two parts of the city, divided by the Euphrates River, belonged to two different eras, the one on the right bank going back to very ancient

فائدة تاريخه دها كوزل ومنقح بر صورتده حاصل ايدلش

اولور • ايته بوخدمتى دخى ايفا المجون (حت) ك

سكرنجى نسخه‌سندن اعتباراً بو'اثار سبعه به تعلق اولان

سورجين واشبو طقوزنجى نسخه‌ده دخى بابل شهرينك

مشهور سور وبنجه‌سى درج اولنمشدر •

عجائب سبعهٔ عالم

(١)

متقدمين عندنده اعظم مصنوعات بشريه‌دن معدود

وهربرى بشـقه بشقه وقايع عجيبه‌يه مستند اولهرق

FIGURE 4.2 Gardens of Babylon, reconstruction drawing. (*Hamiyet* 1, no. 9 [15 Ağustos 1302/August 27, 1886])

times, the one on the left dating from the seventh century BC. The fortifications of the left bank were similar to Egyptian examples; the ones on the right bank included three sets of walls, their heights increasing from the exterior to the interior, hence resembling a pyramid. While the author did not question any of these facts, he expressed his doubts regarding the claims that Babylonians did not know how to construct arches and vaults.[21]

When the ruins could tell more about the original settlement, the descriptions followed the reality on the land in an experiential manner, taking the reader through the city (figure 4.3). Gerasa's 5,800-meter (19,030 ft.)-long fortifications crossed the valley at two points and enclosed a city that was divided by a 916-meter (3,005 ft.)-long straight main street running in a north-south orientation; it was lined by columns, about three to four thousand of which were still in place. The surface was paved in the Roman manner. The main gate was to the north of this avenue, while the round-shaped forum defined by columns was in the south. Another avenue, perpendicu-

جرش خرابه لری

سوریه نك جنوب جهتنده ، شریعه نهری وادیسنك شرق
طرفلرنده قضا مركزی اولان سلطنك شمال شرقیسنده وتقریباً
اوتوز كیلو مترو مسافه سنده وقلعةالزرقاءك شماننده وبورادندن
بته اوتوز كیلو مترو مسافه ده بولنان جرش موقعی شایان دقت
خرابه لری ، قدیماً معمور وبشهرك بقایاسنی حاویدر . بو بلده
قدیمه اسكی یونانلیلر طرفندن تأسیس ایدلمش اولوب اوروبا
كتابلرنده ژراسا (Gerasa) یاد اولنقده در .

یونانستان قدیم صناعتنك آثار متباقیه سنه سوریه نك اكثر
جهتلرنده و اردن نهری حوضه سنده بولنان بلاد قدیمه بقایاسنده
تصادف ایدلمكده اولوب بوجوالیده تصادف اولنان خرابه لرده
یونان معماری قدیمنك ظرافت ونفاستی كوسترزجك كافی آثار
قائمه مشهوددر .

اوروبا سیاحارندن وانارعتیقه وتاریخ منتسبلرندن برقاج ذات
بوخرابه لرده دقیقات اجرا ایتمشلردر . ۱۸۰٦ سنه سنده دوجن؟
و ۱۸۱۰ و۱۸۱۲ تاریخلرنده بوقهارت واحوالیدهكی خرابه لرك
كزهرك بوبلاد قدیمه نك اسكی یونانلیلر طرفندن تأسیس ایدلمش
اولدیغنی اظهار ایلمشلر وبوبلاده لرك تاریخنه دائر خیلی دقیقات
میداننه قوبیلمشلردر .

جرش خرابه لرینك جنوب طرفندن منظره سی

سوریه طرفلرینه قدیم یونانلیلرك شرقی اسكندركیردن
صكره در. بو دوره قدیمده انطاكیه و ، مصر جهتلرنده قدیم یونانلیلرك
تمكن ایتمش بولنوسی سوریه حوالیسنه بهجری تسهیل ایلمشدر .
ابتدا سوریه وفلسطین سواحلندن فلسطینردن وفنیكیلیردن قالمه

جرش خرابه لرنده شمس معبدی

بلاد قدیمه ده براشدكدن صكره یونانلیر داخله طوغرو جكمكه
باشلایه رق بعضی اسكی شهرلری توسیع ایتمك صورتیله بورالرده
تمكن ایتمشلر . یاخود جرش كبی ـ او زمانه كوره ـ یكی شهرلر
تأسیس واحداث ایلمشلردر .

رومالیلر بومیوبوسك قوماندانلیقنده اولهرق بوجوالی یه
كلدكلری زمان یونانلیلرك مؤسساتندن ایلان بلاد ایلشه بیهرك
بونلری ترقی ومعموریتنی ایجاب ایدهجك تدابیر اتخاذ ایلمشلردر .
شریعه نهری حوضه سنده اوزمان تأسیس اولنان شهرلر آره نده
برهنت تشكیل ایدرك بوهجتندن اوروبا تاریخنده ، دهقاپولیس
نامیله وتواریخ اسلامیه ، مدنعشره ، یاد اولنمشدر. مدنعشرهنی
تشكیل ایدن شهرلردن بریده جرش ایدی . الیوم موجوداولان
خرابه لرندن استدلال اولندیغنه كوره جرش وقتیله یك معمور
وبلده ایدی .

رومالیلر زماننده وخرستیانلغك ظهوری صره سنده

FIGURE 4.3 An article on Gerasa, with photographs showing the Temple of the Sun and a general view from the south. (*Servet-i Fünun* 34, no. 882 [6 Mart 1323/March 19, 1907])

lar to this one, cut the city in the east-west direction. A small distance away from the forum, and placed on a hill, a colonnaded temple now in ruins had enjoyed a view of the entire city. Two other temples, one in the proximity of the forum, the other to the west of the main avenue, constituted the main monuments. Their columns were truly elegant, although partially destroyed. Furthermore, the city boasted two theaters, one of which had a total of five thousand seats, surpassing any other theater in the region in scale but also in its "regularity and perfection." The other was dedicated to performances involving "wild animals."[22] The panoramic view showed the entire site, displaying the glory of the settlement.

Miletus, which went back to the eighth–ninth centuries BC and was one of the main commercial centers of the time, boasted four harbors and a

میلت یاخود [میله‌توس'] خرابه‌لرنده تیاترو محلی
[اناطولی‌شاهانه‌ده بولنان اسکی بلده‌لرده حفریات ایله میدانه چیقاریلان تیاترو بنالرینك الكجسیمیدر.]

FIGURE 4.4 Miletus, view of the amphitheater. (*Servet-i Fünun* 35, no. 887 [10 Nisan 1324/April 23, 1908])

100-meter (328 ft.)-long and 11-meter (36 ft.)-wide embankment. Its main avenue was 30 meters (98.4 ft.) wide; a bathhouse and a school were among the buildings along it, and the famous Temple of Apollo stood at its south end. The excavations on this temple, begun in 1899, had revealed its vastness and its elaborately crafted sculptures depicting Apollo and "fairies called 'muses.'" Monuments rich in decoration surrounded the plazas, and with a capacity for twenty-five thousand spectators, Miletus's "perfectly adorned" amphitheater surpassed all ancient theaters in Anatolia. As the accompanying photographs testified, the excavations conveyed the degree of development and architectural stature of this old settlement (figure 4.4).[23]

Again in western Anatolia, Sardis's building remains included a theater, a stadium, baths, a gymnasium, and temples, as well as a basilica from the Byzantine times and fortifications (figure 4.5). Excavations had made it possible to make good sense of the Ionian-style Temple of Artemis, dedicated to the Greek goddess. As a "pseudo-dipteral" type, its shorter façades were lined by two rows of columns, whereas the longer façades had only one

شكل ٥ — آرتميس معبدينك شرقه جبهه‌سى — يافقنده كوردنوسى

شكل ٦ — آرتميس معبدينك شرقه جبهه‌سنده منظره‌سى

FIGURE 4.5 Sardis, views of the Temple of Artemis. (Şehbal [Year 5] 4, no. 86 [15 Teş-rinisani 1329/December 8, 1913])

row. Furthermore, the colonnades of the shorter sides were pulled outward by two columns from the "cella" walls, making the design of the Temple of Artemis unique among the known temples. The two columns, still standing in their original state, were 20 meters (65.6 ft.) tall; other broken ones reached to 9 meters (29.5 ft.). In addition, beautiful Ionic capitals and other fragments, silver objects, and various plaques inscribed in the "Lydian language" were found on the site. Among the latter, one was of "extraordinary scholarly importance," as it included a second language, Aramaic. The excavations had also revealed Persian and Greek-style graves carved into the mountains on the left side of the Paktolos River. The "delicate and rare" artifacts from the graves, now preserved in the Imperial Museum, served as significant documents on the art of jewelry in antiquity.[24]

In a long article, the *Servet-i Fünun* reporter M. Sadık presented Baalbek as consisting of two zones, one constructed under the Phoenicians and Romans, the other (the castle and the mosques) under Arabs. He went through the first section space by space, starting from the main gate, "a gallery of sorts," with its Phoenician walls and Roman-style vaults, and with relief sculptures of Hercules and Diana adorning the vaults; the nature of the decoration gave a clear impression that the stones were put in place first and carved later. The rooms on two sides of this gallery were also decorated skillfully with carvings. The passage led to the main entrance of the temple, which was in a ruinous state. From there, one reached the six-partite hall with rooms in each part, dedicated to priests. Then came the large hall, 112 meters (367.5 ft.) long and 95 meters (311.7 ft.) wide; the reliefs and sculptures in the rooms around it were destroyed. The next space was the Temple of the Sun, the architectural wonder and pride of the city — also much damaged. Of its fifty-eight columns in the Corinthian style that surrounded the façade, only six remained. The Temple of Jupiter to the south of the Temple of the Sun, again delineated by columns on the façades, did not equal the scale and the monumentality of the former. However, architects and antiquity experts considered the Temple of Jupiter the most elegant work of art among all the temple remains in Syria. Aside from this complex, the author wrote about the admirable architectural ingenuity of Arabs evident in the castle, the technological wonders involved in the employment of the vast stones used in the construction of the Temple of Venus, and the mystery of the "single stone" (*seşnekpare*; Europeans described this stone as "cyclopic"), estimated to weigh 1,500,000 kilograms (3,307,000 lbs.).[25]

The Ottoman press reported on the civic art, geometric layouts, impressive hierarchies of main and secondary arteries, and monumental urban spaces of antique settlements with great admiration, associating them with civilization and progress—obsessive pursuits in the late Ottoman Empire. Although not articulated explicitly by the authors, it would not be far-fetched to assume that exposure to these great historic cities would inspire readers to reflect upon the ongoing urban regularization activities and the construction of public buildings in the capital, as well as in all cities of the empire. Starting in the 1860s, a "modern" and technologically advanced practice of urban design, characterized by straight, wide avenues and dotted with open squares had begun changing the fabrics of the old cities. In some cases, as in the widening of Istanbul's main thoroughfare, Divanyolu (the Byzantine *mese*), the links to archaeological remains were obvious, as the interventions valorized historic spaces (for example, the *mese*, the Hippodrome, and the forum in front of Hagia Sophia) and monuments (such as the Column of Constantine) from pre-Ottoman eras. In others, the grids developed outside the old cores (for example, in Damascus and Aleppo) recalled the antique sites in their surrounding geography. These developments constituted some of the main topics in the very same periodicals. Richly illustrated, they presented opportunities to compare contemporary progress with the works of ancient civilizations, including reciprocities between the architectural language of antiquity and the widespread neoclassicism in late-Ottoman architecture.[26]

The attraction of antique ruins for travelers punctuated the value of the heritage and formed another theme. Palmyra had always drawn foreigners, who admired its architecture and wondered how the colossal stones were lifted to such considerable heights. They could get some idea of the prosperity of the city's old civilization from the standing evidence, but attention always turned to the Temple of the Sun.[27] Travel to sites such as Sardis and Baalbek was facilitated by railroad lines, and the financial benefits of tourism were acknowledged; in the case of Baalbek, thousands came every year, spending considerable amounts of money.[28] A new avenue for travel was opened when tourism was oriented toward Ottomans in articles that read like short, inviting travelogues, filled with practical tips. To get to Baalbek, the traveler could take a carriage from Damascus or Beirut and, after a long, rough journey, reach Şatura (Chtaura) in the Baka Valley, famous for its beautiful natural setting and delicious air, in seven hours. After drinking the excellent water and eating the tasty food in the local restaurant, the traveler would hit the road again, passing through a large vineyard on the

FIGURE 4.6 Baalbek, general view. (*Servet-i Fünun* 5, no. 119 [28 Mayıs 1325/June 10, 1909])

mountain slope cultivated by Jesuits and the productive fields of the Baka Valley. As evening approached, the setting sun added further beauty to the changing scenes of the great mountains on both sides, dotted with picturesque villages. The experience was so fulfilling that it could equal a pleasure trip in a rowboat down the Bosporus. As the sun disappeared behind the snow-covered peaks, the small town of Baalbek, complete with its houses, vineyards, gardens, tall trees, and ruins, appeared, as though "under a pink veil" (figure 4.6).[29]

After a delicious dinner at the Hotel Palmyra, including chicken cooked on a coal fire and desserts that combined rich ingredients ranging from pistachios to raisins, and a restful night, the "sweet morning light" woke up the traveler, as it had woken up the city of Baalbek for thousands of years. The excursion to the ruins awed the visitors because of the "progress and prosperity" they broadcast, crystallized in the ornamental carvings and reliefs and the "extraordinary vastness" of the buildings. Travelers, architects, and engineers of "our age of progress and sophisticated machinery and tools" stood before them in wonder, speculating. A French engineer in M. Sadık's party suggested that the huge stones were lifted by the "sloped surface" method, which meant that a hill was built and the stones were carried by hundreds of thousands of workers up the hill to their particular places in the building—a possible, if not proven, explanation, according to the author.

Picking up on his impressions upon approaching Baalbek the previous day, M. Sadık drew another romantic picture of the geographical setting as observed from the top of the entrance on that spring day: in the midst of the emerald-hued gardens that extended throughout the valley and with the Anti-Lebanon Mountains as the backdrop, the monuments in ruins showed the "power of humanity" (*beşeriyetin iktidarı*) amid the beauty of nature.[30]

Adhering to the genre of a travel guidebook, M. Sadık gave facts about the contemporary town as well. Its five thousand inhabitants consisted of Muslims and Christians; among the new Ottoman buildings, the government office and the military barracks stood out; in addition to the Umayyad mosque in ruins, there were other mosques, tombs, and schools; Christians had several churches, but their most striking structure was the English missionary school, with a plaque at the entrance "welcoming everybody." He included a flavor from the human landscape: "innocent and pure village girls" gave small bouquets of flowers to guests. Sadık Bey's voyage to Baalbek was thus completed with the memory of their young, smiling faces offering an interlude to the "philosophical thoughts" invoked by the remains.[31] Tellingly, the author made no reference to the memorial plaque that was hung on the occasion of German emperor Wilhelm II's trip in 1898 on a wall in the Temple of Jupiter. Widely publicized in the press at the time, the event celebrated the Ottoman-German cooperation and the friendship between Wilhelm II and Abdülhamid II.[32] In the climate of the Second Constitutional regime that had overthrown Abdülhamid II, the author's omission was likely intentional, a quiet statement about the regime changes.

An essay on Troy addressed the reader directly and gave straightforward travel tips: "To go to the ruins in Troy, you must tell the carriage drivers in Çanakkale to take you to Hisarlık." The author, Cemal, described the route in detail, which followed the coastline for one hour and thirty minutes and climbed a hill covered with beautiful pine trees, offering a spectacular view of the blue waters of the Dardanelles through the greenery and Çanakkale in the distance and reminding the traveler that this land had been home to many civilizations. After another hour, the carriage would arrive at the village of Eren, where the drivers had the habit of taking a thirty-minute break. The road then went down the hill. Taking a right turn from the paved road, travelers entered the Kumkale plain and in forty-five minutes reached the ruins on a small hill. Unfortunately, there was not much to see, except for a pool believed to date from Roman times, a few broken jugs, and a very deep well. Cemal Bey then gave a brief history of the work done on the site, which had been subjected to numerous excavations and thoroughly searched. The most important of these were by the German explorer Heinrich Schliemann, who had dug 16 meters underground in 1871 and unearthed four different cities built one on top of the other. Not much was known about them except for skeletal facts. The fourth city thus dated to "very ancient times," and the second gave clues about the existence of an advanced civilization (the first and third cities were not mentioned). Around the hill, the foundation stones of the fortifications could be observed. However, the author argued, it seemed unlikely that such a legendary city would have been built only on one hill, and he suggested that this could only have been the location of the palace. The settlement must have surrounded the hill, he speculated, but the area had not been dug yet. The article, passionate about the landscape and neutral, almost disinterested, about the state of the ruins, touched a burning issue that had contributed to the series of laws on antiquities, that is, the issue of looting. In a factual and distanced manner, the author noted that Schliemann had unearthed many antique pieces, among them very rare arms and vases, and had simply taken them away.[33] Curiously, he did not mention the "treasures" and the jewels, which were by then well known through photographs and drawings, published by Schliemann himself.[34]

Reporting on Antiquities Abroad

News pieces from other parts of the world on recently discovered antiquities featured often in the periodicals. In *Servet-i Fünun*, they began appearing from the first year of the publication under the title of "works of antiquity," their lengths limited to a single paragraph in the early days. Not systematic and not necessarily informative, they were fragmented notes addressed to the curious. They did not attempt to establish any connections with the discoveries in the Ottoman lands, but sometimes covered places that hardly made it to the news in any other context, hence helping draw a large world of archaeology. In the Schaffhausen region of Switzerland, excavations had revealed a "considerable number of objects from the old era," valuable for the knowledge they conveyed on the conditions of humanity then;[35] no other explanation was given on these presumably Iron Age remains. A settlement in Caucasus, thought to date from the Sasanian time, was constructed in a large cave and rumored to have many fountains and two- or three-story dwellings. The dreamlike atmosphere was enriched by the stalactites of the natural formations, which glittered under the light of torches.[36] In Tashkent, an excavation had begun on a Scythian site, and fourteen thousand antique objects from Turkistan were sent to the Committee of Antique Works in St. Petersburg. The ruins of a large Aztec settlement in Mexico, discovered during the opening of a canal, consisted of three-story dwellings. Eighteen well-preserved mummies were found on the site as well, altogether offering a good example of the old civilization of the continent, well before the European conquest.[37] In Hungary, three hundred tombs attributed to Hun chevaliers had helmets and arms in them; the faces of the skeletons were turned toward the East. The artifacts were taken to the museum in Budapest.[38] Among the many stones found around the Temple of Dionysus in Athens, one with a relief depicted a sacrificial ceremony. Although it dated from the second or third century AD, several sculptures from the same site belonged to an earlier era.[39] Work on the ruins of Selinunte, Sicily, had resulted in the complete clearing of the inner fortifications, unearthing the plan of the city, which was organized around two large arteries that intersected at right angles. Other important remains, such as the temples of Apollo and Aphrodite and the city gates, had also surfaced. The examination of the stones led to speculations that the inner fortifications were built by local residents prior to the Greek era and that the Greeks had repaired them. The value of the earthenware (pots and statues) found on the site was questionable.[40]

The coverage of some sites deemed more significant acquired more detail. Among these, Egypt and Pompeii stood out. In Egypt, the expedition of the French archaeologist Jacques Jean Marie de Morgan to the Funerary Complex of Dahshur in the vicinity of Memphis for only a few days in 1894 had proven to be much more successful than the work of the former generation of Auguste Mariette and Gaston Maspero. Morgan had cleared one side of the pyramid and revealed a gallery that harbored some sarcophagi, complete with mummies and various objects. Judging from the character of the insignia, the sarcophagi were attributed to the royal family, and they pointed to the likely existence of a much wealthier "treasure" than the present discovery had unearthed. The absence of a large number of valuable objects expected to be found on the site raised again the familiar problem of the looting of antiquities, casually mentioned in the article. What had escaped the eyes of the looters included gold jewelry and precious stones; these priceless objects were taken to the museum in Cairo (a list was included at the end of the article). The author commented on their sociocultural implications: the exquisitely crafted ornaments of the Egyptian gentry showed that four thousand years ago, women were as obsessed with embellishing themselves as they were at the end of the nineteenth century.[41]

The order and the wealth of Pompeii impressed the visitors to this two-thousand-year-old settlement. Thanks to the hard work and generosity of the Italian government, the houses, streets, and official buildings were cleared from the ashes, and an electric tram connected the site to Naples, facilitating tourism. The most amazing revelation was the regularity of all the streets, as they formed a complete iron grid with no crooked thoroughfares among them, even though some were narrower than others. Furthermore, they were lined with sidewalks that sloped from the sides toward the middle to facilitate the flow of water. The organization of the houses recalled that of ones in Damascus: the entrance gate opened to a corridor, which led to a garden or a patio surrounded by rooms. The windows faced this interior open space; there was no fenestration on the outer façades. The dwellings were adorned with marble statues and columns, crafted with refined taste and artistry; discovered during the excavation, they were taken to the Naples Museum. Municipal offices and Roman baths similar to baths in the East could also be identified in the urban fabric, even though their domes had collapsed. Nevertheless, it was the courts that surprised the writer. He argued that no European contemporary courthouse could equal their "perfection."[42]

News from archaeological discoveries in other parts of the world were not linked to the scene at home. Even so, interested readers must have made the associations on their own. At the time that corresponded to the opening of the Imperial Museum, modern European museums did not feature much in the Ottoman journals, and when they did, they were covered only briefly. Similar to the archaeological news from elsewhere, no comparisons were made and no judgments were passed. Two examples from the early years of *Servet-i Fünun* were on the French museums Versailles and the Louvre, glorifying them in generic vocabulary. The museum at Versailles, occupying one part of the palace, was singled out as unique in the world due to the historic prominence of the palace. The short paragraph mentioned the gardens, the ponds, and the waterworks and concluded with a sentence that sent the reader to a travelogue titled *Avrupa'da Ne Gördüm* (What I Saw in Europe).[43] The exposé on the Louvre began with a description of the buildings, giving approximate chronologies and dividing the complex into the "old" and the "new" Louvre, adding that the entire palace was now a museum that people could visit without paying a fee. The museum was so huge that it was impossible to tour it without a plan, and it would take two hours to simply meander through the various halls without stopping to examine the art. The first level sheltered "marble statues and famous antiquities of this sort." With an intellectually dismissive rationale that to comprehend their textual explanations would require close familiarity with the science of archaeology, the author found it useless to give details on the artworks here and cut his account short. He felt compelled, however, to add that the Egyptian section was the most important among the European museums. He added that it would be absurd to even attempt to give information on the entire Egyptian collection in a short article; the important point was that they represented a highly developed society and illustrated its customs and lifestyles. The author completed his tour by surveying the remaining galleries, emphasizing in the jewelry hall on the first floor the superior degree of craftsmanship that had been reached during antiquity. His interest was drawn particularly to the marine museum on the second floor, which displayed, among other things, accurately built models of boats and of military and commercial ports throughout French history.[44]

The author of the travelogue *Avrupa'da Ne Gördüm*, cited in *Servet-i Fünun*, was Ahmed İhsan, the editor of the journal. His 588-page book had been published in 1891, a few months before these articles. Ahmed İhsan's account of his voyage to different European cities is remarkable in many ways and merits a discussion centered on its coverage of European museums. The book's tone is informal, as though the author was in conversation with the reader. The narrative followed a map that charted his route, giving learned information on the history of various places, and day-by-day entries described the structural character and urban forms of particular cities, that is, the primary and secondary streets (down to street furniture), transportation networks, public parks, housing patterns, and the main buildings. He also provided useful tips that would benefit tourists on hotels, restaurants, cafés, and entertainment venues. Ahmed İhsan interlaced history with present-day social and cultural life and illustrated all his highlights with etchings from photographs. His commitment to culture and fine arts became evident in the sections dedicated to museums, classified under "main buildings." Significantly, on his first stop in Europe, he visited the museum in the Palais Longchamps in Marseille. For him, this was the "most perfect" edifice in the city, located in a large and lush garden — "like a forest" — boasting vegetation from different parts of France and a wonderful pond at the entrance. The two doors of the palace led to two museums:

FIGURE 4.7 *The Copyist in the Louvre*, drawing by Charles Stanley Reinhart, published in *Harper's Weekly*, January 4, 1890. This would be the kind of scene Ahmed İhsan encountered in the French museums. (Library of Congress, Cabinet of American Illustration)

the museum of fine arts, filled with exquisite paintings, and the even more impressive museum of natural sciences. In the fine arts section, he observed with curiosity many young women making copies of the paintings. Yet, he added, he became familiar with this scene as he visited other European museums and concluded that it was "an ordinary affair" (figure 4.7).[45]

Ahmed İhsan had excerpted his description of the Louvre in *Avrupa'da Ne Gördüm* anonymously and without any changes in *Servet-i Fünun*; the only difference was in the inclusion of an interior view in the book (figure 4.8).[46] In London, he could not resist the temptation to visit Madame Tussauds, but he also spent a considerable time in the British Museum. The account introduced the latter museum, originating from a generous gift from Hans Sloane to the government (an act that had clearly impressed Ahmed İhsan) and supplemented by the British government's initiative to bring rare artworks from various palaces. The enormous efforts up to the present day had culminated in the well-deserved international reputation of the museum. After listing its different parts, the author proceeded to describe the various halls, starting at the entrance. He summarized his observations in a few mechanical and noncommittal phrases, such as: "We toured the 'Rome' and 'Ancient Greece' sections and looked at the old and rare works from those eras; we then visited the Phoenician, Assyrian, ancient Egypt, [and] Iranian works ... with great attention." The Ethnography (*alem-i en-*

لوور موزه‌سنده آپولو صالونی

FIGURE 4.8 The Louvre Museum, Hall of Apollo. (Ahmed İhsan, *Avrupa'da Ne Gördüm*, 98)

sab) Gallery pleased him the most in its displays of the costumes and every-day utensils of people from all over the world. Curiously ignoring the much-discussed Elgin Marbles, the showpiece of the museum, he kept quiet on the origins of these pieces and their transportation to London. Ahmed İh-san was not prepared for the glamorous library in the museum, which sur-prised him with its beautiful hall and 1.5 million books, not counting the 80,000 extremely rare books; he remarked that every year another 30,000 volumes were added. Dedicating his longest description to the library, he specified that permits were issued to researchers, and during the time of his visit, about 150 were immersed in their studies (figure 4.9).[47]

Ahmed İhsan's excitement over the library and the ethnographic displays could perhaps be explained in terms of his experience in similar institu-tions in the Ottoman Empire. The brand-new Imperial Museum in Istan-bul had familiarized him with the norms of a museum of antiquities, and the illustrated articles he was publishing on that museum in *Servet-i Fü-nun* were charged with the mission of disseminating information about the institution. Yet the Imperial Museum's library was still an ongoing project (see figure 1.10). Another remarkable contribution by Osman Hamdi to late-nineteenth-century Ottoman culture, this elegant space would be fre-quented by only a handful of scholars, echoing the usage of the museum as

FIGURE 4.9 The British Museum, Reading Room; drawing from Edward Edwards, *Memoirs of Libraries*, London, 1859. (Library of Congress, Prints and Photographs)

a whole. As Istanbul did not have any comparable public libraries, Ahmed İhsan seems to have capitalized on the British Library to send a message to his readers, who would have appreciated similar institutions. The closest the Ottoman capital came to an ethnography collection was the "janissaries" section in the Collection of Antique Weapons (Mecma-i Asar-ı Atika), the predecessor of the Imperial Museum, founded in 1846 by Ahmed Fethi Pasha and housed in the church of Hagia Eirene. In addition to displaying the weapons used by the Ottoman army in a chronological order, Ahmed Fethi Pasha, the marshal of the Imperial Arsenal (Tophane-i Amire Müşhiri) and the former ambassador to Vienna and Paris, had ordered 140 mannequins made out of plaster, depicting janissaries of various ranks. Shown engaged in mundane activities and wearing costumes made in Vienna, these figures soon became the most popular part of the military collection. They made a statement about the historical importance of the janissary corps, while reminding the viewers that its abolition in 1826 stood as a symbol of the army's modernization.[48] With its narrow focus, the collection was clearly not comparable to the British Museum's Ethnography Gallery.

In Berlin, Ahmed İhsan visited the museum complex, and pursuing the same format as in the other cities he toured, described the setting and the relationship of the buildings to each other, and gave basic data on their foundation dates and sizes. Of the three, he spent more time in the Altes

Museum, duly admiring the groundbreaking architecture of Karl Friedrich Schinkel but glossing over the collections and referring his readers to the authority of the Baedeker guide, which he had consulted for specific information on each object. For the first and only time during his visits to museums of antiquity, he voiced in the Altes Museum a few words about the places of origin of the displayed pieces: as he slowly walked through the galleries, he noticed in one "very many antique works found and excavated from Pergamon in the province of İzmir."[49] This distanced and aloof acknowledgment of European looting of antiquities from Ottoman lands is difficult to interpret, especially because it gives a glimpse of Ahmed İhsan's awareness of the issue. Nevertheless, his matter-of-fact reporting may still have had a powerful effect on readers in light of the antiquities laws, and especially the 1884 law. The case of the German appropriation of antiquities from Pergamon had indeed played a role in identifying the deficiencies in the 1874 law and clearing the way for tighter measures. Cleverly using the legislation that stipulated the three-part division of the archaeological pieces found on the site between the owner of the property, the excavator, and the Imperial Museum, the German archaeologist Carl Humann had bought the property, increasing his share to two-thirds; he then used personal connections in the Ottoman government to conceal the real value of the discoveries, and managed to avoid sending one-third to the museum in Istanbul.[50] Content with his maneuvering, Humann stated that "scientific research" had unearthed a very rich body of material in Pergamon and the royal museums were enriched by these great treasures.[51] He had thus transported the finds to Berlin, where Ahmed İhsan saw them.

Ahmed İhsan's accounts of the fora in Rome explained the ancient public spaces in an amusing manner, attributing them to the rivalry between emperors, with every new emperor overpowering the forum built by his predecessor in the size and luxury of his own contribution. In his opinion, the resulting complex of fora revealed the vast sums spent on these imperial projects, but their historical value did not match that of the original (republican) forum (figure 4.10).[52] If Ottoman readers expected some parallels to fragments from the same era that dotted the fabric of Istanbul, they did not find them in this book. A link would be made two decades later in *Şehbal* in a short article on the 35-meter (115 ft.)-tall column of Arcadius, erected by the emperor in honor of his father, Theodosius, on a forum known by his own name in "new Rome." Just like Trajan's Column in "old Rome," the one in Constantinople was decorated with reliefs that narrated the famous

FIGURE 4.10 The Roman Forum. (Ahmed İhsan, *Avrupa'da Ne Gördüm*, 505)

wars fought by Theodosius. Damaged in an earthquake, it now stood only 6 meters (19.7 ft.) tall in a neighborhood called "woman's market," where formerly women slaves were sold.[53]

Two decades later than Ahmed İhsan's travelogue, Nazmi Ziya, an Ottoman artist then living in Paris, drew a broad-brush picture of museums and various exhibition halls in Paris with an agenda centered on the role of the state in sponsoring artists and popularizing fine arts for the education and refinement of the public. Stating at the outset that fine arts enhanced the "progress of a nation" and that European governments invested generously in the arts, he added that every European city had a museum, and large cities, more than one. In all corners of France and in Paris, museums opened their doors to the public for free. In other countries, for example in England and Germany, there was not a single small town without a "more or less acceptable" (*iyi kötü*) museum and a library. The glaring example of this government "sacrifice" was the Louvre, which occupied one of the largest buildings in the world right in the center of Paris. The government could have chosen to collect huge taxes from this prime real estate, but, turning its attention instead to "historic and national values," it spent large sums on the museum administration, staff, and maintenance, not including acquisitions. Nazmi Ziya then explained in detail the contemporary art exhibitions in the Grand Palais and the Petit Palais. However, his article included general references to historic "fine arts" as well. He maintained that his goal in presenting the Parisian museums was not to make a simplistic call for "This is the way it is done in France, so we must as well," but rather to acknowledge realistically "our deprivation and underdevelopment" and to work and "sacrifice" to improve the fine arts. He concluded that the government should be held responsible to support culture and fine arts, as Ottomans were more advanced in these fields than "other nations on our level."[54]

A Shift in Focus: The Ottoman Heritage

Upon Osman Hamdi's passing in 1910, his younger brother Halil Edhem took over the directorship of the Imperial Museum. As passionate as his brother about the past, Halil Edhem's main interests were in the Ottoman heritage and the pitiful state of some of the monuments at the time. In a series of richly illustrated articles for Şehbal, he brought his concerns to readers under the now-familiar subtitle of "antique works," choosing many case studies from a range of buildings, some more modest than others. He wrote about the lovely kiosks built by various powerful pashas in the outer gardens of Topkapı Palace for sultans. Most of these had already been destroyed due to the "passage of time," but the Sinan Pasha kiosk, built in 997 (1588) for Sultan Mahmud at the tip of the peninsula, "one of the most beautiful and esteemed locations on earth," was still standing, albeit in a ruinous state (figure 4.11). Halil Edhem documented it with haunting photographs and asked two overarching questions: "Do we know the value of our national and historic works?" and "Shall we ever see this area reflect the prosperity it enjoyed three centuries ago?" Articulated in the language of the Second Constitutional regime, but also rooted in the financial realities of the time, he knew well that restoration projects would not be undertaken, but he continued to hope.[55] The royal boathouses, also part of the Topkapı Palace, were being demolished, and soon this "important part of old Istanbul," at the mouth of the Golden Horn, would disappear completely, together with the boats that belonged to sultans and mothers of sultans. Several photographs showed examples from the exquisite collection in their sad state, the images calling for an urgent appeal to stop the destruction process (figure 4.12).[56]

منارۀ پاشا کورشکۀ مشتمل اولوپ وسایطانۀ مراد خانه ثالثك نائی محتوی بولو نانه خراب جشمه
(موزه مدیری خلیل بك افندینك مقالۀ لرینه عاطف)

آثار ملیه وتاریخیه مزایۀ قیمتی بیلو ورمیز ؟

FIGURE 4.11 A fountain in ruins from the Sinan Pasha kiosk. (*Şehbal* [Year 4] 3, no. 60 [1 Eylül 1328/September 14, 1912])

بدی حقنة نبریل قایغی ایله والده سلطانه خصوصی كوشككلی قایق

كوشككلی سلطنت قایغی .

سلطان محمود ثانی هفرتاریده عطف اولرنانه كوشككلی قایق .

خان و سلطان عبدالعزيز خان حضرتيـله
والـ.ه ساطان علیة الشأنه مخصوص كوشكلی
وتبـديل قایقلری وصوك كوزده ايبه داها
كوجك جاید»، فقط كوشكلی ديكر . قایق
بولوتقده ايدی كه بوك سلطان محد خان
ثانی زمانه عادۀ اولدیغی روایت ایدیلمكـدهـدر.
فی الواقع نوزده‌ڭ مزینافده بر دره
جهبه قدر اعصری ایما ایدهن. داآ خراب
اولان بوقایق بنلك اثنای هدمنده‌بوس‌بوتون
پارجه‌لانذغندن بر جهه تعمیره محتجدر .
نه یالان سویلهیم ، عادات وصنایع

ابتدربلشدر. كتابه‌لك نوستنده سلطان سلیم
ثالث طغراسی و آلتنده اوجاغه معتبردار بر
علامت فارقه‌اولق نوزه‌ره كوشكلی برخنكار
قایغی قارنا اولارق حكوكدر . داخلا مكلف
مطبخ وحمام خرابه‌لری وفوقانی متعدد اوطه
وقوغوشلری و بر مسجدی واردی . قایـدن
كبرینلجه صول‌طرفده غایت جسیم ایكی كوز
قایقخانه‌دن رنجیسنده ایكی سلطنت قایغی
وایكنجیسنده قدیم قادرغا بولو نوردی .
بو تاریخی سفینه‌ه قادرغا دیبوب
كیدیلورز. ارباب وقوفدن بعض كیمسه‌لربونك

Significantly, far-flung places in Anatolia and humble survivors of Ottoman heritage began to appear in the Istanbul periodicals. Among them were a sixteenth-century mosque in Ezine (a small town in the northern Aegean region, not far from Troy), known among the residents as the "Mosque of Olive Trees" (Zeytinli Camii) due to its location in the middle of an olive orchard; the fourteenth-century mausoleum of Ahi Yunus and a *tekke* (Sufi convent) for his followers; and the tombs of two princes from the seventeenth century, not noted previously.[57] The simplicity of the accompanying drawings emphasized their vernacular and sad condition (figure 4.13). Halil Edhem also turned to Anatolia to build some of his strongest arguments. He made a convincing case centered on Konya (central Anatolia), pointing to the fact that the city boasted over sixty buildings of "Islamic antiquity" and each carried a unique historic or artistic importance. Konya's architectural heritage encompassed the Ottoman, Seljuk, and Byzantine periods, sometimes entangled with each other—as in the case of the thirteenth-century Alaeddin Mosque, arguably built on the remains of a Byzantine church in

The Ottoman Reading Public and Antiquities • 121

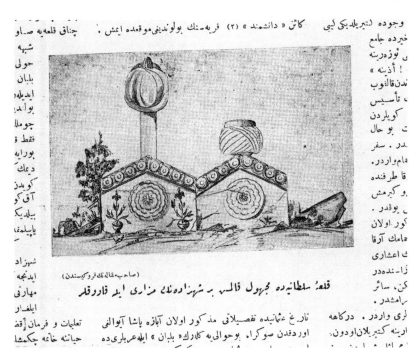

FIGURE 4.13 A prince's tomb in Ezine, near Troy. (*Şehbal* [Year 4] 3, no. 58 [1 Ağustos 1912/August 14, 1912])

the Citadel. The mosque's mihrab tiles and decorative carvings had been partially restored, and its ebony *minbar* was taken to the Imperial Museum in Istanbul. After giving details on different sections of the mosque, Halil Edhem expressed his observations on the general state of the Citadel zone, which had been a glorious sight, dotted with mansions, until two hundred years ago. However, indifference had led to the failure to preserve them, and even the legendary kiosk of Alaeddin had been destroyed "before our very eyes."

The next set of monuments Halil Edhem discussed were in and around Konya: the thirteenth-century Karatay Medresesi (which he called *dar el-fünun*, "university") and Karatay Hanı on the road to Kayseri, and the thirteenth-century works of architecture built under the patronage of Sahib Ata, a powerful Seljuki vizier. Of Sahib Ata's many endowments in Anatolia, Halil Edhem identified İnce Minareli Medrese (literally, "the madrassa with the thin minaret") as a crossroads between Seljuk art and Ottoman art and elaborated on its architecture and decoration, adding that its once very high minaret was demolished during a thunderstorm in 1319 (1903), leaving only

اسلاف اسلامك آثار نفیسه‌سی آراسنده برسیاحت

FIGURE 4.14 İnce Minareli Medrese, Konya. (*Şehbal* [Year 4] 3, no. 59 [15 Ağustos 1328/August 28, 1912])

the present-day squat part in place (figure 4.14). Halil Edhem concluded his article with concerns echoing the ones he had expressed when discussing the state of some buildings from the Ottoman era in Istanbul:

> ... here as elsewhere in our country, consideration of the regrettable condition of old buildings causes deep anxiety. Time passes, no serious initiatives are passed to prevent them from demolition. . . . [A]mong the laws our government passes should be one on the "conservation of national heritage." There is no time left: the most beautiful and the noblest sacred buildings are being ruined day by day.[58]

Halil Edhem outlined his perspectives on "our national antiquities" again in the pages of *Şehbal*, hence appealing to a group of readers already accustomed to articles on the physical remains of heritage. He brought together his records of the extent of historic works in danger of disappearing through neglect, his personal commitment, and the role the government should assume. Addressing his audience in an intimate tone, and hoping they would understand the sincerity of his message, he noted that within a span of two years, he had visited different parts of the country at least once and sometimes twice, examined the buildings together with the objects in them, and taken their photographs. He gave examples, choosing his first exposé from a sixteenth-century mosque designed by the revered Ottoman architect Sinan, the Çoban Mustafa Pasha Mosque in Gebze. Halil Edhem had studied and recorded it with photographs, being especially interested in the four bronze candlesticks, fabricated in Egypt and "exceptionally valuable." Paying a visit to the same mosque complex two years later, he was struck by their absence. He sent his photographs to the Ministry of Pious Foundations, asking for an investigation. He went on in dismay: "Of course, they were not found. Who knows in which museum or antique shop they are now?" Two ivory Koran cases (*mushaf-ı şefif şandukas, coffrets à* Quran) decorated with ebony, made by the architect Ahmed Usta of Egypt, were in the process of rotting. Many other mosques and mausoleums, equipped with similar rare and elegant old lanterns and candlesticks from Egypt, Syria, and Elcezire (Sudan), were all in danger. Two candlesticks from a mosque in Niğde were put in an auction by its trustees; they were saved by a (rather unusual) complaint from a "foreign" (*gavur*) soldier.[59]

The early mausoleums, dispersed throughout central Anatolia, displayed a variety of architectural styles and carried unique importance for the "stylistic history of our ancient architecture." Unfortunately, their deterioration was beyond belief. A lovely square-shaped mausoleum from 629 (1231) near Sivas had fallen into ruins only because the sum of 4,000–5,000 piasters could not be found for its restoration; a few remnants from its mosque were rotting away in the Sivas high school. The mausoleum of Bedreddin in Ilgın, which would require only a small budget for repairs, was also left to its destiny, as was another one from 745 (1345) in Niğde.[60]

Other building types shared their sad destiny. Among them was the *imaret* in Karaman and, next to it, the mausoleum of Karamanoğlu İbrahim Bey. Even in their present state, a guard would have helped stop their total demise. In an unusual acknowledgment of vernacular preservation, Halil Edhem recalled meeting a "poor old man" who resided in the mausoleum and who guarded it without getting paid; upon his death, the delicately carved plaster tombs were broken up in a cruel way. He believed Konya was the most damaged city. Despite the 1,500 piasters invested by the government for the repairs of Beyhekim Mosque, it was too late to save it; its unequaled tile mihrab was now replaced by a "mud" one, its interior looked as if there had been a fire, and even its prayer rugs were stolen. The last remainder of the magnificent palaces in the Konya Citadel, Alaeddin Kiosk had

FIGURE 4.15 Two pages from Halil Edhem's article on the ruined state of various monuments in Anatolia, the photographs showing a range of examples. (*Şehbal* [Year 2], no. 36 [15 Mart 1327/March 30, 1911])

been so damaged that the final desperate efforts to salvage came to naught, as it collapsed totally during the rebuilding. Examples were endless: the state of the thirteenth-century Sahibiye Medresesi brought tears to one's eyes; the wooden sarcophagi, superb samples of Islamic art, were stolen from the mausoleums of Seyyid Mahmud and İbrahim Pasha in Akşehir.[61] Halil Edhem substantiated his claims about all the buildings and the artifacts he mentioned with photographs he had taken personally, carefully composed and distributed on the three pages of text (figure 4.15).

Halil Edhem attributed a main problem to the "strange habit" of entrusting a historic building to one caretaker, who may or may not be available when a visitor showed up. Nevertheless, these individuals were so poorly paid that they should be excused for not doing their jobs properly. In some cases, a huge complex, such as the Sahib Ata complex consisting of a madrassa, a large mosque, a mausoleum, and a *zaviye* (convent) was put under the responsibility of one man, making it impossible for him to adequately carry out the task of protection. Consequently, the buildings were completely looted. Common sense would have dictated two or three guards on duty day and night. Halil Edhem ended his article with a general reminder that all corners of the empire, even villages stretching from Edirne to Iraq, Syria, and Palestine, housed valuable historic works. There was only one action to be taken before their inevitable demise: a new law aimed at their preservation.[62]

The looting of Islamic antiquities was not only on Halil Edhem's mind. The architect Mukbil Kemal dedicated an entire article to the topic, positing it as one of the "moral and social" troubles of the country. He compared the responses to art theft in Europe and in the Ottoman Empire, favorably for the former, where in the case of a reported theft from a museum, the national press would disseminate the news, security forces would be called on to comb through the whole country, and telegraphs would notify foreign governments, asking for their cooperation. The situation at home was diametrically opposite. For example, a mosque, much admired for its beautiful Kütahya tiles, would be targeted by thieves of Islamic antiquities; quick research would reveal the nights the building would be empty; entering it at that time, a group of expert workers would remove the tiles without damaging them, put them carefully into sacks and crates, and after this hourslong operation, take them away. "Where to?" the architect asked, and his reply was "Where else? ... to European museums." Indeed, he concluded, most Islamic artifacts displayed in European museums today had been accumulated by "the looting method."[63]

Like Halil Edhem, Mukbil Kemal wrote about the widespread nature of the problem throughout the Ottoman Empire. He cited a letter that described the consequences of urban interventions in Aleppo: during the widening of a road, many old houses, their ceilings and walls decorated with beautiful paintings and inscriptions, were demolished, but the artwork on the ceilings was taken down in pieces, without any damage. While they would have made an invaluable contribution to the Museum of Pious Foundations in Istanbul, there was no doubt they would end up in the hands of foreigners, who were already in the process of bargaining with the owners. During the same renovation operation, a historic fountain was broken down. The director of the Education Department was able to remove a few stones, which were taken to the Imperial High School in Aleppo. The architect bemoaned the missed opportunity to reconstruct the fountain in the gardens of the Museum of Pious Foundations. The looting had indeed escalated in the Aleppo region, he continued, and foreigners stole every beautiful tombstone and every piece of railing from old tombs, a process facilitated by locals eager to make quick gains. Alas, the new and extensive railroads served this "illegal trade" well, as they smoothly allowed the transportation of the stolen objects to European museums, whereas in the past, their removal and transportation would have been noticed more readily and reported to the authorities.[64]

Halil Edhem and Mukbil Kemal's shared passion for Ottoman and pre-Ottoman Islamic art and architecture, almost at the expense of classical antiquity, was a timely development connected to the change in political power. The Second Constitutional regime differed from the Hamidian era in its investment in nationalism, echoed in the agenda and language of the discourse that associated Islamic works with the new official ideology. The Ottoman claim to classical antiquity could be explained in part by the effort to bring the empire into parity with Western modernity and, in particular, by Osman Hamdi's own investment and participation in contemporary archaeological scholarship. Under Osman Hamdi, the Imperial Museum sheltered some objects from the empire's Islamic era, but they remained peripheral to the main collection. Halil Edhem maintained the agenda of the Imperial Museum, but pulled the Islamic collections to the Museum of Pious Foundations.

The Museum of Pious Foundations may have eerily harked back to Salomon Reinach's call to Osman Hamdi in 1883 to abandon spending huge sums on classical antiquity, leave that heritage to Europeans culturally rooted in it, and valorize instead the Islamic heritage that truly belonged to Ottomans.[65] However, it was the product of other key developments in the empire and outside, that is, the establishment of a museum culture; the passage of laws regarding the antiquities; the inevitable, if slow, inclusion of Islamic works in the Imperial Museum; the interest of foreign collectors; and the change in the political atmosphere. In an evaluation of the Museum of Pious Foundations after its first five years, Ahmed Cemal marked it as a turning point in the conservation and exhibition of Islamic arts. The shift was from an old "Turkish practice," which centered on the donation of valuable artifacts to mausoleums, libraries, and sacred buildings — rather different from European "museum methods." As these were public buildings, the artifacts were viewed by many people.[66] However, their current decrepit conditions showed the abuse they were subjected to and facilitated their looting. They belonged in protected museum settings.

Osman Hamdi had succeeded in introducing the concept of a European-style museum into the "Turkish mentality" with the Imperial Museum. The Museum of Pious Foundations followed suit. On a larger scale, it reflected a global phenomenon: nation-states had been willing to spend great sums on the acquisition of Greek and Roman antiquities for their museums earlier in the century, but "national" antiquities had soon found their places in either specialized museums or departments within the existing ones.[67] Four years after the foundation of the Museum of Pious Foundations, an article evaluated its status. During this short span, the museum had been endowed with valuable and rare historic artworks collected from various mosques, mausoleums, *zaviyes*, and libraries; more could be gathered from the provinces by relegating the selection to officers of the Ministry of Pious Foundations (Nezaret-i Evkaf). In its current form, the museum occupied a building in the Süleymaniye Külliye, and the contents included rugs, china, pottery, sarcophagi, and various tools and devices, as well as several decorative panels and a model of the Yeni Camii in Istanbul (some of them transported from the Islamic collections in the Imperial Museum). Unique among the other museums of the capital, namely the Imperial Museum, the Topkapı Museum, and the Military Museum, the Museum of Pious Foundations could become one of the most beneficial cultural institutions, especially with a better classification system.[68]

A Literary Episode: Sardanapalus from London to Istanbul

Arguing for broadening the sources for the history of archaeology beyond the texts of travelers and explorers, Michael Seymour emphasizes that "it is important that the history of archaeology is one of intellectual development as well as physical exploration" before he delves into a detailed study of literary works that converged on Babylon.[69] Intertwined with the new interest in Mesopotamia and the gradual filling of the major European museums with objects from Mesopotamian civilizations, artists and writers engaged in metaphorical uses of Sardanapalus, the doomed Assyrian King. *The Death of Sardanapalus*, Eugène Delacroix's monumental painting (1827), and the best known among the many Sardanapaluses of the time, represented an Eastern monarch as he took all his entourage with him to his disastrous end and stood for a decadent Orient in ruins, reiterating one of the favorite themes of Orientalist discourse.[70] In music, Hector Berlioz's cantata *La dernière nuit de Sardanapale* (1830) and operas by Franz Liszt (1845–1852), Victorin de Joncières (1867), and Victor-Alphonse Duvernoy (1884), all titled *Sardanapale*, brought the story of the last Assyrian king to the stage. Nevertheless, the pioneering Sardanapalus was Lord [George Gordon] Byron's play (1821) by the same name, and it is commonly credited as the source for the surge of interest in the story in various artistic productions.[71]

The Ottoman playwright Abdülhak Hamid started writing his version of *Sardanapal* in 1876 during the heyday of this European passion, although it was published much later, in 1919. In a career that drew upon a range of historic figures, it is not surprising that Sardanapalus entered the repertoire of Abdülhak Hamid's plays.[72] On diplomatic mission to various European countries (as well as India) and well versed in European cultures, the author must have been inspired by Byron's play. However, his manipulation of the characters and the events has other interpretations, and the structure of his play is quite different from Byron's. While Byron's Sardanapalus is a gentle, tired, self-indulgent, and effeminate soul not drawn to the violent pastimes of his compatriots and ancestors but a symbol of the demise of the Eastern power, Abdülhak Hamid's Sardanapal is representative of absolute authoritarianism and was used to criticize the Ottoman Sultans Abdülaziz (r. 1861–1876) and Abdülhamid II (r. 1876–1909).

A literary comparison of Byron's and Abdülhak Hamid's plays falls beyond the scope of this book and has been lucidly achieved by İnci Erginün.[73] Due to the accessibility of Mesopotamian artifacts in the British Museum in London and the Imperial Museum in Istanbul, as well as the dissemination of visual information through illustrations in various publications in both contexts, the links between the two plays provide an unusual angle to the penetration of Mesopotamian antiquities into nineteenth-century cross-cultural exchanges.

When Byron wrote his play, not much was known about Mesopotamian antiquities. The whole scene changed with the publication of Austen Henry Layard's *Nineveh and Its Remains* in 1849, followed by the significant acquisitions brought to the British Museum. It should therefore not come as a surprise that the sets Byron described in 1821 were sketchy. For example, Act I took place simply in "A Hall in the Palace"; Act II was in front of "the portal of the same Hall of the Palace"; in Act III, "the Hall of the Palace [was] Illuminated"; Act IV opened with "Sardanapalus sleeping upon a couch"; and the play ended in Act V in "the same Hall." When Charles Kean staged the play at the Princess Theatre in London in 1853, he had a lot more to work with in terms of stage design, as "he had been permitted to link together the momentous discoveries of one renowned Englishman [Layard] with the poetic labors of another," in his own words. He claimed to have "diligently sought for the *truth*" in his use of "the costume, architecture, and customs of the ancient Assyrian people, verified by the bas reliefs ..."[74]

Charles Calvert's sumptuous production at Booth Theater in New York also relied on Layard's discoveries. In the 1876 edition of the play, which was published on the occasion of this production, Calvert substituted the ambiguity of Byron's sets with precise detail. He made the point clearly in his introduction:

> The luxurious reign and tragic end of Sardanapalus, chronicled in the magic lines of Byron, have now the proof of history, and the astonishing discoveries recently made and now progressing on the banks of the ancient Tigris give an additional interest to this work.... Our museums contain many of the sculptured slabs, scorched and calcined by the fire that ended the Assyrian Empire.[75]

Calvert explained that to create a "successful stage representation," he "studiously labored to give it a setting worthy of its merit," gratifying at the same time "the student of art and history" through the representation of "the surpassing splendor of [Assyria's] regal life, its wealth, and early glory; its high, though remote civilization." He acknowledged the help of George Smith (of the Department of Oriental Antiquities at the British Museum), who had offered his expertise in the design of the scenery.[76] Act I showed "the Royal Palace of Nineveh, from the opposite bank of the Tigris, the forepart of the stage represent[ing] a Terrace in the Pleasure Gardens." Along the way he moved the sets from the Euphrates to the Tigris and corrected Byron's error—as Kean had done before him. He explained in a note that the scene was from Layard's *Nineveh*, relying on "that eminent authority to convey a general idea of the exterior appearance of the palace as it stood on the platforms washed by the river Tigris." He added that the set was constructed by using the plans and drawings of the remains and gave further details to punctuate its authenticity: the tower in the distance was the tomb of the king, the small building beneath the tomb was a temple, and the replica palace showed some of the "principal Assyrian sculptures, now so highly prized in the British Museum."[77] The same claim to integrate scholarship into stage design surfaced in Act II, now duplicating the "Summer Palace, called the Pavilion":

This scene is a restoration from actual remains and from fragments discovered in the ruins. The paneling of sculptured alabaster slabs covered with inscriptions in the cuneiform character, and the entrances formed by the winged human-headed hons, still existing entire in some of the buildings uncovered.

A reference to Layard about the painted nature of the bas-reliefs and sculptures, as well as the ornaments of the plastered walls, strengthened the claim to historical faithfulness.[78]

The "Hall of the Palace" in Act III was made more specific by Calvert as "the Grand Hall of Nimrod," in its "luxurious splendor," where the alabaster steps led to "various thrones" of crystal, ivory, and gold. The roof was constructed of inlaid cedar beams and "supported by huge winged lions with human heads." The specification of "illumination" in Byron was realized by "suspended lamps and large censors of burning fragrant incense." An opening in the back showed "in perspective the long wing of the Palace and part of the city of Nineveh, by moonlight."[79] In its entirety, the sets complemented Layard's imaginary construction of the dream palace on the banks of the Tigris, itself curiously accepted as scholarly.[80] They even went further and brought the Orientalist fantasies in three dimensions to broader audiences.

From the date Abdülhak Hamid started to write his play to its final publication, he lived on and off in various European capitals, and considering his keen interest in history, it is reasonable to assume that he must have visited the major museums, acquiring some familiarity with the Mesopotamian artifacts. The Mesopotamian collections in the Imperial Museum had also expanded during these decades, again allowing the speculation that the author may have spent some time studying the wealth of the museum in his hometown. If originally he may have been inspired by the London productions, his personal firsthand encounters with the objects must have played some role in the richness of the sets he described in *Sardanapal*. In fact, Abdülhak Hamid's *Sardanapal* shifts scenes twelve times, each one depicting a different image inside and outside the palace, while extending over a longer time span than Byron's tragedy, which takes place in one day.[81]

Abdülhak Hamid's sets varied in detail. The play opens in a state office in Babylon, followed by a moonlit outdoor view, and then moves to a date orchard near Nineveh, with historic ruins, such as those of an Assyrian palace, dotting the distance.[82] The scenery in the fourth act becomes much

FIGURE 4.16 Nisroch, an Assyrian god, drawing. (*Tarih-i Umumi*, Istanbul, 1285 [1868])

more elaborate in detailing the chief astrologer's vast room in a temple, focused on a divan at the center. Statues of gods and idols in gold and stone are placed on the plaster walls, as observed in the greatest Assyrian temple, the Temple of Baal; they are described, for example, as having human bodies with eagle heads and wings or human heads on bulls' or horses' bodies.[83] The sets of the fifth and seventh acts take place in another luxuriously furnished room in the royal palace in Nineveh. This is a long and narrow space surrounded by divans and lighted by candles the size of chandeliers, with doors carved out of ivory and precious woods; the paintings on the glittering back wall show the emperor and various ceremonies.[84] From then on, the descriptions become bare bones, such as "Sardanapal's bedroom, dark" (scene 7), "a simple room in Sardanapal's palace, lighted by a dim candle" (Act 8), and a "simple, desolate space" (Act 9). Nonetheless, to reflect the story's increasing tragedy, the sets in the seventh and ninth acts are enlivened by repeated lightning strikes, the lightning in the seventh act appearing "tied to a chain."[85] Act ten takes place "outside the walls of Nineveh," and the play concludes in a longitudinal hall in Sardanapal's palace, where the entire palace population is gathered, as lightning reflects on the windows and rain batters them.[86]

The reaction of Ottoman readers to the setting of the play, which has not been staged to date, could perhaps best be understood in light of the growing literature on the history of Mesopotamia in the late nineteenth century. The coverage ranged from general history books (*tarih-i umumi*) to scattered reports in periodicals on archaeological excavations in Mesopotamia and the antiquities from the region (figure 4.16). While the Ottoman context cannot be compared with the scale and intensity of the information and discourse that nineteenth-century British readers and theater audiences would be familiar with, it distantly echoes the British scene. The greater parallel was the actual antiquities from Mesopotamia displayed in the British Museum and the Imperial Museum, even though the numbers of visitors differed enormously to the great advantage of the British Museum. Nevertheless, it is not unrealistic to suggest that the handful of readers of Abdülhak Hamid's *Sardanapal* had visited the Imperial Museum and had made the association.

CHAPTER FIVE

THE LANDSCAPE OF LABOR

The Workforce

A CHAPTER that has been conspicuously absent from histories of archaeology is the landscape of labor. Archaeological work always depended on a large labor force drawn from local populations that could seasonally reach hundreds of workers every day (figure 5.1). While the relationship between archaeologists and fieldworkers was indispensable and intimate, it does not emerge in either the contemporaneous accounts or in later scholarship, which features the former as the heroes of scientific discovery among a primitive human sea. In his lonely and pioneering book on the topic, Stephen Quirke explores a shared genealogy between archaeology and European imperialism, with methods and attitudes borrowed by the archaeologists from the British military. During their "seasonal campaigns," he suggests, each excavation site turned into a battleground, with Europeans who had "no knowledge of local language or customs beyond the needs of manpower recruitment" in charge.[1] As powerful as Quirke's metaphor is, it was not a vision shared by the archaeologists themselves. On the contrary, they saw themselves as informed and insightful observers of local societies and cultures. Furthermore, they confidently reported on current political struggles and conflicts, offering their opinions in authoritarian tones. It may not always be possible to test these accounts, speckled with colorful and personal anecdotes, on their historic and ethnographic accuracy, but situat-

FIGURE 5.1 Nippur, general view. Joseph Meyer qualified Nippur as "our Babylonian Pompeii." (UPMAAA, Nippur 5814)

ing them in their own social, cultural, and political contexts helps us understand something about their conditions of production.

Perhaps Quirke is too quick in his portrayal of the greater scene and ends up glossing over the possible nuances and differences from site to site, from archaeologist to archaeologist. Nevertheless, his diagnosis calls for the urge to open up alternative narratives. He does this by undertaking a detailed examination of the British archaeologist Sir William Matthew Flinders Petrie's notebooks, which include extensive information about the workers, cited by their names and discussed in terms of issues ranging from their ages and genders to salaries and their habits, as well as his relationships with them as individuals. Quirke deciphers Petrie's journals to convey intimate details about daily life on the excavation sites, creatively reading through their imperial baggage.

Firsthand accounts of archaeological research always conveyed information on the mundane quotidian events and human relationships on the excavation sites, even though this aspect of the history of archaeology had not interested scholars until Quirke's inquiry. The overlooked social history of the sites introduces new lenses into imperial ambitions and presumptions, cultural entitlements, and the inseparable entanglements of the discipline with politics. At the same time, it may finally restore some overdue recognition of the multitude of faces and bodies routinely featured textually and visually in the background of archaeological accounts.

If the historiography of the field celebrated only the great scientists and discoverers, it is through the words of those very men that we can attempt to piece together the stories of the workers and the complex human landscape they formed. In effect, accounts by archaeologists, ranging from Austen Henry Layard and Hormuzd Rassam to John Punnett Peters and Osman Hamdi, mixed scholarship with ethnographic and anthropological data, local conflicts, and larger political struggles. The names of individuals were cited, and many vignettes were narrated about selected personalities; these included Ottoman governors and officers, guides, translators, tribal and religious leaders, foremen, and skilled and unskilled peasants, as well as their families.

The blurry masses of archaeology's past did not remain faceless. They inserted themselves visually, if inadvertently, into the discipline through photographs meant to document the scholarly achievements. In photograph after photograph, the laborers appear engaged in their work as individuals and as groups, sometimes with their European bosses, sometimes in patterns that show the organization of labor on various sites. To take two random examples, one photograph from the excavation site in Babylon conveys the plurality of the characters involved: three Europeans (a committee of German scientists — according to the caption), an Ottoman officer (an inspector?), and laborers in local attires. The active work scene depicted in the frame points to the use of technology in the form of carts on rails being pushed by workers under the eyes of the controllers, and the distance between the carts attests to a serial and efficient organization that recalls a factory-like production (figure 5.2). A second photograph from Sardis shows a moment of pause by an American archaeologist and his workers in front of the camera. The pushcarts on rails shine once more in the midst of the ruins. A group of workers on the hill gives clues about the simultaneous digs at different points of the site, while the huts in the background reveal the spontaneous growth of a workers' settlement around the excavation zone (figure 5.3).

با اراده يه خانه يوكلارى بالاى قلاربزه بر الماں هيئت علميى لحرفينرى وموعودلاں حفريات

FIGURE 5.2 Babylon, view of the excavation site showing the committee of German scientists in charge of the operation. (İÜMK 90573)

FIGURE 5.3 Sardis, excavation of the south wall of cella near the east end. The archaeologist is on the left. (Butler, *Sardis*, 70, illus. 62)

The most common, and the most impersonal, data on workers were given by archaeologists in straight numbers, with high numbers broadcasting the importance of the particular operation. As personal log books, journals, and explorers' accounts do not have systematic formats, it is not always possible to collect consistent information. Based on his excavations in the late 1860s and the early 1870s, the accounts of General Luigi Palma di Cesnola, the U.S. consul in Cyprus whose collection forms the foundations of the Metropolitan Museum of Art's antiquities department, offer a good case study regarding the nature and variety of information that can be found in site reports. Cesnola referred possessively to the work done in first-person singular, the majestic "I" crediting himself throughout. He reported, for example, that during the course of one summer, *he* had opened "several hundred tombs" in Dali. Elsewhere, he hinted at the presence of workers, when he noted that he "had made borings in the places where the men had excavated," or *his* "men unearth[ed] the base of a colossal statue of Hercules." His tone got more punctuated as he mentioned the "four men busily at work extracting *my* [Assyrian-style] statue" of 6 feet 3 inches (1.9 m) in Golgoi. In a more matter-of-fact manner, he gave the total number of workers in Golgoi as 110 men and the scope of work carried out by them as unearthing 228 sculptures. But, later on, in a chilling account of the digging conditions in wells 40 (12.2 m) to 55 feet (16.8 m) underground, accompanied by a sensational drawing, he would describe how 15 men were employed for two days "to remove the fragments of sarcophagi, human remains and rubbish" in Amathus (figure 5.4).[2]

Depending on the funding of the enterprise, the size of the workforce varied significantly. Reviewing one hundred years of archaeological work, Adolf Michaelis, a professor at the University of Strasbourg, mentioned only the earliest operations, setting the scene for what was to come. Hence, in Lord Elgin's venture in Athens, "300–400 workmen were kept busy for a year carrying off the decorative sculptures of the Parthenon" in 1801, whereas a relatively small number of 30 workmen were engaged in Aegina in April 1811 for sixteen days, and 60–120 in Andritsena on July 12, 1812.[3] Austen Henry Layard's groundbreaking Mesopotamian enterprise (November 1845–April 1847) started with a modest workforce of "6 Arabs ... and 5 Turcomans, attracted by the regular wages." When he began to dig on the mount of Koyuncuk, he employed 30 "Arabs," who became more and more engaged in the discoveries of the "bearded men" they considered jinns and who expressed their excitement by tribal war cries. Their sentiments were reflected

How Tombs are excavated, and with what Tools.

FIGURE 5.4 Golgoi, excavation of tombs. (Cesnola, *Cyprus*, 255)

in one of the most popular engravings in the book, which shows peasants standing in awe in front of the huge statue of a "bearded" head just discovered—a curious scene considering that these men had lived with the antiquities for centuries (figure 5.5). When Layard was finally funded by the British Museum (noted begrudgingly, as it was only a fraction of what his French rival Paul-Émile Botta had received for the excavations at Khorsabad alone) and accepted the position of the superintendent, he was able to hire a larger group of Bedouins, who camped with their families around the site. In addition to about 80 "Arabs," who could remove the earth but who were

DISCOVERY OF THE GIGANTIC HEAD.

FIGURE 5.5 Nineveh, "Discovery of a Gigantic Head," showing the "natives" in awe of Layard's discovery. (Layard, *Nineveh and Its Remains*, 1:72)

not strong enough to dig, 50 "Nestorian Chaldaeans" were hired to carry out the harder work.[4]

The dramatic frontispieces to Layard's two volumes conveyed the changing sizes of the labor force, as well as the tough working conditions — the rigor of the pulling and the pushing involved. They also relayed other stories. The creative procedures developed specifically for the transportation of the immense statues point to the intelligence of the few European men on the site, underlined by their body language and commanding positions above the "natives" expressing superiority and power. The exoticism of the locals,

FIGURE 5.6 Nineveh, excavation site, lifting of the statues. (Layard, *Nineveh and Its Remains*, 1: frontispiece)

FIGURE 5.7 Nineveh, transportation of statues. (Layard, *Nineveh and Its Remains*, 2: frontispiece)

FIGURE 5.8 Ephesus, a group of workmen with their superintendents. (Wood, *Discoveries at Ephesus*, 1877)

indicated by their costumes and skin color, was in close harmony with Orientalist depictions of the time. The indispensable spears and camels played up to popular expectations (figures 5.6 and 5.7).

James T. Wood began his eleven-year-long expedition in Ephesus in 1863 also with a very small crew: 5 Turkish workmen he had found at the train station in Ayazoluk on the day of his arrival and who had just been discharged by the railway officials. During the following months, he could increase this number only to 20. However, his workforce grew impressively, to 200 men in spring 1873 and to more than 300 in fall 1873; for 300 workers he had 7 superintendents. The workmen consisted of Turks from neighboring villages and beyond and Arabs (about 100 of them), who would pitch their camel-hair tents on the lowlands near the excavation site with their wives and children. The two groups complemented each other, even though they often got into conflicts: Turkish men were strong and could carry huge weights, whereas Arabs were agile but had the shortcoming of being "exceedingly quarrelsome." Wood had serious reservations about Greeks: although quick and intelligent, they were lazy. He thus would hire only 3 or 4.[5] A group photograph of some workers with their superintendents did not reflect the problems, but showed them as a multiethnic crew, disciplined by Wood, and neatly lined up for the camera (figure 5.8).

The high number of workers often indicated the impoverishment of local economic conditions, which served the archaeologists. In Mesopotamia, Hormuzd Rassam reported employing 400–500 laborers per day in 1882 in Koyuncuk and Nimrud and pointed to the attraction of the work as evidenced by men who showed up in high numbers year after year during the excavation season.[6] Robert Koldewey hired around 200–250 workmen in Babylon in 1899.[7] John Punnett Peters's figures in his field notes from 1889 provide a precise account of the gradual growth of the force day by day from the beginning of the excavation. Every entry in his journal began with the number of men on the site. To give a random sample, on the first day, February 7, work had begun with 32 men at six points close together; on February 11, it had gone up to 56; on February 18, to 92; on February 28, to 125; on March 16, to 144. After this date, Peters stopped recording the number of laborers, with the indication that they had stabilized.[8] His notes from 1890 reveal a much larger labor force from the first day, when he "commenced work with 14 gangs" (gangs were groups of laborers assigned to specific tasks under a leader; their sizes varied), increased to "exactly 200 men, 4 overseers, and 21 gangs" in ten days, with 50 more men added in four more days.[9] In 1899, the same site in Nippur "recorded during the week 1800 days of labor marking an average of 300 men employed each day"[10] (figures 5.9 and 5.10). The photographs Peters, Hilprecht, and Koldewey published only showed fragments of the workforce. Related to specific corners of the expedition sites, these group images nonetheless convey ideas about the larger numbers, as well as the organization of labor.

In comparison to large extraction sites, which required a high level of organization and supervision, many sites remained relatively small. For example, the modest mission of the American Archaeological Institute in Assos in 1882 and 1883 relied on a workforce that shifted between 12 and 45 men, the majority of which came from the island of Lesbos across the water.[11] In Sardis, the season of 1910 started with only 30 workers (pickmen who loosened the soil, shovelers, and basket carriers), but, in a notable increase, during the season of 1911, the number was 250.[12]

In some cases, archaeologists recorded the numbers assigned to specific tasks. In Nemrud Dağı, Osman Hamdi and Osgan Efendi relied on "about 15" men to open up a dozen tombs in the necropolis of Grynium; to sweep the snow off the monument on the northern slope of the mountain, they needed 30 to 40 workers, whereas for the same task in the southwest, they hired on subsequent days from Saturday to Tuesday, 18, 13, 33, and 34 men.[13]

FIGURE 5.9 Nippur, excavation site showing workers carrying baskets. (UPMAAA, Nippur 5555)

FIGURE 5.10 Nippur, group of workmen at lunch break. (UPMAAA, Nippur 5323)

To cut out one trench that led to three caves of sarcophagi, Osman Hamdi's workforce in Sidon was composed of 25 men; gendarmes who had to keep guard day and night added a few more to the crew. The extraction of one of the larger sarcophagi required the efforts of 50 to 60 men.[14]

Labor was commonly organized in groups called "gangs" in the archaeological vocabulary. Some accounts referred to them in numbers and provided insights into the nature of the work. For example, Rassam's gangs in Kalaa-Shirgat (60 miles from Mosul) were composed of 7 men, and there were eight to ten gangs.[15] Koldewey's gangs in Babylon were formed of 16 workers. Each gang was supervised by a leader, who broke up the ground with a pickax; 3 filled baskets with earth; and the rest would carry the loads to carts on rails. The hierarchy was reflected in the salaries, with the leader receiving five piasters, the fillers four, and the carriers three.[16]

Peters described in more detail an organizational pattern in Nippur that was similar to Koldewey's. The "heads of the gangs" were responsible for digging the earth carefully, without damaging the objects that may have been in it; they were paid the highest wage of six piasters a day. The "heads" were handpicked from Jimjimeh and Hillah because of their profound expertise and remarkable skill in "burrowing for antiquities ... in the payment of Chaldaean and Jewish antiquity dealers of Baghdad." Their duties included supervising the ordinary pickmen, who received four piasters. Each pickman worked with a scrapeman, who scraped up the earth and put it in baskets; he was paid three piasters. Then came the lowest on the ladder, the basket carriers, grouped in gangs of 5 to 10 "wild Arabs of the neighborhood," who were paid two and a half piasters. Admittedly, this system of transportation was not the choice of the archaeologist, who preferred wheelbarrows. However, as it took great patience to teach the Arabs how to use them, they had to revert back to the primitive method of carrying the earth in "small baskets supported on hips, after the manner of the country."[17] In 1894, Joseph Andrew Meyer, an MIT-trained architect hired by John Henry Haynes to document the findings at Nippur with drawings, detailed the process in his diary, with sketches of the tools inserted in his text (figure 5.11).

> The chief of the gang wields a pick and is an expert excavator brought from Hillah. His immediate assistant fills the baskets with a small hoe. Each such gang has a number of basket carriers, who bears his basket on his hip with his hand under the basket and behind him. [He] carries it

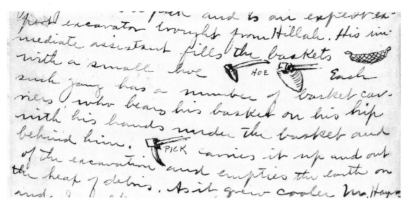

FIGURE 5.11 Nippur, Meyer's sketch of the tools used in the excavation. (SPHC)

up and out of the excavation and empties the earth on the heap of the debris.[18]

Meyer also listed the salaries as 13 cents for basketmen and 23 cents for pickmen for a workday of eleven hours.[19]

Peters's journal from 1890 displays a more intimate relationship with the workers, especially the foremen, than his book conveys. He gives their names (Hussein, Abbas Davud, Mousa, Ismail, Mehmet Turki, and others) and describes their responsibilities and the work achieved by them. The entry from February 4 records, for example, that "Mousa el-Jerwani had been working for two days in the third room of the Hebrew house," "Hamud el-Hajji had reached the bottom of the walls of his room to the east of the ziggurat," "Hassan has found that the second of his rooms rests against the step-like wall which seems to be a part of the terrace," and "Mousa el Qadhim is excavating another set of rooms further out on westward." The next day, among other discoveries, "Hisbat ha[d] found an immense fine looking wall of mudbrick in step-like work," "Dhaki ha[d] found a doorless room on the wall he is excavating," and "Abbas ha[d] found a room of brick to the south of Ismail's." Peters's account gave even further authority to the workforce when he mapped the site, showing the different locations of the excavation, numbering each location and linking the number with the names of the workers: in area 1, Hussein Davud "is digging out rooms on the outer face, west of breach," whereas "Dhaki is digging out rooms on the east of the breach on the inside"; in area 2, "Hussein el Khalif is digging out old brick wall on slope of plateau," and "Abdullah el Ouadah is descending

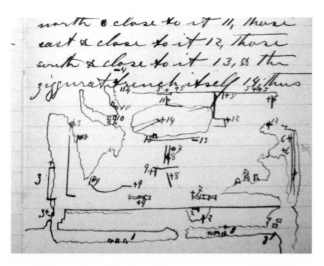

FIGURE 5.12 Nippur, plan of a section of the excavation site, drawn by John Punnett Peters and showing the division of labor. (UPMAAA)

to foundation of long wall by its first buttress east of center," and so forth (figure 5.12).[20]

The presentation and the language of the journal diverge significantly from Peters's book. In the journal, "Arabs" gain agency, they become individualized, and they participate actively in the excavation. Responsible for a particular part of the site, they make their own finds, and Peters's journal entries and diagrams acknowledge their contributions. The journal thus seems to reflect a closer version of the everyday realities of the site that helps reconstruct the intricate relationship between the archaeologist and the laborers. In this private medium, Peters did not have to appeal to an audience with certain expectations about a distant land and its exotic people, but earnestly logged the progress of daily work. The same attitude is reflected in Meyer's diary, where the architect also cites the workmen, especially the gang leaders, by their names.

Archaeologists' journals did not all share the same attitude. Howard Crosby Butler's 1910 entries in his Sardis journal lacked any references to individuals, giving only numbers in a casual manner: on the first day there were 18 laborers, and on the sixth there were 54; Butler did not mention any numbers after that day.[21] Nevertheless, the orderly presentation of photographs taken day by day showed the growth of the workforce (figures 5.13 and 5.14). Some data about the ethnic origins of the workers were implicitly

FIGURE 5.13 Sardis, first day on the excavation site. The Americans are in the second row to the right. (PUAA, Sardis, A.9)

FIGURE 5.14 Sardis, workers at the east bank of Paktolos. The photograph registers the growth of the workforce. The field house is in the background. (PUAA, Sardis, A.83.b)

conveyed by the variety of their costumes (figure 5.15). The nature of the relationship between the American archaeologists; the Turkish supervisor, Yakub Bey; and the workers could be glimpsed in the photographs. An attempt to bring efficiency to transportation by horse carts, which had arrived on the fourth day from Salihli, was proudly documented as well (figure 5.16).[22]

Other important data about the labor landscape entered the archaeologists' description. For example, to summarize the vast scope of the work accomplished, Peters sarcastically referred to the low wages:

> In praise of our ten-cent workmen it should be said, moreover, that the amount of earth removed by them in the six months of excavations was really very large, so that in cubic feet of the earth excavated, and size and depth of trenches, ours far surpassed any excavations ever undertaken in Babylonia; and de Serzac's work at Tello, which represented six seasons and thereabouts.[23]

Sometimes, schedules for a regular workday were given. In Nippur, work would start at sunrise and end at sunset, with an hour's rest for lunch. Before lunch and at the end of the day, the team leaders would report to the archaeologist their finds and progress. Payments were issued on Saturday afternoons, followed by a feast if the work had been good.[24] A noon break for lunch and rest, announced by a call for "paidos" (break), was also set into the daily routine of Osman Hamdi's workers in Sidon. However, the days could be long and draining, depending on the difficulty of the tasks. On one specific day, Osman Hamdi reported having spent eleven consecutive hours in a crypt with his workers.[25] In Sardis, "sunshine" marked the beginning of the workday, which was interrupted for breakfast for thirty minutes at 8:30 a.m. and for an hour at noon, and continued "until sunset."[26]

Foreign Archaeologists and Ottoman Officers

After obtaining their permits from the Ottoman government, foreign archaeologists were in charge of the excavations. However, the laws complicated the hierarchies on the sites, requiring their supervision by Ottoman officers. The 1874 law had designated local authorities in the provinces to control the activities of foreigners holding permissions and verify that they conformed to the specified conditions.[27] The 1884 law inserted another level of supervision by implementing "a delegate of the Government, ac-

FIGURE 5.15 Sardis, a "native" child. (PUAA, Sardis, B.107)

FIGURE 5.16 Sardis, excavation site at the beginning of the second week, with the newly acquired horses. Note the security forces standing at the top. (PUAA, Sardis, A.17)

quainted with the necessary knowledge,... [to] assist on excavation sites."[28] This soon turned into an inconvenience for foreign teams on several levels. One article, particularly hostile to Osman Hamdi's "strict surveillance of antiquities," argued that Ottoman public servants in the provinces could "be bought for money" on any occasion, except on the subject of antiquities. The consequences were sad for scholarly societies like the American Institute, ready to spend "thousands on the excavation at Babylon [and] be expected to be content with the honor and glory of enriching Hamdi's museum without acquiring one iota for themselves."[29] In the *New York Times*'s relatively more temperate language, for the American team working in Nippur, "the most disagreeable thing was that a Turkish official had to accompany any expedition to take charge of all objects found."[30] Foreign archaeologists now had to accommodate an individual whose unique job was to watch their activities. Inevitably, the relationship became quite intimate, as the officer had to be provided with rooms in the archaeologists' compound, taking part in all their daily activities, including meals.

Ottoman efforts to make foreign archaeologists abide by the laws had mixed results. Cases of disobedience would prompt the government to search for additional measures. A document from 1899 reveals the scale of the operation. Upon figuring out that the German archaeologist Karl Lehmann, who worked with a permit in Nimrud, had taken four pieces from the excavation site to Mosul without permission from the authorities, the Ottoman government expanded its supervision network. Until then, the directors of education, the highest officers of the Ministry of Education in the provinces, were held responsible for keeping an eye on the activities of foreigners and reporting to the Ministry of Education. However, as these public servants worked in cities, they could not successfully carry out their duty on many sites. The net was cast much wider, now including civil service personnel such as governors and district head officials (*kaymakam*), as well as high school principals in larger settlements, middle-school teachers in smaller towns, directors of sub-districts, and police and gendarmes.[31] It is thus not surprising that during the first two months of his excavation in Sardis in 1910, Butler was visited twice by the *kaymakam* of Salihli, on April 5 and May 20, the first visit also bringing the imperial commissioner Yakub Efendi, while the second was initiated on *bayram*, a religious holiday (figure 5.17). The American archaeologist resented the *kaymakam*'s visits for wasting his time on both occasions and for being obligated to entertain him.[32] Even worse, all antique sites were guarded by government appoint-

FIGURE 5.17 Sardis, *kaymakam*'s visit; photograph taken at the northeast corner of the excavation site. (PUAA, Sardis, A.202.a)

ees. A regulation about their duties and responsibilities shows the intended level of supervision on foreigners: the guards were to accompany the visitors during the entirety of their time on the grounds and make sure they did not take even the "smallest of stones," did not photograph the site and the old fragments, and did not make casts.[33] As if to display the effectiveness of the Ottoman control on all archaeological activity in the empire, a yearbook on public education in 1903, prepared by the Ministry of Education, gave a complete list of the excavation work done in the past, as well as the present day. If the archaeologists were foreigners, their names and their affiliations with various universities and museums were provided and the fact that they had government permits was highlighted.[34]

At the end of the century, the social dynamics of archaeology revolved around three distinct entities: foreign archaeologists, Ottoman public servants, and local laborers, each one keeping a close eye on the others for different reasons. The hierarchical structure on the excavation site became blurred as Ottoman supervisors, representing the imperial government, now exerted their power over the Western teams. Tensions were charged on multiple levels: between the representatives of the Ottoman state and the foreigners, between the archaeologists and the local workers, between the Ottoman officers who represented the central authority and the local laborers, not to mention the internal struggles within each group itself. Many scenarios can be imagined. Foreign archaeologists, cautious about the kind of Ottoman supervision they were subjected to, must have watched their supervisors carefully to retain some control over their own activities; they must have also observed these bureaucrats to satisfy their curiosity about Ottoman middle classes. Of course, they must have kept a very close eye on the workers to maintain the efficient functioning of the excavation and prevent any "suspect" behavior. Ottoman bureaucrats, lonesome among foreign teams with whom they were forced to live, had to do their official jobs, which required considerable effort, given the extent of the sites being dug. As government representatives well aware of the ethnic and tribal conflicts in the region, they must have surveyed the relationships between the groups of workers. The recurring complaints of foreign archaeologists point to the gaze of the workers focused on them; the unfamiliar lifestyles and customs of the patrons must have constituted a major element in their curiosity. The workers probably scrutinized the Ottoman supervisors, who represented the state, even more than the foreigners. On yet another level, it is reasonable to imagine different tribal and ethnic groups watching each other in the close quarters of their work and living environments. To complicate the relations even further, archaeologists could expect visits even from military officers, as on May 30, 1894, when a "lieutenant or captain" called on the excavation in Nippur, accompanied by about twenty-five soldiers, encamping in the vicinity.[35]

Undoubtedly, the Ottoman measures operated against the hopes and expectations of foreign archaeologists, who continued to search for alternative ways to procure objects. Peters, for example, had bought tablets from local antique dealers, who had guaranteed their illegal transportation to London, from where they were shipped to New York. To avoid "Oriental regulations," Hilprecht was also inclined to stock the American museums with objects from the black market in Baghdad.[36] In any case, the concerted Ottoman struggle against the smuggling of antiquities seems to have been a lost cause on the eve of World War I. In the summer of 1914, the Minister of Education appealed to the Minister of Interior Affairs, reminding him of the "pillaging" of Nineveh and Khorsabad by the British and the French half a century ago, and of the "historic land of Assyria" during the past decade by the Germans, and urged the ministry not to issue any excavation permits.[37] Three weeks later, Süleyman Nazif, the governor of Mosul, wrote to the Ministry of Interior Affairs, explaining that it had become impossible to stop the illegal activities of even those granted official excavation permits. In an act of desperation, the governor pointed out that despite all the attention, the situation had not been controlled for over fifty years and pleaded with the ministry to stop all archaeological work by foreigners until the time when "experts are trained in our country" (*bizde ashab-ı ihtisasi yetişene kadar*).[38]

Tools and Technology

Archaeological work was delicate, labor intensive, and slow. Nothing explains better the work conditions than two dramatic drawings in Cesnola's account (see figure 5.4) that depict how the tombs were excavated. The first shows a narrow well, one of several, with two workers squeezed into a situation comparable to that of mines. On the ground level, other workers pull the baskets up; the "primitive" tools are rendered in an artistic composition on the right. The second image zooms in on a tomb chamber accessed through the well. The heat level is indicated by the half-naked laborer, carrying a torch, the latter also giving an idea of the darkness and even the thrill of the discovery; skeletons and various artifacts are strewn on the ground.[39] In some cases, clues are offered by unlikely sources. A seemingly neutral cross section from Osman Hamdi and Théodore Reinach's *Une nécropole royale à Sidon* exposes the conditions of labor. The extraction of the Sarcophagus of the Mourning Women, seen pulled on rails in the drawing, took place in a tunnel about 1.60 meters (5.2 ft.) high. The sensitive nature of the operation must have necessitated hours of work in a very uncomfortable setting, something not mentioned in the narrative of the discovery (figure 5.18).

Bringing new tools and new technology to the excavation field increased efficiency, especially in terms of transportation, but it was never possible to modernize the working methods entirely. In some cases, this stemmed from the unwillingness of the laborers to change their ways. In the 1870s, Cesnola complained of resistance from his workers, the Greek peasants in Cyprus, to adopt iron spades for digging and wheelbarrows for carrying the debris. He reported with resentment that they insisted on "removing the excavated earth by means of the native basket slung over the shoulder by a rope," their "persistent" refusal slowing down the process.[40]

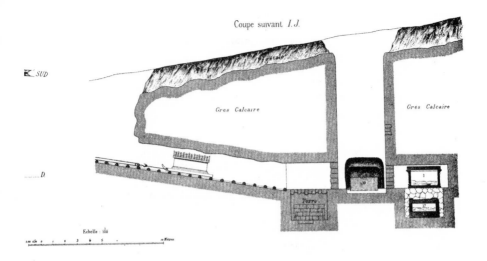

FIGURE 5.18 Sidon, section drawing of excavation site showing extraction route of a sarcophagus. (O. Hamdy Bey and Théodore Reinach, *Une nécropole royale à Sidon*)

In time, rail transportation became indispensable at all major sites. In Koldewey's account, rails had to be built as a first necessary step before the excavation could even begin at the Ishtar Gate in Babylon.[41] In Sardis, a train was essential in order "to move the heavy crane from place to place," while the "heavy crane" lifted and carried the huge blocks of marble abundant on this site. Yet, bringing the train to the site in Sardis proved to be a bureaucratic challenge. The American archaeologists had to maneuver around a possible conflict with the government, as "even a small and temporary railway [between the town of Sard and the village near the ruins] would interfere with the Turkish railway Régie" according to the regulations of concessions given by the state to the railway company. To avoid "interminable troubles," only about 100-meter (328 ft.) stretches were constructed at one time, making the transportation process cumbersome and fragmented:

> The engineering staff of the excavations, without any outside assistance, constructed the road bed along the Paktolos from Sart to the excavations, assembled the parts of the locomotive and the crane, put the wagons together, made up a train and loaded it with the extra rails and other equipment. This train ... was moved forward a little over an hundred metres; then the labourers would pick up the line in long sections and move them in front of the train ... Exactly ten days were consumed in

FIGURE 5.19 Sardis, "The Engine." (PUAA, Sardis, C.7.4)

this entire operation, and on the eleventh the locomotive, adorned by the labourers with evergreens and flowers, brought the train triumphantly into the excavations.[42]

Despite the hardships, the rails, the wagons, and the crane, documented by photographs, increased the scale and the speed of the excavation, requiring a workforce of 250 (figure 5.19).[43]

Ethnographic Entanglements, Orientalist Mind-sets

Numerical and factual data were useful in conveying the scale of the operations and the numbers of local people who would be involved in the excavation work. Such straightforward information was complemented by proto-ethnographic and anthropological narratives, which offer additional insights into the workforce — although framed by the archaeologists and the world they belonged to.[44] The social, cultural, and ideological mind-sets of the era, shaped by imperialism, colonialism, and Orientalism at their peaks, reflected on the arrogance of the Western archaeologists, confident in their status as representatives of progress and civilization. Hilprecht went as far as associating their work with a version of the colonial *mission civilisatrice*:

"Through their continued exploration of the ruins these foreign excavators have introduced new ideas into the country, made the people acquainted with important inventions, and, above all, taught them the value of time and work."[45] The self-assured attitude of archaeologists peeks through many images taken at different times at different sites. There is a continuous line from the lithographs of Layard commanding the workers from the top of the hill (see figure 5.6) to photographs of the archaeologists supervising the work in Sardis from heights six decades later (figures 5.20 and 5.21).

Ottoman archaeologists (counting Hormuzd Rassam with Osman Hamdi and Osgan Efendi) shared the overall visions of their foreign colleagues in their perceptions of local people, thereby doing away with the Eastern-Western dichotomy, but making class difference and educational background more pronounced. A widely reproduced photograph of Osman Hamdi at Nemrud Dağı epitomizes this position: the archaeologist is carefully cleaning an old object as a worker stands behind him in a static posture, like a sculpture frozen in time, holding a plate for his findings. Osgan Efendi also appears as the skilled archaeologist in action, watched by a local man on a neighboring rock.[46] When Osman Hamdi showed up among his laborers in photographs, he occupied the center of the scene, his body language expressing possession over the heritage and his hands placed protectively over the antique fragments (figure 5.22).

Archaeologists expressed their views on local peoples liberally and with authority. Their accounts were loaded, unsurprisingly, with the familiar clichés well engrained in European discourses by the end of the nineteenth century. With few lapses here and there, their close daily relationships with the workers in the intimate conditions of the excavation sites did not seem to have allowed them to break through the established formulas. Whole volumes could be written on the coverage of the "natives" in archaeological accounts, but that exercise would only add familiar observations on the hierarchical thinking of the time. Yet overlooking it altogether would also be misleading, as the dynamics of the working conditions were deeply impacted by archaeologists' unconditional pronouncements on the character and the intelligence of local residents. A few examples from the mid-nineteenth century to the first decades of the twentieth century will suffice to set the tone.

Layard made a distinction between the laborers who worked with him: Chaldeans from the mountains were "strong and hardy men" who could dig, whereas physically weaker Arabs could only be used to carry away the

FIGURE 5.20 Sardis, archaeologists supervising the workers. (Butler, *Sardis*, 1:43, illus. 30)

FIGURE 5.21 Sardis, archaeologists supervising the workers. (Butler, *Sardis*, 1:48, illus. 38)

FIGURE 5.22 Osman Hamdi claiming the ruins. (İÜMK 91525-0002)

earth—a categorization repeated by others during the following decades. Paying a visit to the leader of the Abou Salman Arabs, who had camped around Nimrud, Layard seems to have met an Arab exceptional in appearance and character: handsome, "tall, robust, and well-made, with a countenance in which intelligence was no less marked than courage and resolution." Furthermore, in an un-Arab manner, the sheik had shaved his beard. His tent, crowded with women, as well as two mares and a colt, was an object of curiosity not only in terms of its occupants but also because of its carpets and cushions, and the fire of camel's dung at the center, used by a "half-naked" Arab to make coffee. Unlike the sheik, the men in the tent were "of the most motley appearance." Continuing in a semiethnographic tone, Layard gave a sarcastic account of a group of Kurdish men, "dressed in the height of fashion" in "every color" conceivable, and whose weapons "were of very superior design and workmanship, their turbans of adequate height and capacity."[47] He supported his verbal descriptions with engravings that depicted large views of the landscape, dotted with tents, people in rich costumes, and camels (figures 5.23 and 5.24). Although not presented or argued in a methodical manner, observation of local dress was quite common by archaeologists, as testified by a color drawing of "A Turkish Brigand," with a gun in his hand, a spear, and three knives tucked in his belt, in Wood's *Dis-*

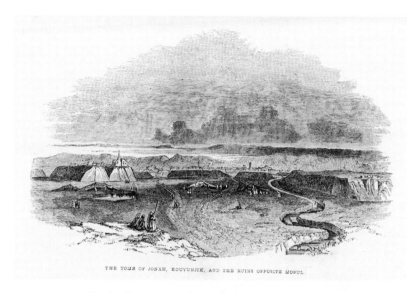

THE TOMB OF JONAH, KOUYUNJIK, AND THE RUINS OPPOSITE MOSUL.

FIGURE 5.23 The landscape around Mosul. The tribes and the tents provide some ethnographic data. (Layard, *Nineveh and Its Remains*, 1:123)

coveries at Ephesus; the unique figure of this genre in the volume, its loneliness makes the impact all the more striking.[48] The tradition continued for decades, appearing, for example, in the work of Peters and Hilprecht. Peters used local figures next to discovered pieces to indicate scale, but also to display the range of their costumes from fully dressed (even with a gun) to half naked.[49]

Women, a main subject of European fascination, surfaced often in Layard's book. Indeed, Layard knew well the lure of Oriental women for his audience and stated it clearly. "I must endeavor to convey to the reader some idea of the domestic establishment of a great Arab Sheik," he wrote, and continued by alluding to the sexual appetite of Sheik Sofouk, who would take a new wife every month, divorcing her at the end of the month and marrying a new one — in an endless cycle. His current wives had made strong impressions on Layard. Beautiful and noble Amsha was celebrated "in the song of every Arab in the desert." She reclined on cushions and carpets, supervising "fifty handmaidens" busy baking bread, while her three children, "naked little urchins, black with sun and mud, and adorned with a long tail hanging from the crown of their heads," rolled around.[50]

Nevertheless, it was the sheik's second wife, Hatem, tall, fair, and dark eyed, who represented the notion of "perfection" to Arabs.[51] In fact, "all

TEL AFER.

FIGURE 5.24 Tel Affar, general view. "Natives," camels, and tents provide some ethnographic data. (Layard, *Nineveh and Its Remains*, 1:256)

the resources of their art had been exhausted to complete what nature had begun," in a most exotic manner:

> Her lips were dyed deep blue, her eyebrows were continued in indigo until they united over the nose, her cheeks and forehead were spotted with beauty marks, her eyelashes darkened by kohl; and on her legs and bosom could be seen the tattooed ends of flowers and fanciful ornaments, which were carried in festoons and network over her whole body.[52]

Layard's presentation of her jewelry was unmatched by any Orientalist painting or text:

> Hanging from each ear, and reaching down to her waist, was an enormous ear-ring of gold, terminating in a tablet of the same material, carved

FIGURE 5.25 "Shammar lady on a camel." (Layard, *Nineveh and Its Remains*, 1:283)

and ornamented with four turquoises. Her nose was also adorned with a prodigious gold ring, set with jewels, of such ample dimensions that it covered the mouth and was to be removed when the lady ate. Ponderous rows of strung beads, Assyrian cylinders, fragments of coral, agates, and parti-colored stones, hung from her neck; loose silver rings encircled her wrists and ankles.[53]

His provocative descriptions were not accompanied by visual representations. Indeed, women were not shown at all, although the figure of a "Shammar lady on a camel" was meant to trigger the imagination to place Hatem traveling in the desert in the small chamber on the camel's back (figure 5.25).

Layard's book, so rich in its exotic sidetracks, claimed to be a scientific documentation and was abundantly illustrated with drawings of the antiquities, ranging from site plans to the smallest object, such as a drinking cup. Cesnola used the book to evoke awe in the Cypriot peasants in another favorite theme common to many accounts: the stupidity of local folk. To convince some peasants "with tact and manoeuvring" to hand the antique pieces in their possession to him, the American consul impressed them with a volume of *Nineveh and Its Remains*. Showing a peasant a page on which figures of an object resembling the one owned by him (about which he was privately informed), Cesnola informed him that this was a book of divination, which led him to discover whether or not he was in possession of antiquities. The peasant's reaction, followed by a cry of astonishment, was "'Panagia mou!' [my Blessed Virgin!] He has a book telling everything." It was duly followed by the handing over of the hidden antiquities.[54] The stupidity of the Greek peasant was only matched by the laziness of the Turks in Cyprus. Cesnola reported that all the areas on the island where the Turks lived were "dirty, miserable, and showing every sign of decay." He was not surprised, as "this degenerate race" did not "know or care to learn any profession and handicraft," but spent its time "in idleness at the cafés, drinking and smoking."[55] The urge to draw comparisons between the Greek and Turkish characters emerges again in Joseph Thacher Clarke's descriptions of the labor force at Assos: "The Greeks were light-spirited, and even somewhat fool-hardy ... ; but the Turks, while of greater strength and bravery, were more quiet and careful." Although Greeks were greatly superstitious, their "love of money" was such that they would work on Sundays, feast days, and even on Christmas.[56]

Such assumptions pale compared to the ones about Arabs. Like those before and after his, Peters's tales about local tribes are adorned with the usual qualifications: they were warriors and fought with each other constantly; they were ignorant and mystified by the knowledge of Westerners (Peters's medical know-how became legendary among them), and they were stuck in the past but unappreciative of the historic heritage surrounding them. Their only interest in antiquities was geared toward finding treasures. They shared a lust for stealing and a particular love for gold. Indeed, the archaeologist's gold tooth crown had raised so much curiosity that "groups of them would come and squat in front of me and watch until I should open my mouth." Peters feared for his life because of this crown![57]

Hilprecht characterized his employees simply as "fickle Arabs, whose principal 'virtues' seemed to consist in lying, stealing, murdering, and lasciviousness." They were irrationally warrior-like: "At the slightest provocation and frequently without any apparent reason they threw their scrapers and baskets away and commenced the war-dance, brandishing their spears or guns in the air and chanting some defiant sentence especially made up for the occasion ..." They were "simple-minded children of the desert and ... half-naked peasants of the marshes" who claimed the archaeologists' lifestyle was "strange." Their intellectual capacities were so limited that they believed foreigners carried great magical powers and could bring upon their enemies diseases like cholera.[58]

Hormuzd Rassam, an insider and an outsider to both worlds, claimed at the outset that he had a different outlook toward local people, a "dissent from the opinions of some travelers and historians." He found it easy to get along with the "Arabs, Koords and Turcomans," and in an explicit criticism of his European and American peers, emphasized the importance of not treating them with "unbecoming hauteur and conceit." His depictions, although echoing the Western archaeologists in their formulaic vocabulary and overall tone, conveyed more fluctuating messages. In his words, the locals were "true, loyal, and most hospitable." Even their women, set by Rassam in ethnographic frames, were ready to "assist and entertain" the strangers.[59] His descriptions of the four wives of his host in Tirmaneen (two Turkomans, one Arab, and a Circassian) coalesce into a mini account of the region's diversity of traditions through the lens of costume — albeit one tainted by Orientalist condescension and sarcasm:

> The Arab will wear no drawers, because it is a disgrace to do so; and the other races must wear them because it is considered a disgrace to appear in public without them. The former do not consider it unbecoming to expose their bare legs, but they think it most improper to show their breast, and will cover it with any dirty rag, sooner than let it be seen, or even take up the lower part of their skirt at the expense of exposing their legs up to the knees to cover it; the latter, on the contrary do not mind walking about with part of the breast uncovered, though their legs and feet must be quite concealed.[60]

At the same time, Hormuzd Rassam displayed an understanding of local dress, the changing habits, and the Western inability to relate to them even "in these days of constant communication between the East and the West." Criticizing Wilfrid Scawen Blunt and Lady Anne Blunt, dressed in the "Arab fashion," he pointed to the fact that European-style attires were commonly adopted by the "Turks, native officials, and other respectable classes in Turkey" and that "the wearing of that old-fashioned and clumsy dress by an English lady and gentleman seemed quite whimsical."[61]

Hormuzd Rassam's ethnographic interest extended to local dishes and their preparation. He detailed, for example, the preparation of "pillaw," the rice dish with fried almonds and raisins, and, more impressively, "dolma," that is, "any vegetable stuffed with rice and minced mutton, seasoned with onions, peppers, and salt, and boiled in water made acid with sour grape or lemon juice, or a berry called 'simmock'" (sumac).[62] It is reasonable to attribute Hormuzd Rassam's delight in the deliciousness of this food to his local roots; for him this was not an acquired taste. However, the language he used gave the dishes an otherness, fulfilling the expectations of the audience he addressed.

Osman Hamdi's paternalistic, Orientalist, and quasi-colonial attitude toward local people has already been examined by Edhem Eldem in two contexts, in reference to Arabs and Bedouins of Iraq in the late 1860s (in letters written by Osman Hamdi to his father) and in reference to Kurds during his archaeological expedition in Nemrud Dağı in 1883 (in Osman Hamdi's notebooks).[63] The hospitality of the Kurdish tribes, "found in all people in the Orient," was a theme that occurred repeatedly in the accounts; their feasts were accompanied by dances, music, and all kinds of celebrations. In one instance, when the archaeologists relied on the services of a local tribe to cross Göksu River, they saw "dervishes, playing large tambourines and chanting ... some entirely nude and others only wearing shirts"; they constituted a "most amusing and most picturesque" spectacle as they shouted "ardent prayers to God and his saints" to allow for smooth passage. When Osman Hamdi and Osgan Efendi reached the military headquarters in Adıyaman, treating the Ottoman archaeologists as though they were foreign tourists, the major organized an "indigenous" feast in their honor, and "Kurdish soldiers" performed their "national dance."[64]

Osman Hamdi's accounts of his workers in Sidon in 1892 reveal some shifts in attitude from the Nemrud Dağı expedition, which can be explained by the differences in the contexts. In Nemrud Dağı, Osman Hamdi and Osgan Efendi had ventured into the wilderness of southeastern Anatolia, away from all "civilization," whereas Sidon was close to Beirut, a major cosmopolitan Ottoman port city equipped with modern amenities. The self-awareness of the two refined gentlemen as bearers of high universal culture might have colored their reactions to the local human landscape in Nemrud Dağı, accentuating their Orientalist tendencies—as compared to the few slippages in Sidon. In Sidon, Osman Hamdi diverted from Western accounts to some degree, and, when relating similar episodes as his Western colleagues, he filtered them through some understanding of local culture. Hence, during the festivities celebrating the joining of two underground galleries, the workers cried out "hourrahs" and sang "Arab airs" (not war cries, as foreign archaeologists would qualify them) to a flute made of rush. In another instance, while they failed to grasp the archaeologist's great joy at the discovery of a "magnificent anthropoid sarcophagus in black marble," the Arab workers figured out that "something happy" had taken place and started dancing and shouting "frenetic hourrahs" (again, not war cries). Osman Hamdi pointed out that according to the custom of the place, when lifting a great weight, both Muslim and Christian workers chanted asking for help from God. He heard the words "Ya! Rabb-il-Beït," meaning "Oh God of the house." While "Beït" referred among Muslims also to Kaaba, here it was used by Christians as well as Muslims. He concluded that the reference could not be to the "God of the Kaaba," but perhaps revealed an "unconscious remnant of primitive cults, a confused memory of the Lares gods."[65] Returning to one of the most obstinate Orientalist associations, Osman Hamdi placed the local culture in an obscure and fixed past.

The photographs of the Sidon expeditions depict the working process and the actors, both laborers and supervisors (figure 5.26). Two engravings from these photographs, published in *Une nécropole royale à Sidon*, show the extraction of the sarcophagi from the caves; the Ottoman officers are clearly identified in their dark costumes and supervising roles. A third image, a rather poorly reproduced photograph, focuses on the loading of the "Grand Sarcophagus" onto a barge. The photographs of locals from Nemrud Dağı pursue a different theme: as argued by Eldem, they describe ethnic characteristics, complemented by the rough and exotic landscapes; a few highlight Osman Hamdi and Osgan Efendi as the two "white" men amid Orientalist "tableaux vivants."[66]

Against the Grain

There is no corollary to archaeologists' opinions and observations on local people from the other side, only a complete lack of records. The body language and the gazes of the workers who crowd the photographs may sometimes tempt one to construct scenarios, but the historian's métier is more restricted than that of the fiction writer and the artist, who could take, for example, the photograph of Babylon (discussed above; see figure 5.2) and give the individuals in it imagined lives. The drawing that shows the section of a well in Golgoi can hardly be viewed without empathizing with the feelings and the thoughts of the worker who had to spend eight hours a day in that hole (see figure 5.4). However, history writing has its conventions even in the present-day climate that is increasingly open to interpretation. If the historian is curious about the missing perspective, she will have to take methodologically risky paths and turn to archaeologists' accounts and attempt to read them against the grain. Despite the recurring clichés on the

FIGURE 5.26 Sidon, extraction of a sarcophagus showing local workers and Ottoman officials. (İÜMK 91533-0002)

customs, character, social norms, and habits of local people, it may be misleading to flatten these accounts into a broad and homogeneous discourse. As every vignette is open to multiple interpretations, if read between the lines, they can be stretched to tell alternative stories. An interpretative position of this nature works against "the once-admirable principle of not saying more than we know," in the words of Michael Woods, but invites us "to say what we feel or think," a position that is expected from the scholar today.[67] It is not that scholars invent new meanings irresponsibly, but they can enjoy some flexibility to treat the evidence more freely and more acrobatically, with the hope of engaging the reader in a more active response.

Power relationships are among the themes that can be gleaned from the accounts, and examining these dismantles the lopsided assumptions and disrupts the position of the Western archaeologists deemed in charge. There is no question that excavations provided new means of income for peasants—a major "pull," given the dire economic conditions of the agricultural sector. Benefiting from this situation, archaeologists kept the wages low in order to make their funds last longer, but they could still gather the workforce they needed. Nevertheless, they could not always control the schedules. J. T. Wood complained bitterly about not being able to keep a sufficient number of workers at Ephesus in springtime, when the workforce dwindled down to 35 men. Nothing Wood offered them "had the least effect on them"; they returned to tend their farms and homesteads. In Wood's words, "They declared most positively that they would not stay for a thousand piasters a day"—an ironic and desperate statement, considering that they were paid ten piasters a day.[68] Hilprecht encountered the same phenomenon on the excavation site of Nippur, where the "native Arabs" quit the trenches in mid-April "to harvest their barley and to look after their agricultural interests."[69] A similar situation took place in Sardis: labor grew scarce as "as the harvest ripened," forcing the excavation work to stop; a small number of skilled workers who remained behind concentrated on the construction of the excavation house.[70] In the end, then, it was the workers who made the crucial decision about the length of the excavation season, not the archaeologists.

Archaeologists shared a widespread opinion on the frozen status of the local culture and its lack of dynamism and change, in some cases illustrating it with similarities in dress "now and then"—as in Cesnola's "modern priest" and "a stone head," one of his recent discoveries from Golgoi, wearing similar caps (figure 5.27). John Garstang stretched the notion to physical characteristics and, describing Turcomans as "descendants of wanderers

Modern Priest.   Stone head from Golgoi.

FIGURE 5.27 Golgoi, drawings of a modern priest and a stone head. (Cesnola, *Cyprus*, 180)

from the East," stated that "there is something in their faces reminiscent of Hittite portraits, suggested generally in the women, and marked strongly in some of the men." He included a photograph and a drawing, both in profile, displaying "a strong nose in line with the receding forehead, the round protrusion of the head behind, the heavy lips and beard, and the stolid look. The figure is short and thickset, betokening stamina and strength" (figure 5.28).[71] In other instances, the formal similarity of contemporary objects to historic ones was shown, throwing a quick ethnographic light on archaeological knowledge. The lines of a coffin and a burial urn were echoed in the design of a basket held by a woman from Nippur (figure 5.29). Peters jotted down in his journal that the "copper ball ... composed of two more plaths, [and with] a small ring for attachment," was "the same as are now used for playthings by the Arab children."[72]

The continuity between the past and the present was not a resolved issue for archaeologists. On the one hand, they used the link to attribute backwardness and resistance to change in indigenous societies; on the other hand, they repeatedly wrote about local residents' disrespect for the past. The construction materials and the architecture of the old and the new houses, as well as the pottery and utensils found in the houses and graves,

I. A LIVING AMORITE.

2. SURVIVING HITTITE TYPE.
From a sketch by Mr. Horst Schliephack.
(See p. 16, note 2, and cf. p. 48.)

PLATE LXXXIV

FIGURE 5.28 Similarities between "Turcomans" and Hittites. (Garstang, *The Land of the Hittites*, 320)

FIGURE 5.29 Similarities between contemporary and historic objects. (Hilprecht, *The Excavations in Assyria and Babylonia*, 336)

were so similar in the region around Nippur that Peters admitted the immense difficulty of identifying the dates—a phenomenon that displays a powerful attachment to the past. Two stories, both from Peters's excavation account of Nippur, help shed some light on his intriguing and conflicting opinions. In one episode, Peters admitted to being "hopelessly mystified" by the meaning of some "small, round, rectangular, or octagonal objects of clay" he had found in a booth in front of the great Temple of Baal at Nippur. The mystery was resolved thanks to contemporary pilgrim tokens sold at the gates of mosques in Nejef and Kerbela: not only their sizes and shapes were the same but also their decorative elements, marked by the image of a hand or simply a circle—intended to be touched to the forehead. Peters commented on this continuity as a sign of people "living the same life [as the Babylonians had four thousand years ago], excepting only for the modifications introduced by the use of coffee and tobacco," emphasizing their stubborn inability to keep up with the times.[73] Another reading, which argues for the power of "indigenous archaeologies," as proposed by Yannis Hamilakis in deconstructing Western conceptions that the ancient civilizations carried no meaning for the local residents, would draw a diametrically opposed conclusion from Peters's observations and would see the phenomenon as evidence of the attachment to and the value placed on history.[74] From this perspective, the visits of "hosts of Arabs, sometimes a whole tribe at a time," to the tunnels, wells, and galleries of the excavation site, which Peters reported, could perhaps be understood as a genuine interest in the history of the land, rather than a display of foreigners' ingenuity that left the natives in awe—as the archaeologist believed. Then again, Peters contradicted himself, as he likened the visits to those "we would [to] a museum."[75] Given their continuity with the past (as described by the archaeologist), would it be unreasonable to suggest that local crowds felt curiosity and pride in history rather than a helpless admiration for Western knowledge and technology?

Osman Hamdi approached the local interest in the sarcophagi he had unearthed at Sidon from a more broad-minded angle. The desire to observe them was so keen among residents, as well as travelers, that Osman Hamdi was prompted to create a "true Museum," "a garden of antiquities," in a citrus grove where the "artistic wonders" were being temporarily stored. Open to the public on Friday and Sunday mornings, the displays attracted large crowds.[76] Simultaneously, the excavation site itself turned into a platform for festivities. On one single day toward the end of the excavation process that was marked by the discovery of yet another beautiful sarcophagus, Osman Hamdi invited a group of musicians upon the wishes of the workers. Music accompanied the work, and a crowd of "four to five hundred" people that had gathered around the trench joined the workers in a "spontaneous outburst" of excitement when the sarcophagus was taken out.[77] We may never know who these musicians were and what kind of music they played, but we can only imagine that the vernacular tunes and chants were most likely not in accord with Osman Hamdi's own taste in classical European music. Yet the joy of local residents in their land and their past added to the archaeologist's pride in his discovery.

Locals' interest in small objects found on the site was attributed to their desire to smuggle them to antique dealers. However, archaeologists' own records show some other reasons. Peters wrote about peasant women who searched for small antique objects and seal cylinders around Warka. To his awe, Arab women collected them "for their own persons." Especially after rainstorms, they engaged in searches, and "when they find signs of a coffin, they dig a hole with their fingers, as deftly and savagely as real hyenas, tear out the contents,... and appropriate the ornaments ..." He continued, "Every woman wears strings of beads and curious odds and ends gathered by her own resurrectionary industry, or bequeathed by ghoulish ancestors."[78] The practice, most likely uninterrupted through millennia, testifies to the aesthetic appreciation of the artifacts of older civilizations and the ingenuity of local women in restringing them to create their own contemporary jewelry. How distanced is this from the jewelry inspired by historic examples sold at museum shops today?

CHAPTER SIX

DUAL SETTLEMENTS

The Past and the Present among the Ruins

DESCRIBING THE RUINS OF Palmyra in the 1780s, Constantin-François Volney noted a "spectacle" in the courtyard of the Temple of Baal (Temple of the Sun) that he considered "even more interesting [than the temple] for a philosopher":

> That is, to see on these sacred ruins [showing] the magnificence of a powerful and refined people, about thirty mud huts, where as many peasant families live in misery … All the industry of these Arabs depends on cultivating a few olive trees, and a little wheat that they need for living; all their richness has been reduced to a few goats and a few sheep which they graze in the desert.[1]

The glory of the past civilization, associated with the foundations of European civilization, and the misery of the current village, inhabited by backward people, presented a dichotomy that would be described repeatedly by others. Palmyra appeared in a book written in 1825 for young adults to introduce them to the wonders of the world, from the Great Wall of China to Niagara Falls and the steam engine. The author described "the remarkable ruins" in detail, pointing out with pride that they were discovered by "two Englishmen, Messrs. [James] Wood and [Robert] Dawkins," who wrote *Ruins of Palmyra* and drew the contemporary scene, repeating Volney's message:

This once splendid city is now inhabited by about thirty Arab families, who have built their huts in the court of the great temple. The intervals between these magnificent ruins being laid out in wretched plantations of corn and olives, inclosed with mud walls.[2]

A detailed report on the huts was provided by Charles G. Addison, who traveled to Syria in the 1830s. Regretting that the great temple was "surrounded and disfigured by the mud huts of the village, through the interior rooms of which you are obliged to walk to get to the different parts of the building," he narrated how he entered the villagers' homes in order to reach his destinations. This close experience allowed him to make some observations about the architecture of the Arab village: "square hovels of mud mixed with chopped straw, roofed with earth, leaves, and dry sticks." At the southern end of the temple, he noticed the village mosque, "fantastically ornamented and set off with passages from the Koran written round the walls." The village nestled in the Roman ruins impressed Addison to note "the striking contrast of the magnificence of bygone times with the poverty and meanness of the present day."[3]

In the following decades, many more travelers recorded comments on the village in the ruins and photographers documented the site, exposing a rather picturesque general view (figures 6.1, 6.2, and 6.3). The layout of the indigenous settlement adhered to an order, with some straight streets (the main streets). The awareness and appreciation of the unique setting in which the peasants placed their village are glimpsed in the axial relationship of one street (described as "a mean street" by one traveler in 1906) to an entrance of the temple, but also in the decision to remain on the lower level, perhaps taken consciously so as not to intrude in the monumentality of the ruins. Many of the houses ("more like wasps' nests than any other thing," according to the same traveler) had walled gardens and decorative details.[4] Examining these images against the background of travelers' remarks opens another point of view, one that presents a village that is proud of its location, its connection to history, and its own aesthetic conventions. In an exceptional case, a European traveler even acknowledged that the residents "respected" the antique site by not treating it as a quarry, a fortunate affair also due to the fact that their houses were built of "dust mixed with water."[5] Yet the possibility of a harmonious relationship between peasants and the past of their land was not conceivable to the European mind at the time — as expressed in the following passage:

FIGURE 6.1 Palmyra, village among the ruins, ca. 1900–1920. (Library of Congress, Prints and Photographs)

FIGURE 6.2 Palmyra, main street of the village among the ruins, ca. 1900–1920. (Library of Congress, Prints and Photographs)

FIGURE 6.3 Palmyra, a house built among the ruins, 1929. (Library of Congress, Prints and Photographs)

The people evidently feel no sense of incongruity between past and present. To them the buildings of nobler men of old are but part of the world as they found it, like the mountains and the water-springs. Indeed, so little reverence have they for the ancient buildings, that they are to be seen driving donkeys among the ruins ...[6]

However, stemming largely from the demands of foreign travelers and the increasingly strict Ottoman laws that specified heavy penalties on contraband activity, the villagers were acutely aware of the past they literally lived on and exploited for financial gain. Peters reported that as he walked through the streets within the limits of the temple, many doors opened and the villagers offered him "very good Palmyrene pieces," which they had hidden under the floors, in ovens, and in gardens.[7]

Commentary on the duality between the past and the present was not reserved to Western observers. Writing on the glamour of the antique city of Gerasa in 1911, İsmail Fazıl Pasha, the governor of Syria at the time, shared the viewpoint, revealing the distanced position of the Ottoman elite from the region and their firm belief in a social and cultural hierarchy that placed them above the local populations. He stated that the remains of the old settlement testified to the prosperity of the older civilizations. But, he continued, in the twentieth century, those magnificent works had been replaced by black tents and hovels resembling mole nests, made out of earth and inhabited by nomads and shepherds. A photograph of the governor inside one of the tents, being feasted by a tribe, marked his difference from the "natives" and reiterated this message (figure 6.4).[8]

Duality on the Excavation Site

The contrast between the glamour of the past and the misery of the present, observed by travelers, found a parallel in another duality on excavation sites, this time between the quarters of the archaeologists and those of the laborers. Archaeologists needed spaces that responded to their particular lifestyles, albeit within the restrictions of local resources, including materials and construction techniques. Nevertheless, the facilities they built for themselves and to store the objects they discovered tended to stand out from their surroundings, namely, the workers' camps that mushroomed on sites that were not within commuting distance from existing villages. The seasonal migration of the workforce involved entire families, who brought

عبد الله عشيرلى طرفنده سوريه واليسى اسماعيل فاضل پاشا اشاء وربله ضيافت

FIGURE 6.4 İsmail Fazıl Pasha (in the middle) and Ottoman officers feasted by the villagers. (*Şehbal* 2, no. 45 [15 Teşrinisani 1327/October 28, 1911])

their own ways of life to the excavation grounds. The resulting duality evoked the physical structure of colonial cities, where the colonizer and the colonized lived separately but next to each other in architecturally differing settings. This pattern went back to the earliest excavation sites. For example, in 1812, having obtained a permit from Veli Pasha, the governor of Morea, to work on the Temple of Bassae in Peloponnese, the German archaeologists Otto Magnus Stackelberg and Carl Freiherr Haller von Hallerstein had created a temporary camp of tents and huts for the fourteen Europeans involved in the work. The locals immediately coined it "the Franks' Town."[9]

Austen Henry Layard's popular accounts of his Mesopotamian explorations owed much to the lively descriptions of the people of the land, the tribes of different ethnic and religious groups, their customs and habits, down to their costumes and living environments. The role played by Layard's imagination in these proto-ethnographic accounts may have been significant, but they raised an interest in the human scene, presented in a multidimensional and colorful manner; furthermore, they provided intelligence data for British expansion projects in the region.[10] The village that developed near Layard's excavation site in Khorsabad, crowded with women and children, was an impromptu "native town." Nearby but separate were the units of the archaeology compound: storage tents protected by guards and a house for Layard, his immediate entourage (his translator and servants), and his frequent guests. Layard was careful not to make his house a controversial structure that would stand out. He thus filled in the equidistant narrow windows originally built by his construction workers, arguing that they gave the building the appearance of a fortress, which could be interpreted by the locals as "making a permanent Frank settlement in the country."[11] In light of Layard's close association with British imperial ambitions and his intelligence work, this act was a clever political move to assure a degree of obscurity rather than a thoughtful response to local sensibilities.

Of course, not all archaeologists were able to build comfortable homes for themselves, nor did all temporary workers erect their own sheds or tents. To give one example, Joseph Thacher Clarke and his colleagues, digging in Assos, had to find shelter in a "badly built house" in the village nearby (Behram), where the bitter winter cold was "decidedly uncomfortable." Although they had the advantage of glazed windows in the two rooms the expedition occupied, it was impossible to heat them with a *mangal*, or charcoal brazier. The Greek workmen from Mytilene (Lesbos), all immigrants, were accommodated in four small houses on the waterfront, "which were at the same time cafés, shops, and bakeries." In the winter months, "they slept, closely packed together upon the dais of the cafés, or stowed away upon the shelves of the forcers and bakers."[12] As Clarke implies, even the difficult conditions were not equally difficult for all.

It is in the later wealthier, longer, and larger excavations that the archaeologists were able to be housed in comfort and convenience. The American Society for the Excavation of Sardis, founded by Howard Crosby Butler in 1909 with support from wealthy New York philanthropists and art collectors, including some members of the Metropolitan Museum of Art, was a privileged organization, affording good living conditions for the team. Even the tents of the 1910 first season reflected the attention paid to the archaeologists' well-being. The "camp site," on high ground above the Valley of Paktolos, enjoyed views of the ruins, as well as the cool air. Set up in a tight cluster, the compound was separated by some distance from the peasant houses below it, marking the first step in the separation of the two communities (figure 6.5). It was composed of five sections: a double tent for living purposes, a smaller tent to be used as an office by the engineers, three sleeping tents (two for regular members, one for assistants), a kitchen

FIGURE 6.5 Sardis, general view showing the archaeological site, archaeologists' tents, and the village. (PUAA, Sardis, A.13.b)

tent, and another sleeping tent for visitors. All tents had wooden floors and wooden racks for books, equipment, and small objects found on the site (figure 6.6).[13]

The construction of the expedition house began in the first season. During the second month of work, Butler negotiated with the *kaymakam* of Salihli for the price of the land on the hill to the east of the temple, which enjoyed panoramic views of the surrounding landscape and the ruins below, dramatic with the two famous columns standing alone. To facilitate the building process, a branch of the railway was directed toward the site.[14] The house was organized around a courtyard, with the one–story-high living quarters in the front, overlooking the excavation site to the west. On the east, in the back, there was a storehouse, again one story high. The two other sides of the courtyard were defined by a wing of bedrooms on the north and the kitchen and servants' quarters on the south—both two stories high; the north side was expanded during the next season for the accommodation of the military guard, which consisted of a sergeant and two privates (figures 6.7 and 6.8).[15]

An arched loggia in front of the living room connected the two wings on

FIGURE 6.6 Sardis, interior of a tent in the archaeologists' compound. (PUAA, Sardis, C.7.5d)

FIGURE 6.7 Sardis, general view with the field house ("Villa Omphale") in the background. (PUAA, Sardis, A.247)

FIGURE 6.8 Sardis, interior view of the field house. (PUAA, Sardis, Butler Archive Album, 3b)

the north and the south, dominating the main façade in a manner foreign to the region. Yet in terms of formal characteristics and construction techniques, the American team had made a decision to use local sources and local unskilled labor. Stones from the riverbed were laid in mud plaster on the exterior walls of the first level, while all other walls were in mud brick. The structural system of the upper floors was timber skeleton as used in the architecture of the area; overhangs endowed the building with another regionalist flavor. Skilled labor proved necessary only in the construction of the loggia and the interiors. For these tasks, Greek and Cretan workers were hired from the nearby town of Salihli[16] (figures 6.9–6.12).

The archaeologists named the new building "Villa Omphale," after the queen of Lydia in Greek mythology, "the most distinguished of the mythical heroines whose history was bound up with that of ancient Lydia." They also acknowledged an irony in their choice of local architectural concepts, which were not received as such by the workers, all showing "greatest interest and enthusiasm" in the building: "They thought that they were building a truly American palace, while we thought we were planning a very Oriental but simple habitation."[17] In effect, the expedition house was a modern

FIGURE 6.9 Sardis, front view of the field house. (PUAA, Sardis, C.7.7.f)

FIGURE 6.10 Sardis, back view of the field house. (PUAA, Sardis, C.7.7.h)

experiment in a proto-regionalist style, not unlike the architecture of contemporary official buildings ranging from government palaces to schools and hospitals throughout the empire.[18] Its location emphasized its scale and made a statement of power: it dominated the surrounding landscape and established supremacy over everything in sight. It appeared in the background of innumerable photographs of the expedition as a constant reminder of the American presence.

FIGURE 6.11 Sardis, the field house during construction, showing the use of local materials and techniques. (PUAA, Sardis, C.7.7.c)

Laborers came to the site from the surrounding countryside, as well as from Salihli. However, a small settlement of about a dozen households also developed in the valley, on the northern edge of the antique site (see figure 6.5). Photographs depict their houses as rather well-built structures, which seem to have grown into a permanent village rather than a seasonal abode. Yet the scale of the buildings, their architecture, and the informal manner in which they occupied the land formed a contrast to the archaeologists' villa

FIGURE 6.12 Sardis, courtyard of the field house. (PUAA, Sardis, B.524)

on the hill, the distance between the two attesting to the separation of the two communities. The American interest in the ethnographic dimensions of the local community was reflected in photographs of individuals that showed them in their exotic costumes, but these did not make up a comprehensive survey (see figure 5.15).

Considering this seasonal compound in its broader setting may give a better understanding of the way it operated at the time. The ruins were about 5 miles from Salihli, the largest settlement nearby. Salihli was a village of about fifty households prior to the opening of the railway between İzmir and Alaşehir in 1869. Due to its strategic location on the line that connected the large and cosmopolitan port on the Aegean to points inland, Salihli grew significantly, boasting a population of 24,374 in 1891 and 28,836 in 1914. An Ottoman yearbook summarized Salihli's participation in the modern world by the sixty-two petroleum gaslights that illuminated its streets.[19] The trains from İzmir took four hours and stopped in the small village of Sard in the vicinity of the ruins. With its mixed population of Muslims (the largest group), Greeks, Armenians, and Jews, in the midst of a fertile agricultural area, and on a main transportation conduit, Salihli (and, of course, İzmir itself) offered a wealth of services and products, which must have contributed to the quality of the everyday life of the American archaeologists, as well as their working conditions.

Nippur: The Archaeologists' Castle

Compared to Sardis, Nippur, the site excavated by John Punnett Peters, Hermann Volrath Hilprecht, and John Henry Haynes of the University of Pennsylvania in four seasons between 1889 and 1900, occupied a more obscure location in Mesopotamia, creating serious challenges. The team's trip from Baghdad to the site during the last expedition took several days from late January to February 4, 1899. Its details convey much about the size of the crew, the distances covered, the hardships endured, and the equipment that needed to be taken along. The caravan that left Baghdad consisted of sixty-two camels and several mules, all loaded with equipment. In Hillah, this load was transferred to six large "native boats," together with "the staff and the Ottoman commissioner, half-a-dozen servants, about 150 of [the] former workmen from the vicinity of Babylon with their families and supplies, and six *zabtiye* furnished by the government as a guard." The boats sailed down the Euphrates, through the Daghara Canal and Khor el Afej to Nippur.[20]

The Ottoman yearbooks describe Nippur as being about "one hour's distance" from the village of Souk al Afaq in the subprovince (*sancak*) of Diwaniyah, and at "four hours' distance" from it; Diwaniyah itself was 160 kilometers (99.4 miles) to the southeast of Baghdad on the left bank of the Euphrates River. In the 1890s, the town of Diwaniyah had 484 small mudbrick houses (described by Peters as "a miserable little collection of mud hovels"),[21] 200 shops, eight coffee shops, one *mescid* (small mosque), three schools for young children, four khans, two baths, four wholesale markets, one telegraph office, and military barracks. There were about four thousand palm trees within and in the vicinity of the settlement, with a few vegetable and fruit gardens as well. Most of the residents were tradesmen and artisans. The village of Souk al Afaq was named so because it had more shops (130 shops and two coffee shops) than houses. The tribes living in this area, who engaged in agriculture and animal husbandry, came to the village to shop but chose to live on their lands in the countryside.[22]

Hillah, on the Euphrates and about 70 kilometers (43.5 miles) to the north of Diwaniyah and 95 kilometers (59 miles) to the south of Baghdad, was one of the major settlements in the region, dependent on a rich agricultural hinterland that produced wheat, barley, rice, beans, sesame seeds, and dates. Its population in 1911 was about thirty thousand, and it had 2,626 houses, thirty coffee houses, eighteen khans (the "best in Hille [Hillah]" was qualified by Peters as "a miserable place"),[23] a large warehouse, 120 markets, and 3,126 shops. The list of official buildings indicated the degree to which Hillah had been affected by the Ottoman centralization and modernization programs, reflecting especially the investment made in the Arab provinces under the reign of Abdülhamid II: government palace, telegraph office, pharmacy, *gazhane* (gas factory for street lighting), slaughterhouse, two warehouses for grains, military barracks, military hospital, military police headquarters, one high school, thirty traditional elementary schools (*mekteb-i sibyan*, with a curriculum of literacy, mathematics, and Koran studies), and two modern elementary schools (*mekteb-i ibtidai*), as well as an old, large mosque and twenty-eight *mescids*. The architecture of the military barracks and the government palace was noted as "large and orderly," and the telegraph office, the pharmacy, and the two modern elementary schools — all built in 1900 (1318) — were "perfect" structures.[24] According to Peters, the government palace was "built for the most part of bricks bearing the Nebuchadrezzar stamp, and evidently taken from the ruins of Babylon."[25]

American archaeologists used the facilities and resources of Diwaniyah and Hillah, as well as conducting business with the government officers there.[26] Not only did they rely on local labor, but the *kaymakam* of Diwaniyah gave them security forces on the orders of the Ministry of the Interior, which stipulated that local administrations were to maintain safe conditions on excavation sites throughout the empire.[27] Food supplies came from the region, and the archaeologists depended on local transportation means (boats, carriages, camels, mules, and horses), as well as the modern communication systems (figure 6.13). Arranging for the weekly dispatch of mail and

FIGURE 6.13 "The carriage which brought our [Haynes'] party from Baghdad to Hille." The photograph shows the security forces that accompanied them during the journey. (UPMAAA, Nippur 6957)

telegraphs from Diwaniyah to the excavation site, Peters stated that "during the whole course of our work at Nippur, we were thus in comparatively close connection, through mail and telegraph, with the rest of the world."[28] Nevertheless, Nippur's lonely location in the middle of the desert played a big role in the development of a true village, near the excavation site, with the expedition house dominating it.

Upon their arrival to Nippur on their first expedition (1888–1889), the American archaeologists pitched their tents at the highest point on the site, to the southwest of the ruins. Haynes, who had made this decision, argued for the advantages of this location: unobstructed views of the swamps and the desert and protection against malaria as well as "possible attacks from the Arabs." The tents formed the core of a larger compound, surrounded by small structures built around them in a square plan. They consisted of stables; storerooms for food, equipment, and antiquities; servants' rooms (for thirty-two workmen, six with families); a hut for guards; workshops; a kitchen; and a dining room. The commissioner, Bedri Bey, and Haynes preferred sleeping in huts rather than tents. Haynes's hut was connected to a photographic workroom. Constructed by local workmen using bunches of reeds arched together and covered with palm-leaf mats, these "native huts" were replicas of dwellings called *sarifas*. They were intended to screen the tents from sandstorms and form a layer of security from "the thievish inclinations of the children of the desert." Nevertheless, the resulting unusual village, with the tents in the center, surrounded by the recycled huts in the tried-and-true local architectural forms and construction techniques, proved to be "a great mistake." Its high location made it open to hot winds and sandstorms and called the attention of "every loiterer and marauder in the neighborhood." Despite the presence of the *zabtiye*, the Arabs wandered around the site, even entering the tents and examining the contents, "like a crowd of naughty boys." The end of the expedition came with the unplanned end of the settlement. After the tents were taken down and the entire team was ready to leave on the early morning of April 18, a fire (set secretly by an "Arab") demolished the whole camp in five minutes. Three horses, including Peters's own horse, "were roasted to death."[29]

The archaeologists applied the lessons learned from the first expedition in their second expedition (1889–1890) and set up their camp in the plain "to the south of the western half of the ruins."[30] Photographs from 1890 show a rigidly ordered settlement on flat land, with four tents at the center and again surrounded by "native huts" with various facilities serving the team—none of which provided protection from the "diluvial downpours." This formed an inner compound in a square plan, buffered by open spaces on four sides, then separated from the surroundings by a 3-foot (0.9 m)-tall wall made of ancient bricks dug from the site (figures 6.14 and 6.15). Farther out, but still part of the settlement, was the workers' village in the reed and palm-leaf architecture, neatly lined at right angles around a large open court in an unprecedented layout for the region. This pattern was dictated by the Americans, based on their conviction that it would "render the destruction by fire less possible."[31] A similar intervention from the fourth expedition adhered to the archaeologists' continued preference for orderly arrangements. Haynes wrote in his field notes that in order to help the workers who were having problems in plotting their settlement, he had "to adjust the difficulties by taking full direction and adopting a plan, laid out a street and caused all who would move their houses to conform to it." Likening the "revengeful native" to the "untrained irritable child," he added: "Rightly handled, they respond quickly and sometimes very gladly to discipline from a rightful source."[32]

The imposition of a "considerable distance" between the workers' village

FIGURE 6.14 Nippur, view of the camp at the excavation site. (UPMAAA, Nippur 5302)

FIGURE 6.15 Nippur, a nearer view of the camp at the excavation site. (UPMAAA, Nippur 5303)

and the archaeologists' headquarters was a deliberate strategy. The latter had only one entrance on the east side, facing away from the native compound, and thus enabling the team "to guard the better against treachery." Meanwhile, unfamiliar as it must have been to peasants in its formal character, the open area in the middle of the village was appropriated for customary uses, notably for cooking and for informal gatherings.[33] The "circus" for exercising horses was also located here. At the opposite end, just outside the "inner camp," a guest house was built. The American *mudhif*, as these accommodations were called, thus repeated a common feature of the villages in the region, exactly "in the fashion of the country." Nevertheless, it was not copied without modification: its placement reflected strategic thinking, as the visitors were thus "prevented from over-running our camp and spying out our equipment."[34]

During the second expedition, the archaeologists struggled to improve their daily life in Nippur. In addition to better living conditions, special measures were taken for the provision of food supplies. In order not to encounter a shortage of meat as in the previous expedition, Americans bought a flock of sheep and hired a shepherd, enabling them to eat "excellent mutton." They also purchased chickens and benefited from a fully stocked chicken coop. Haynes's attempt to grow a vegetable garden seems to have failed, but the idea would reemerge and succeed during the later expeditions. Green produce remained rare in 1889–1890 and had to be brought from Hillah. Nonetheless, meals had gotten much better in the camp, owing to the "marvelous" Chaldean cook, fat Gerghiz, who served sumptuous dinners. On one important occasion, the visit of the French military attaché from the embassy in Constantinople, Gerghiz cooked a memorable twelve-course dinner.[35] A common Sunday dinner would include "soup, a baked pot-pie, rice, stewed cucumbers, cucumber salad, sour milk curd."[36]

A big step was taken during the third expedition (1893–1896), marking the American presence permanently in the landscape by means of a prominent structure (figure 6.16). In the accustomed way, the season began with four tents, which sheltered the officers, security forces, and the servants. The boxes and bales that contained the provisions, implements, and equipment were placed in the quadrangular space enclosed by the tents. Haynes wrote in this journal that because "the Arab imagination, as fanciful as of yore, filled the boxes with gold and silver," it was essential to keep them out of sight of this "robber people." In effect, the valuable instruments used in photography and surveying needed better storage than "a tent on the shift-

FIGURE 6.16 Nippur, view of the "Castle." (UPMAAA, Nippur 6025)

ing, drifting sands of a burning desert." Furthermore, "it was much more necessary to secure the shelter and protection of walls and roofs for those born and bred in cooler climates."[37] As the third expedition was expected to be considerably longer than the previous ones, two to three consecutive years as compared to two and a half months and four months, the archaeologists opted for an expedition house, built according to their particular needs, instead of tents and sarifas. This structure would provide protection from the harsh climate (the heat, the sandstorms, and the rainstorms), as well as from the "thievish inclinations of the Arabs."[38] In addition, it had to emanate "the appearance of strength" to convey a message about the power and status of the archaeological team, while "excluding the people round about us [them] from its precincts. The "defensible or fortified" building had a complicated program, composed of three main features: a castle, a storehouse, and a residence.[39]

Haynes, in charge of the entire operation, had decided on a site close to the one chosen by Peters in the second expedition, on the plain to the south of the ruins. Relying on his knowledge of the "ancient structures" in the region, Haynes oriented the building toward the cardinal points of the compass in order to secure a direct breeze through it in summer when the wind blew steadily from the northwest. It occupied a total area of 70 feet (21.3 m) by 50 feet (15.2 m) and had a courtyard in the center that measured 20 feet (6 m) by 35 feet (10.6 m). The ground floor consisted of storage spaces for provisions and antiquities, as well as a kitchen and rooms for servants and security forces; the security forces were placed next to the doorway, "within which the Arabs were not admitted." The rooms on the second story on the southeastern part belonged to the director of the expedition; the Turkish inspector, Bedri Bey, also lived on this floor. Another room on the same level was relegated to the drying of tablets. Haynes thought of the flat roof covering the second story as an "excellent" sleeping area for summer months. In the courtyard, a well was dug and a pump was inserted to be used only in emergency cases, as the water from the well was too salty. Just as for the second expedition, a chicken coop was built again in the courtyard.[40] Meyer's plans, included in his diary, indicate how these functions continued to be accommodated the same way in the "Castle" in 1894; by then, the Turkish inspector, Bedri Bey, was replaced by Saleh (Salih) Bey (figures 6.17 and 6.18). During the fourth expedition another story was added to address the need for more rooms; it included a new dining room and guest rooms. As the building had remained empty for three years, the damages it suffered from the harsh winter and summer weather had to be repaired during the first weeks of the excavation season.[41]

Haynes relied on workers from Hillah, who were excavating the mounds in Nippur. Only one among them was a bricklayer; the rest were skilled only "in searching the graves and habitations of antiquity." Haynes himself served as the carpenter and fabricated the few doors out of small poplar poles and old boxes. The building was finished after an intensive construction period of twenty days. The exterior walls of clay, 7 feet (2.1 m) thick at the bottom, were laid up in layers; they gradually diminished in thickness, creating slanting façades. To enhance protection, there were no large windows on the external façades and only one door; all other openings were onto the courtyard. The 2-foot (0.6 m)-thick partition walls were made of kiln-burned bricks, just like the bricks made in Ur 4,500 years ago. They were made on the site, whereas palm logs were transported from Hillah, and reed mats, used to cover the floors and roofs of clay cement, were bought from Arabs in the vicinity.[42] Meyer appreciated the response of the house to climatic conditions, as "the walls are thick and what breeze there is flows into the court and the rooms," even on a day when the temperature struck

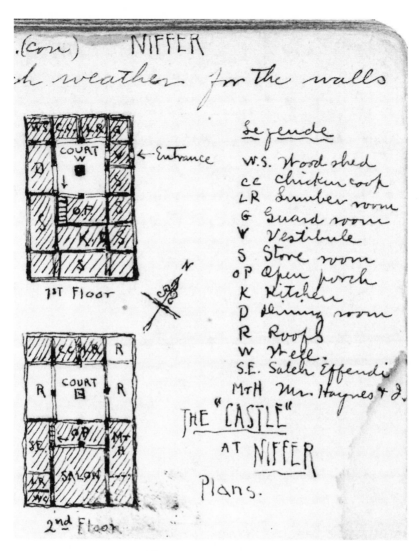

FIGURE 6.17 Nippur, plans for the "Castle," drawn by Joseph Meyer and showing the first and second stories. (SPHC)

100 degrees in the shade. The construction of a roof over the courtyard, covered by "horizontal laths of reeds" on which mats were placed, helped further reduce the heat in the building in the afternoons.[43]

The dig house stood proudly in the landscape, higher than everything else around it. Admittedly "rudely and roughly built," it nevertheless attracted much attention from the neighboring tribes and was named "the

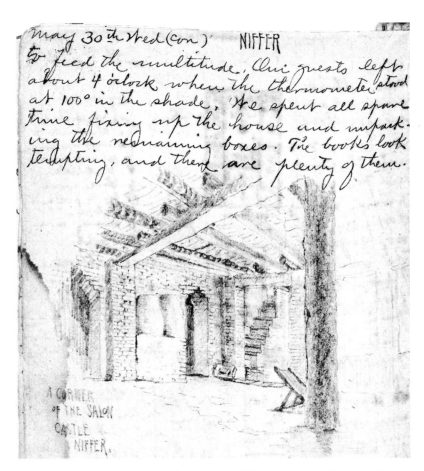

FIGURE 6.18 Nippur, the "Castle," a corner of the salon; sketch by Joseph Meyer. (SPHC)

Castle" (or, the Kala) by the Arabs — a name adopted by the Americans. With its imposing scale, fortresslike exterior walls, and few small openings (most likely made to provide cross-ventilation throughout the building), it merited the title. However, constructed out of local materials and in adherence to the architectural forms of the region, it also recalled the residences of local families of wealth and status in nearby settlements. Meyer described the "Arab forts" as built of "crude brick or merely of mud, . . . nearly always square, tall and tapering." The corners sometimes had square pinnacles, and the few windows were filled with latticework in wood.[44] His sketches situated them in their idyllic contexts, as described by the architect: "picturesquely placed on a reedlined canal in a beautiful garden of dates, figs and

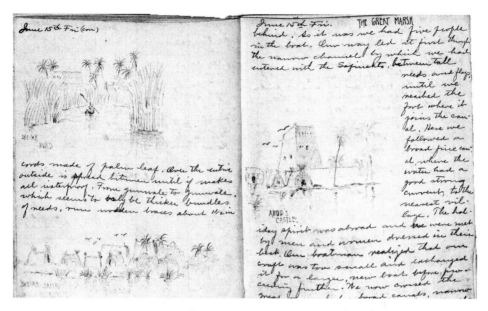

FIGURE 6.19 Nippur, "Arab forts," sketches by Joseph Meyer. (SPHC)

pomegranates" (figure 6.19).[45] Haynes was similarly drawn to these houses: several of his photographs depict "Abdel Hamid's Castle" and "the more attractive houses at Anah," suggesting that they served as inspiration for the architecture of the American Castle.

Haynes associated the Castle with the success of the excavations, linking it to the well-being of the archaeologists; the shelter and protection it gave to the team members assured their health during the difficult summer months they spent in Nippur. Moreover, "the fortified dwelling" had finally blocked the party from the "crowds of curious and covetous idlers always thronging about the tents." The "fortress home" gave them privacy; it was a "sacred shelter of peace even among a robber people."[46] Daily life also improved a great deal with the new building. A walled garden adjacent to the house produced vegetables and fruits; its first harvest of eggplant, lemna, cucumber, and melons in 1899 was registered with much delight.[47] Chickens and sheep, again owned by the expedition team, contributed to the preparation of balanced meals.[48] The rooftop turned into a pleasant dining area, but only before sunset, as the insects made the use of lamps inconvenient when the light faded.[49] Sleeping here "in the cooler strata of the sultry night" and the comfortable rooms that allowed for a midday rest further improved the lifestyle of the archaeologists.[50]

Meyer gave a romantic description of the exotic

> view from the roof over the wide plain—yellow here and there with ripe
> grain, or showing the course of a distant canal by a long line of trees,—
> and towards the great mysterious mounts to the north that hides nobody
> knows what...we [are] cut off from civilization by the long stretch of the
> desert and marsh that separates us from Hilleh.[51]

He reiterated the poetry of the land a couple of weeks later, this time describing it during dinnertime:

> My favorite view is from the castle roof in the early evening when the sun
> sets behind the south end of the long range of Niffer mounds, which here
> ends in the reed-grown marsh. Just beyond is a sheet of water, and the
> whole looks like the picture book view of Babylonia.[52]

The drastic changes in the living conditions owed much to the arrival of
Mrs. Haynes, who seems to have brought "a true homelike atmosphere" to
the Castle. Cassandria Haynes served as her husband's private secretary,
and having acquired some knowledge of Mesopotamian history, she kept
meticulous notes of the daily work on the expedition site. However, she
was most appreciated for taking "complete charge of the household of the
expedition in an admirable manner" and providing the members of the expedition and their frequent guests with "remarkable comfort." Hilprecht
remarked that the conditions were so different than 1889 that he could
"almost imagine himself transplanted to one of the watering-places of the
Arab caliphs in the desert," referencing Qasr Amra, the early-eighth-century
palace built by the Umayyad caliph Walid (now in Jordan).[53]

Nippur: The Native Village

Several photographs of the American Castle in Nippur show in the foreground a village of considerable size composed of huts typical to the region, recalling Meyer's sketches of "Arab forts" surrounded by huts (see
figure 6.19). Others taken from the roof terrace give general views of the
settlement, conveying a clear idea of its overall image, organizational pattern, and open spaces, as well as the people engaged in numerous activities that crowded it. Even though similar compounds accompanied the first
two expeditions, the albums from the third and fourth expeditions depict
the more substantial nature of the villages and, judging only from the sheer

numbers of photographs and the wording of their captions, demonstrate a rise in an ethnographic curiosity among the archaeologists. As the numbers of workers recorded were around three hundred for these years, and as each worker came with his family, the population would easily reach fifteen hundred people—much larger than many permanent villages. Not only the architecture but also the lifestyle brought to the expedition site reflected the residents' places of origin, especially in terms of daily activities ranging from the preparation of food to weaving, family customs, child rearing, music, and various celebrations. The difference was in the employment of men in excavations rather than farmwork and animal husbandry.

The "huts for the people," built by the workforce upon the order of the archaeologists, created an unlikely cousin of the indigenous villages common to the universal expositions held in European and North American cities in the late nineteenth century.[54] Assembled in part as exotic curiosities, in part as ethnographic tableaux vivants, these precursors of theme parks served as venues to acquaint European and American crowds with "other" people in a hierarchical order, loaded with notions of civilizational superiority, colonial power, and race-thinking. Their extreme popularity drew large crowds, and information about them was disseminated through various publications, endowing them with great visibility.[55] The archaeologists in Nippur, undoubtedly familiar with the phenomenon (at least in its version at the World's Columbian Exposition in Chicago held in 1893), must have been intrigued and amused to realize that they had something akin to that in their front yard. In light of the pervasive interest in ethnography at the time, the "native village" (as it was named by the archaeologists) called for analysis and documentation—duly carried out by Haynes.

From Wood to Layard, Hormuzd Rassam, Osman Hamdi, and Peters, archaeologists had always written about the people who lived in the places where they worked. As seen in the previous chapter, these observations often carried an Orientalist flavor and were shaped by the sociocultural and political contexts of the chroniclers. Remaining with the case of Nippur, Peters's accounts of the early expeditions, for example, are speckled with anecdotal information on the character, customs, houses, and lifestyles of the locals. To refer randomly to a few of his observations, the villages of "Affech Arabs" consisted of "a few huts of marsh reeds and palm mats, with a guest house, of *muthif*, of the same, grouped around a mud castle," hence establishing a model for the excavation Castle and village, but on a more modest scale; the "universal" house in the region was "a hut of mats of grass spread on arched columns of bundles of reed tied together"; coffee, flavored with myrrh, was prepared by a "negro slave" in several copper pots, drained from the largest to the smallest; the "war songs" of Arabs were "threatening and uncomplimentary."[56]

During the third and fourth expeditions, Haynes, the new director of the team, engaged in disciplined ethnographic research and documentation, most likely enhanced by the longer excavation seasons, the panoramic view of a complete village below the Castle, and the emphasis placed by the University of Pennsylvania on photographic documentation, as well as its financial backing. Unhappy with his own failure at using the camera, Peters had underlined the importance of its convenience to document "the work in the trenches frequently and systematically, and photographing objects found *in situ*, ... with numbers corresponding to those used in the notebooks and catalogues."[57] Haynes took the assignment seriously and carried it beyond archaeological research, giving a comprehensive record of the "native village."

The University of Pennsylvania endorsed the ethnographic project, as evidenced by a letter from George Brown Goode, the assistant secretary of the Smithsonian (see chapter 1), to William Pepper, the provost of the university from 1881 to 1894. In this letter, written in 1889, Goode expressed the Smithsonian's desire to have "a costume of a Mesopotamian chief, or of his wife, or both, with photographs which will enable our preparators to make lay figure for the display of the costumes" and urged Peters, then the director of the expedition, to secure this item. He also conveyed a wish list from the museum:

> Any illustration of the methods employed in spinning, weaving, dyeing, working with metal or wood, would be exceedingly valuable to us, especially if accompanied by illustrative photographs. Any musical instruments, especially the cruder and simpler forms, and simple lamps, or appliances for making fire, or heating, would also be immediately available.[58]

Goode hence outlined a rough methodological guideline, which was followed by Haynes. Haynes's field notes were dotted here and there with casual ethnographic observations. He wrote, for example, about the first day of the "Moslem feast called 'Bairam' ... [as] a day of rejoicing and feasting." It was an occasion for acquiring new costumes or at least "one garment." The "supremely happy" crowd celebrated by chanting "most lustily

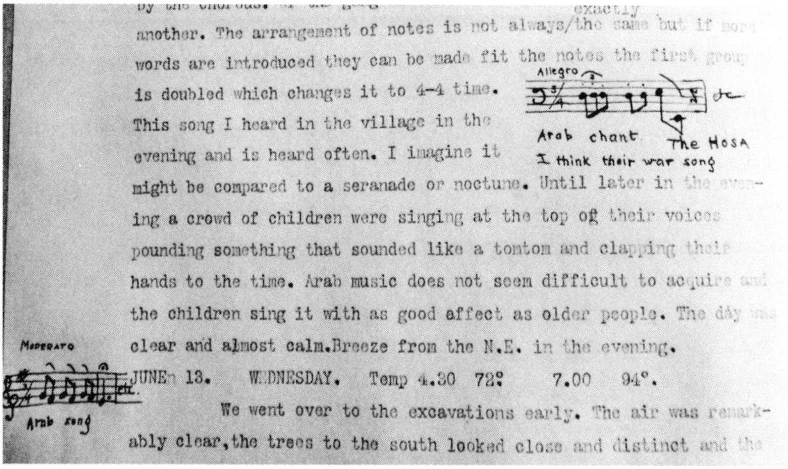

another. The arrangement of notes is not always/the same but if more
words are introduced they can be made fit the notes the first group
is doubled which changes it to 4-4 time.
This song I heard in the village in the
evening and is heard often. I imagine it
might be compared to a seranade or noctune. Until later in the evening a crowd of children were singing at the top of their voices
pounding something that sounded like a tomtom and clapping their
hands to the time. Arab music does not seem difficult to acquire and
the children sing it with as good affect as older people. The day was
clear and almost calm.Breeze from the N.E. in the evening.
JUNE 13.   WEDNESDAY.   Temp 4.30 72°   7.00   94°.
We went over to the excavations early. The air was remarkably clear,the trees to the south looked close and distinct and the

FIGURE 6.20 Nippur, page from Joseph Meyer's diaries with notes on music in the
margins. (UPMAAA, diaries or daybook of Mr. Joseph Meyer)

their hosas" spontaneously.[59] Meyer described the special holiday from a
visually livelier angle. Women and children danced, clapping their hands
to "one of their characteristic songs." Their holiday clothes were black with
pale red and green motifs; colors were reserved for the headgear. However,
"the children were rainbow hued all over."[60] In contrast to the casual tone
of Haynes's notes on the music played in the village, Meyer gave informed
data and added an amateur musicologist's skill to enrich the ethnographic
documentation—not surprising, given that he had studied violin, piano,
and composition.[61] Supplemented by notes in the margins of his diaries (in
one instance writing that he thought the "Arab chant" he was listening to
was "their war song"), his descriptions of the songs he heard from the rooftop of the Castle gave some detail (figure 6.20):

> A leader improvises words and sings them alone ... to be answered in
> the same words by the chorus. Or the gang divides into two parties who
> answer one another. The arrangement of notes is not always the same but
> more words are introduced [so] they can be made fit the notes. The first
> group is doubled which changes it to 4–4 time.

In another instance, he recorded a tune that was in "a descending group of
a minor diameter—three notes in a triplet time nearly always accompanied
by a down." He also made short entries on the musical instruments he heard
without seeing them: an instrument that was pounded on that "sounded

like a tomtom," and another one that "sounded like a pipe." Furthermore, Meyer noted when and why the workers played music and sang. Likening them to "serenades and or nocturnes," he reported that songs were "evening diversions," and continued: "Towards the evening, our arabs begin to be lively." He believed that music played a role as relief and relaxation from the fatigue the laborers felt at the end of the day and, referring back to the excavation work, observed that they shifted to a "lively chant" when making a physical effort, such as pulling a rope and lifting a weight. Listening to a crowd of children singing, he concluded that Arab music did not seem difficult and that the children sang it with "as good affect as older people."[62]

The ethnographic record in Nippur is most striking in the photographs taken during the last two expeditions. Haynes continued to cover the more traditional topics of archaeological photography with shots of the digs on a regular basis, framed from larger views down to single artifacts. "Natives" featured in many of these photographs, digging the earth, carrying the debris and the finds, sitting around in groups on lunch breaks, and posed against the ruins and next to antique objects (see figures 5.1, 5.9, and 5.10). In the conventions of the discipline, they were used to show the impressive operations, give a quick idea of scale, and introduce an exotic human touch. Another collection of photographs, which belonged to a different genre, zoomed in on the "native village." It is through these photographs that Haynes came close to scholarly ethnographic research and to responding to the guidelines sent by Goode.

Several photographs depict general views of the village and convey its organization in clusters. Each group of dwellings has its own courtyard, which serves as a communal open space, used for work as well as for socializing. In one, titled "Scene in the Village," the houses are under construction, with mats and reeds scattered around the site; yet these shells are inhabited — as gleaned from the household activities carried out in the shared open space and the storage jars and baskets (figure 6.21). Others show similar scenes, now taken from the roof of the Castle and zooming in on clusters, again under construction (figure 6.22). As the huts are in different stages of construction, the photographs paint a complete picture of the process. The overall views focus on completed houses against impressive backgrounds. Photographs taken from the ground level, with the mass of the Castle behind, emphasize the duality in the built fabric, whereas frames from the rooftop toward the "mounds of Niffer" situate the village in its topographic and historic context, creating another contrast.

FIGURE 6.21 Nippur, scene in the village. (UPMAAA, Nippur 5748)

FIGURE 6.22 Nippur, general view of workmen's huts as seen from the roof of the "Castle." (UPMAAA, Nippur 5904)

Presented in large scale, the characteristics of the indigenous houses, their construction techniques, and their materials constitute another genre in Haynes's photographs. They cover the construction process in all its phases, from the building of the frame, to the filling in of the walls, the covering of the roof, and finally to the finished unit with a single low door and no fenestration (figures 6.23–6.26). "Natives," shown putting their own houses together, help explain the nature of the work while indicating the scale. One caption accompanying a photograph of a hut in an "advanced stage" and another in the "skeleton" phase in the background, titled "House Building in Niffer," outlined the construction process of the structure: "The architect and chief builder is twisting several moistened flags, or in other words, is making ropes to be used (in place of nails) to build the parts of the structure together."[63] Although the choice of the word "architect" may not be accurate, the information provided in this instance complements the photographs that are labeled as "Building Workman's Hut," "House Building in Nippur," "Houses under Construction," and so forth. Adding his architectural expertise to his ethnographic observations, Meyer also recorded the construction techniques of reed houses in fine detail, illustrating his text with explanatory sketches (figure 6.27). They were built "by means of large arches made by binding together two bundles of reeds, binding their tops together, and planting their ends in the earth. The arches, "either for appearance of for some constructive reason," took the "horseshoe form and nearly always [had] the 'Ctesiphon' oval crown." They were set placed about 10–15 feet (3.0–4.5 m) apart, bound by longitudinal ribs and covered by reed mats. The ends were closed by a frame made of poplar poles, which were covered by mats, with space for doors left in the middle. Mats would also be spread out on the floor.[64]

The third genre is about daily life and shows the villagers carrying out their "typical" activities against the backdrop of their new settlement. Men are commonly portrayed building their houses, with some exceptions: for example, one photograph shows a group of four men, two weaving baskets, two cleaning "a brace of pistols" (figure 6.28); another is about "two brothers engaged in a sham fight" (figure 6.29). Women's work centers around food production: they pound rice to remove the husk from the kernel (figure 6.30), and in many views, they prepare meals squatting on the ground in small groups and using the ovens in the courtyards. An uncharacteristically long caption focuses on one woman "patiently building up a storage jar of clay which only requires drying in the sun to complete it for

FIGURE 6.23 Nippur, construction of a hut, preparation of bundles of reeds to form the frame. (UPMAAA, Nippur 5751)

FIGURE 6.24 Nippur, construction of a hut, assembling the frame. (UPMAAA, Nippur 7003)

FIGURE 6.25 Nippur, completing the construction of a hut. (UPMAAA, Nippur 5574)

FIGURE 6.26 Nippur, a completed hut. (UPMAAA, Nippur 6969)

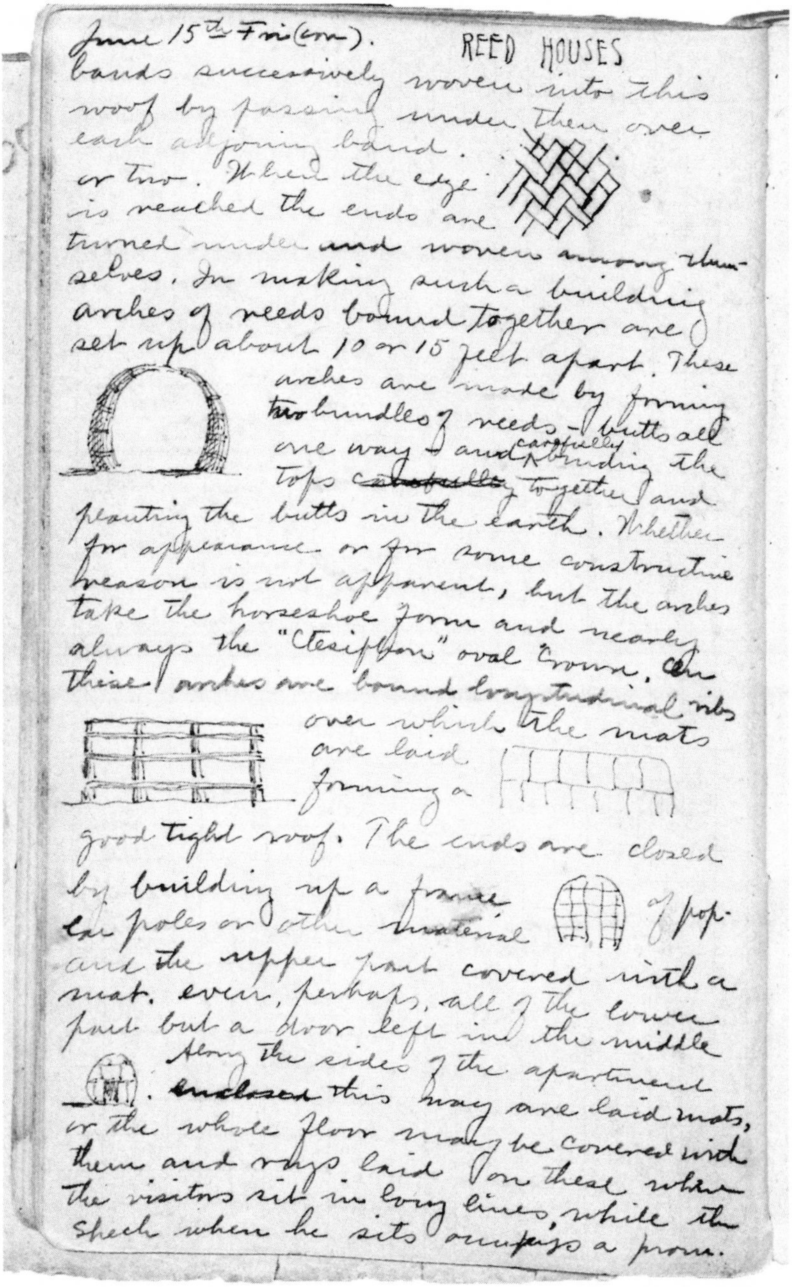

June 15th Fri (con). REED HOUSES

bands successively woven into this woof by passing under then over each adjoining band. or two. When the edge is reached the ends are turned under and woven among themselves. In making such a building arches of reeds bound together are set up about 10 or 15 feet apart. These arches are made by forming ~~two~~ bundles of reeds – butts all one way – and carefully binding the tops ~~carefully~~ together and planting the butts in the earth. Whether for appearance or for some constructive reason is not apparent, but the arches take the horseshoe form and nearly always the "Ctesiphon" oval crown. On these arches are bound longitudinal ribs over which the mats are laid forming a good tight roof. The ends are closed by building up a frame of poplar poles or other material and the upper part covered with a mat. even, perhaps, all of the lower part but a door left in the middle. Along the sides of the apartment enclosed this way are laid mats, or the whole floor may be covered with them and rugs laid on these where the visitors sit in long lines, while the Sheck when he sits occupies a prom.

FIGURE 6.27 Nippur, Joseph Meyer's notes and sketches on the construction techniques of a reed hut. (SPHC)

FIGURE 6.28 Nippur, a group of men engaged in "authentic" activities. (UPMAAA, Nippur 6911)

FIGURE 6.29 Nippur, "two brothers engaged in a sham fight." (UPMAAA, Nippur 6998)

FIGURE 6.30 Nippur, women's activities. (UPMAAA, Nippur 6912)

use." Several household implements lie about "in usual confusion," including "another jar in process of formation and to be made in three sections of set three different times, it being necessary to partially dry each section before another section can be built upon it."[65]

Celebrations were also captured by Haynes. He shot communal events, for example, Bairam (eid) scenes, among them groups of women celebrating and performing "the native dance" in clusters of dark figures that coalesce into an amorphous mass. He also documented private celebrations: in one photograph, a foreman exhibits his youngest son, only ten days old, to a small audience of women clad in long garments and covering their faces; another young boy, nude, stands by him (figure 6.31). In rare instances, names of the subjects were given. The foreman with the newborn was called Hassan Sahab. The women of Haji Tarfa's household from a neighboring village were also identified with their proper names. Fatima, the first wife and the "mistress of the harem"; Hatija, the second; and Lira, "the youngest of Haji Tarfa's three wives" (figure 6.32). Not much can be seen in this rather poor photograph of three figures clad from head to toe in dark costumes. Facing the camera directly, they still remain hidden from the photographer's gaze. These women, belonging to a higher social and economic standing than their hardworking sisters in the excavation village, seem to be less accessible

FIGURE 6.31 Nippur, a celebration. (UPMAAA, Nippur 6913)

FIGURE 6.32 Nippur, the three wives of Haji Tarfa. (UPMAAA, Nippur 234211)

to the ethnographer/archaeologist. Nevertheless, they helped the photographer to complement the ethnographic scenery with Orientalist color.

The life in the village narrated by the archaeologists in text and image was "crude and simple," to recall Goode's specifications. It presented a picture that was not reconcilable with what went on inside the big house — so near and yet so far. The reservation, the mistrust, and the fear expressed by the Americans derived from their awareness of this difference, which increased expedition by expedition as they improved their own living standards from tents to a Castle with living rooms, dining rooms, studies, and photography laboratories, and from diets short on meats and vegetables to multicourse dinners with "excellent mutton" and an array of fresh vegetables.

Relying on the archaeologists' fragmented ethnographic data, it may be worthwhile to take a risky detour and attempt to construct some aspects of the life in the camp from the villagers' perspective. Such imagined scenarios are limited (and desperate) exercises to empathize with the "silent" men, women, and children of Mesopotamia from a distance of over a century. The first question that comes to mind is what it must have meant to accept employment on the excavation. While regular pay must have been the main attraction, the seasonal nature of the job created certain problems. As the site was isolated, lodging and meals had to be provided, necessitating support from families. Added to the likely anxiety about leaving women and children behind, this must have led to the difficult decision to move entire households to Nippur. The fact that the same laborers returned to the expedition season after season affirms the acceptance of this pattern of temporary life for monetary gain.[66] Once settled, everyday activities seem to have followed a set pattern, without major shifts from the original villages. The difference was in the long work hours of the men; during the daytime, the village was occupied only by women and children. Among one of the hardest chores was the provision of water, brought from the marshes and full of "animal life" as reported by Hilprecht.[67] We learn from Meyer that music was a leisurely evening pastime that engaged the community at large.

The big novelty for the "natives" was the presence of a group of foreigners living in the midst of them according to their own peculiar customs. The curiosity of the locals manifested itself in their persistent sneaking into archaeologists' tents—to the endless complaints of the members of the team, which led to the construction of the Arab-proof "Castle." They knew the architectural organization of the rooms, built by workers from the excavation, who likely passed on the information to the village residents. They also had some access to the house on special occasions. On paydays, they came to the entrance, where Haynes and Meyer sat at "the place of judgment ... with a small table and many little piles of Persian silver, Indian rupees, and Turkish gold." The common laborers were paid one by one, their fees depending on the quality of the work they had done. Afterward, the "principal men" were invited to the courtyard to receive their salaries.[68] To celebrate Kurban Bayramı (Eid al-Adha), first a group of women and children visited the Castle and performed a dance in the courtyard; they were followed by workmen who offered their good wishes for the special holiday.[69]

However, with few exceptions (house cleaners, servants, cooks), the house was protected from the workers. Life in the forbidden Castle must have remained an infinite source of speculation, ranging from the simple everyday routines of the foreigners to the manner in which they entertained their guests. The peasants had some idea of the food provisions and the quantities, but could they peek into a dining party with male and female guests and many courses served (including wine from Syria)? What did they think about their clothes—and their hats? What did they make of Mrs. Haynes, who had her own gender-based role at home, but who also took notes on the site as her husband's assistant? How did they react to being photographed by Haynes? Did Haynes show them any photographs or give them copies for keeps? What would an ethnographic record kept by the "natives" on Americans reveal? Such questions will never be answered, but asking them provokes the imagination in critical ways.

EPILOGUE:

ENDURING DILEMMAS

THIRTEEN DECADES have passed since the construction of the Imperial Museum's new building that proudly housed the Sidon sarcophagi and the passing of the Ottoman laws of antiquities that restricted the activities of foreign archaeologists, putting them under the scrutiny of the museum administration, and hence the Ottoman state. Yet the debates and controversies on the possession of antiquities persist today on a global scale with the rigor and passion of the nineteenth century.[1] Indeed, they have intensified under recent pressure from modern nation-states, coined "source" countries (among them, Italy, Greece, Turkey, Egypt, Cambodia, China, and Peru), which demand that Western museums return the ancient works illegally smuggled out and appeal to courts if their requests are not met. With the directors of some prominent Western institutions in the vanguard, the laws have been labeled as "retentionist cultural property laws," "challenging the very basis of encyclopedic art museums," and the museums throughout the world have been divided into two main categories: "encyclopedic" (or "humanistic") and "nationalistic." The first are considered products of the Enlightenment, humanist in their missions, inclusive of "the full diversity of human artistic industry," and drawing "direct attention to different cultures, asking visitors to respect the values of others and seek connections between cultures."[2] They were founded "to think differently about the world"; for example, the British Museum was "established very specifically for everybody, for the whole world,... [as] a way of creating a new kind of citizen for the world," in the words of its former director.[3] In contrast, "nationalist museums" served as instruments "in the formation of national narratives"; they told stories about a nation's past and confirmed its present importance.[4] According to this discourse, they were created by "individual national governments" to suit "their own self-interested decisions," and, keeping antiquities within the borders of national states, they "segregated" them.[5] In their hands, antiquities became politicized in order to support "modern, national cultural politics."[6]

There is, of course, validity to the claims about the political agendas behind the museums in the "source countries," although flattening their intentions into one simple rationale is problematic. Furthermore, to endow Western museums with histories cleansed of political agendas is not convincing in light of recent revisionist literature, as well as the discussions put forward in this book. On the contrary, these institutions and the archaeological research that enabled them to amass their riches were deeply rooted in politics, carried ideological meanings, and contributed to imperial and national identity building from their beginnings. This was not unusual, as the past had always been used in history for political empowerment. An obvious reminder on the architectural appropriations and interpretations of classical Greek architecture in a myriad of ideological twists from the Roman era to the present day should suffice to make the case. Viewed from the long-term perspective, neither the charged histories of the European museums nor the exploitative uses and abuses of antiquities by "modern national states," whether Greek, Iraqi, Peruvian, Turkish, or Chinese, should come as a surprise.[7] In short, the present-day bickering on the good and bad uses of antiquities appears to be a way to conceal the practical question of returning the objects illegally obtained by Western museums.

The group of museum directors and scholars, passionate defenders of the "humanistic" myth, attempt to make a case based on who the real possessors of the artifacts are. They approach the issue from two angles. The first is by a general argument on which all parties would agree: the ancient past is important for "all of us." This is followed by the definitive claim that more people will see them in "international" museums.[8] A 2013 *New York Times* article criticized American museums for being intimidated by "baseless lawsuits by foreign governments" and for agreeing to return some artifacts, claiming that "recent restitution of antiquities makes ancient art less available for the public."[9] Thus, the key questions of the debate that call for reflection are Who is "all of us"? and Who is "the public"?

The second angle answers the questions by designating who does *not* have the cultural right to own antiquities—a thesis that goes back to tired nineteenth-century precedents, with Salomon Reinach's 1883 article "Le vandalisme moderne en Orient" at the forefront.[10] In an attempt to situate the attitudes toward antiquities, James F. Goode claims that "members of traditional societies rarely approached their ancient history and monuments as scientists" and that they "recited mythical tales of glorious ancestors, without the need to tie these to specialized study of surviving sites and monuments."[11] Robin F. Rhodes endorses Goode and maintains further that ownership should be related to preservation, especially because certain "nations ... do little to live up to the responsibilities of protection of cultural heritage," and he asks: "Is it the modern Greeks alone who are cultural heirs to the art and architecture ... of the classical Greeks, or is it the western world as a whole?"[12] James Cuno complements Goode and Rhodes by citing "a Lebanese man," who had expressed his identity through Lebanon, the prophet Mohammad, Imam Ali, and cedar trees, and not through "ancient Roman ruins or antiquities within Lebanese borders." To remedy the situation, controlled by "nationalist retentionist cultural property laws," and to stop "the world's ancient artistic legacy ... [from] being held hostage to the nationalist ambitions of nation-state governments," he proposes "a principle of shared stewardship of our common heritage" and the distribution of antiquities "to better ensure their preservation, broaden our knowledge of them, and increase the world's access to them." He advocates the reestablishment of the "practice of partage," which the Ottoman state had eliminated in 1884, but which had been salvaged, for example, in Iraq in 1924 under the British Mandate.[13]

To facilitate the process of repatriation, Dennis Doordan appeals to "international stewardship" and suggests the substitution of the term "country of origin" for "culture of origin." This, he claims, would enable us to identify "a lineal cultural relationship to these artifacts," rather than accepting their possession by political entities "designated" as the source countries.[14] The debates find a widespread echo in the popular press. To give one example, the New York Times states that "patrimony claims too often serve nationalist ends these days" and, linking the issue to globalism, reformulates the same question in a syntax that includes the answer "Why should any objects necessarily reside in the modern nation-state controlling the plot of land where, at one time, perhaps thousands of years earlier, they came from?"[15]

Requests abound from "countries of origin" to Western museums for the return of antiquities deemed looted, and courts are busy trying to resolve the many related lawsuits. The Greek government's tireless efforts to repatriate the Elgin Marbles, wrapped in shifting political agendas and still continuing in the refueled climate following the opening of the New Acropolis Museum in 2009, stand as the ultimate symbol of these demands. The Greek claims are attributed to "pride and justice," but even more to "nationalistic and symbolic" values. They are also counterbalanced by the special place the "marbles" occupy in British culture: "After 200 years the Elgin marbles have a history that roots them in the British Museum as well as in Athens."[16] Regardless of practical solutions, the high visibility of the enduring controversy serves a meaningful purpose. In Mary Beard's words: "The Parthenon controversy continues because it reflects a real and important conflict about the role of cultural heritage, the responsibility for the classical past and the function of symbolic monuments."[17]

The focus of this book urges a brief look at the demands of the Turkish Republic directed at Western museums. The Turkish claims are reported in the Western media in a terminology that conveys a combative attitude, as exemplified in a 2012 article with phrases such as "Turkey jolts museums," "in their latest salvo Turkish officials filed a criminal complaint," or "Turkey's aggressive tactics." They are also inflicted with political innuendos such as Turkey's "asserting itself in the Middle East in the wake of the Arab spring" and possible penalizing threats for the demands, among them risking and harming relationships with European countries at a time when Turkey seeks to join the European Union.[18] Turkey's response is moralistically self-assured and self-congratulatory. The sheer numbers of artifacts deemed smuggled and recently brought back thanks to hard negotiations by the Turkish government are presented to give an idea of the scale of the operation: 4,519 between 1998 and 2011, according to the then Minister of Culture and Tourism, Ertuğrul Günay.[19] Rejoicing that the Turkish position was finally beginning to be taken seriously by the American museums, the daily newspaper *Milliyet* credited the *Los Angeles Times* for reporting "for the first time" a list of the objects believed to be illegally taken out of the country and now in the J. Paul Getty Museum, the Metropolitan Museum of Art, the Cleveland Museum of Art, and Harvard University's Dumbarton Oaks Research Library and Collection.[20]

The contested antiquities in the American museums included ten from the Getty, twenty-one from Cleveland, eighteen from the Norbert Schimmel Collection at the Metropolitan, and the Sion Treasure at Dumbarton

Oaks. The long struggles with these powerful institutions contributed to the Turkish victimization syndrome that has dominated the scene since the late nineteenth century. The Turkish government's request for the return of a number of objects from the Getty goes back to the 1990s and from Dumbarton Oaks to 1986; none had been repatriated by 2012. The Metropolitan was asked to return the Schimmel antiquities in September 2012; after first denying the receipt of the request, the museum declared that it had reported to Recep Tayyip Erdoğan, prime minister at the time, about the provenance of the pieces and froze the process. Among the Turkish success stories was the return of the Lydian Hoard from the Metropolitan after a thorny process that involved an initial rejection in 1986, followed by legal proceedings, and ended in the museum's agreement to return the collection in 1993.[21]

Perhaps the most spectacular of the recent restitutions to Turkey was that of the upper part of the Weary Herakles statue, transported to Turkey in Erdoğan's official jet as he returned from a United Nations meeting in New York on September 25, 2011. Much publicized by government agencies and widely covered in the press, the highly politicized event celebrated the growing power of the Turkish government on the international scene. The battle over Weary Herakles between the Museum of Fine Arts in Boston and the Turkish officials had been especially difficult. A second-century AD copy of the fourth-century BC original by Lysippos, the upper part of the statue had been exhibited at the MFA since 1981 and was held in half ownership between the museum and the husband-and-wife collectors Shelby White and Leon Levy. Upon the discovery of the lower part in 1980 in an excavation in Perge (southern Anatolia), the Turkish government had filed an inquiry to Boston. After a debate on whether the two halves belonged to the same statue, a cast of the Turkish counterpart was sent to Boston in 1992 and the issue was resolved. However, the museum continued to deny the allegations that it was looted and did not acknowledge Turkey's ownership until negotiations were reopened in 2006, finally resulting in the return of the partial statue to join its missing body.[22]

Weary Herakles, placed in the Antalya Museum, received 406,510 visitors during the first one thousand days of its exhibition life, that is, from October 9, 2011, to July 14, 2014. The curiosity about this symbol of political clout was obvious from the first wave of visitors, with a count of 20,629 between October and December 2011; it reached 173,843 in 2012, but receded to 136,587 in 2013.[23] Despite the decrease, these are significant numbers for a provincial Turkish museum, and they are clearly linked to the statue's publicized story. Nonetheless, the interest must signify something beyond simple associations, revealing the integration of classical antiquity into local culture to some degree.

Picking up on that issue, I conclude this book with two personal vignettes, which, I believe, complicate the question "Who owns antiquity?" My first story takes me to a Sunday morning in May 2001, when with a colleague I went to Kerkouane in Cape Bon, Tunisia. This Punic-Phoenician town (sixth century BC–second century BC) has no glorious standing monuments (such as Dougga and El-Djem) and no legendary history associated with it (like Carthage), but its ruins reveal a fascinating urban fabric that is deciphered with some close attention. My own prejudices had led me to believe that I would be a lone visitor, maybe with a few other tourists. I was wrong. The place was swarming with local families — examining the site, reading the labels, discussing the street pattern and the house plans — and parents explaining to their children what they were looking at. My second story is that of a forty-five-year-old woman and her neighbors from the small town of Burhaniye in northwestern Anatolia. Working seasonally as a housekeeper for vacationers and as an olive picker, Esma, along with her husband and their friends, began to use the off-season for local excursions to historic sites in the late 1990s. Organizing free accommodations in various madrassas and traveling in a van borrowed from the Burhaniye municipality, they visited year after year the monuments, museums, and archaeological sites abundant in the region. They prepared for their excursions with some basic research and went to pre-Islamic and Islamic ruins, including some modest structures from the Ottoman centuries that have been overlooked by architectural historians. Hearing Esma's impressions of Anatolian museums — underfinanced, understaffed, and subjects of harsh criticism from scholars, yet each housing important works — was a humbling experience. These incidents gave me glimpses of the value ordinary Tunisians and Anatolians attached to the remains of the cultural heritage in their own backyards, cautioning me on the utter inaccessibility of the magnificent "encyclopedic" museums of the Western world to them.

Understanding history from different perspectives and casting a wide net can destabilize unilateral claims and provoke further questions. This is what I tried to do in this book.

Postscript

As I prepare *About Antiquities* for production, the destruction of antiquities by the Islamic State (ISIS or ISIL) has opened a painful episode. The familiar actors surface in the debates on the ownership of antiquities, with Cuno now acknowledging that calamity could happen anywhere and hence antiquities should not have been "concentrated," but "distributed." He is joined by many others, including the directors of several museums, as well as Boris Johnson, the mayor of London, who connects today's destruction to the wisdom of salvaging the Elgin Marbles two centuries ago. Many scholars, archaeologists, and lawyers are bringing back the idea of repartition, which they describe as a valuable, albeit "discredited" practice.[24]

On the Middle Eastern front, ISIS's involvement in antiquities reveals ugly stories on multiple fronts — cultural, religious, political, and economic. Focusing on its activities in Nabil Yunus, the hilltop shrine of Jonah in Mosul, Ahmed Kamel Mohammed, the director of the National Museum of Iraq in Baghdad, is reported as saying: "They are digging, not just destroying." Nicholas Pelham emphasizes that the widely screened ISIS videos documenting the destruction of antiquities were in fact designed to show and market what was *not* destroyed, hence what was for sale. He concludes that the "caliphate" is estimated to have made hundreds of millions of dollars from Assyrian antiquities thanks to "ISIS zealots," who double as "petty tomb-raiders."[25]

NOTES

Introduction

1. For the story of Venus of Milo, see Jockey, "The Venus de Milo," 237–255; for the Elgin Marbles, see Casey, "'Grecian Grandeurs,'" 30–62.

2. Malley, "The Layard Enterprise," 99–123.

3. See chapter 4 herein. The last point was made by Ahmed Süreyya in "Evkaf-ı İslamiye Müzesi," *İslam Mecmuası* 4, no. 56 (15 Cemaziyelahir 1335/March 28, 1918), 1112–1113. Imperial Museum is today's Istanbul Archaeological Museum.

4. Diaz-Andreu, *A World History of Nineteenth-Century Archaeology*, 3.

5. Hamilakis, "Indigenous Archaeologies in Ottoman Greece," 49–69.

6. Following a decision I had made in writing *Empire, Architecture, and the City*, and encouraged by the feedback I received, I chose not to include any references to theoretical sources. Again, this is "not because I disown the myriad influences that shaped my thinking (they will be obvious to many of my readers), but because I did not want to burden the narrative with transparent reminders that often risk turning into repetitive lists of familiar names and texts" (Çelik, *Empire, Architecture, and the City*, 274n2).

7. Trigger, "Alternative Archaeologies," 355. See also Trigger, *A History of Archaeological Thought*.

8. See, for example, Schnapp, *La conquête du passé*, and Kohl and Fawcett, *Nationalism, Politics and the Practice of Archaeology*.

9. Bohrer, *Orientalism and Visual Culture*, 190.

10. Quirke, *Hidden Hands*, vii.

11. Historians noted the presence of workers sporadically, albeit in passing. For example, in his analysis of archaeological photography, Bohrer highlights a few instances and reads them critically to depict the power landscape on the excavation site. He maintains that in a photograph taken in Delphi in 1904, "workers are posed in a way as if realizing the importance of the excavation and the unimportance of their own history."

In another, a Turkish peasant standing on a column drum in Troy in 1915 testifies to the position of the "Western viewer as archaeological spectator." Bohrer, *Photography and Archaeology*, 74, 121–122. Robert Ousterhout briefly notes that "in the final season at Nippur, [John Henry] Haynes became increasingly interested in the lives of local tribes" and that his photographs became more "anthropological, as he attempted to capture aspects of the lives of the local tribes." Ousterhout, *John Henry Haynes*, 133, 142.

12. Bahrani, Çelik, and Eldem, "Introduction," 13–43, and Çelik, "Defining Empire's Patrimony," 454–474.

13. Çelik, *Empire, Architecture, and the City*, 18–21.

14. For the proceedings of a conference on the topic, see Rona, *Osman Hamdi Bey ve Dönemi*.

15. See chapter 6 herein.

16. Ginzburg, *The Cheese and the Worms*; Davis, *Fiction in the Archives*.

17. Habel, *"When All of Rome Was under Construction,"* 1.

One • Beginnings: The Nineteenth-Century Museum

1. Pierpont Morgan Library Archives, Morgan Collections Correspondence, 1887–1948. Although the original attribution of the most spectacular sarcophagus found in Sidon to Alexander the Great was soon proved to be wrong, the sarcophagus continued to be called "the Sarcophagus of Alexander." For practical reasons, I will continue referring to it as the Sarcophagus of Alexander throughout this book.

2. Shaw, *Possessors and Possessed*, 126.

3. "Müzemizin Kıymet ve Ehemmiyeti," *İçtihad* 23, no. 235 (September 1, 1927): 4473, 4475.

4. Istanbul Archaeological Museums Archive (hereafter cited as İAMA), Müze-i Hümayun, letter from Müze-i Hümayun to Şehremanet-i Celilesi (27 Temmuz 1311/ August 8, 1897). The letter mentions a similar earlier request on 30 Eylül 1309 (October 12, 1893).

5. İAMA, Müze-i Hümayun, letter from Maarif-i Umumiye Nazırı to "Müze-i Hümayun Müdiriyet-i Aliyesi" (2 Teşrinievvel 1315/October 14, 1899).

6. İAMA, Müze-i Hümayun, letter to "Vilayat-i Malumeye Hususi" (not dated).

7. İAMA, Müze-i Hümayun, letter to "Topkapı Saray-ı Hümayunu Kumandanlığı Canib-i Valasına" (23 Ağustos 1315/September 4, 1899).

8. İAMA, letter from the Nezaret-i Maarif-i Umumiye to "Müze-i Hümayun Müdiriyet-i Aliyesine" (17 Teşrinievvel 1315/October 29, 1899).

9. For the curriculum of the School of Fine Arts, see *Salname-i Nezaret-i Maarif-i Umumiye* (Istanbul: Matbaa-i Amire, 1318 [1900]): 105–112.

10. "Müze-i Hümayun'da bir Şube-i Cedide-i Sanat," *Osmanlı Ressamlar Cemiyeti Gazetesi* 2, no. 11 (25 Mart 1328/April 7, 1912): 97. This collection formed the basis of the Museum of Paintings and Sculptures, which opened in 1937. It is known as "Elvah-ı Nakşiye Koleksiyonu." A catalogue of the collection, *Elvah-ı Nakşiye Koleksiyonu*, was published by Halil Edhem in 1924. According to him, the special budget for copies of European master paintings had been subsumed into the total budget of the museum

in 1916, with the result that the number of copies stopped at forty-two. Halil Edhem, *Elvah-ı Nakşiye*, 40. For the regulation and list of the works exhibited, see Halil Edhem, *Elvah-ı Nakşiye*, 51–68.

11. Ibid., 42.

12. "Müzemizin Kıymet ve Ehemmiyeti," 4475; Halil Edhem, *Elvah-ı Nakşiye*, 42. The School of Fine Arts was moved to the Lisan Mektebi (School of Languages) building in nearby Cağaloğlu.

13. İhsan Şerif, "Müze-i Hümayun'da Bir Ders," *Tedrisat* 4, no. 24 (9 Nisan 1330/ April 22, 1914): 211.

14. Ahmed Süreyya, "Evkaf-i İslamiye Müzesi," *İslam Mecmuası* 4, no. 56 (15 Cemaziyelahir 1336/March 28, 1918): 1116.

15. Preyer, *Art of the Metropolitan Museum*, 8.

16. Howe, *History of the Metropolitan Museum*, 170.

17. Halil Edhem, *Elvah-ı Nakşiye* (1970), 20.

18. Letter from Mr. Straus to Mr. Bayard, *Papers Relating to the Foreign Relations of the United States, Transmitted to Congress*, December 3, 1888, Part II.

19. "Americans in Babylonia," *New York Times*, July 3, 1897.

20. "The Museum of Constantinople," *New York Times*, April 24, 1897.

21. See, for example, "Sarcophagi of Sidon," *New York Times*, August 6, 1898.

22. Caillard, "The Imperial Ottoman Museum," 137.

23. Emerson, *Account of Recent Progress*, 18.

24. This sarcophagus is known under many names: the Pleureuses, the Weeping Women, the Weepers, the Mourning Women, and, in Turkish, Nevhakeran Lahdi. I will refer to it as the Sarcophagus of the Mourning Women throughout this book.

25. "The Late Hamid [*sic*] Bey, the Ottoman Museum He Founded and One of Its Greek Treasures," *New York Times*, December 18, 1910. Osman Hamdi's name is misspelled throughout the article as "Hamid." The image of Osman Hamdi as an anomaly in Ottoman culture had been broadcast to Americans. Consider, for example, the following sentences from the American archaeologist John P. Peters: "... it has been only by personal interest, and an incessant struggle against obstacles almost inconcernable to an Occidental, that [the Museum has] been established ... The principal credit for this result is due to O. Hamdy Bey ..." John P. Peters, "An Impetus in Turkey," *The Century: Illustrated Monthly Magazine, November 1892 to April 1893* 45, new series 13 (New York: The Century Co., and London: Fisher Unwin, 1893), 546.

26. Ahmed Refik, *Büyük Tarih-i Umumi*, passim.

27. BOA, MF.MKT, Dosya 33, Gömlek 103 (27 Zilkade 1292/December 25, 1875); BOA, MF.MKT, Dosya 34, Gömlek 23 (23 Muharrem 1293/December 19, 1876); BOA, MF.MKT, Dosya 38, Gömlek 28 (27 Cemazeyilahir 1293/July 20, 1876); BOA, MF.MKT, Dosya 45, Gömlek 101 (15 Zilkade 1293/December 2, 1876); BOA, MF.MKT, Dosya 51, Gömlek 169 (26 Cemazeyilevvel 1294/June 8, 1877).

28. Cesnola, *An Address*, 22.

29. Howe, *History of the Metropolitan Museum*, 153–154.

30. UPMAAA. John P. Peters, "Biblical Antiquities," *Evening Post, Supplement: New York* (Saturday, May 1884), press clipping.

31. Emerson, *Account of Recent Progress*, 19.

32. Sterrett, *A Plea for Research*, 145.

33. Ibid., 180.

34. "Müze-i Hümayun—Avrupa Matbuatı," *Servet-i Fünun* 1, no. 49 (6 Şubat 1307/ February 18, 1892): 266. This article is also quoted by Wendy M. K. Shaw in *Possessors and Possessed*.

35. "İstanbul Postası—Müze-i Hümayun," *Servet-i Fünun* 1, no. 13 (1307/1891).

36. Howe, *History of the Metropolitan Museum*, 40.

37. *The Metropolitan Museum of Art*, 3.

38. Preyer, *Art of the Metropolitan Museum*, 1–2.

39. Joseph H. Choate, quoted in Howe, *History of the Metropolitan Museum*, 196.

40. Cesnola, *An Address*, 17, 22.

41. *A Memorial of George Brown Goode*, 72–73.

42. Preyer, *Art of the Metropolitan Museum*, 2.

43. "Art Museum's Progress: Twenty-fifth Annual Report of the Trustees," *New York Times*, March 8, 1895.

44. Young, *Corps de droit ottoman*, 2:388.

45. Quoted in Ahmet Mumcu, "Eski Eserler Hukuku ve Türkiye," *Ankara Üniversitesi Hukuk Fakültesi Dergisi* (1971): 68.

46. Serbestoğlu and Açık, "Osmanlı Devleti'nde Modern Bir Okul Projesi," 163–164.

47. Articles 1 and 3 are quoted in Young, *Corps de droit ottoman*, 389.

48. Quoted in Caillard, "The Imperial Ottoman Museum," 150.

49. "Müze-i Hümayun—Avrupa Matbuatı," 266.

50. "Cümle-i Müessesat-ı İlmiyye-i Cenab-ı Padişahiden Müze-i Hümayun," *Servet-i Fünun* 26, no. 672 (26 Şubat 1319/March 10, 1904): 338.

51. "Müze-i Osmani Müdür-i Sabıkı Merhum Osman Hamdi Bey," *Osmanlı Ressamlar Cemiyeti Gazetesi* 2, no. 11 (25 Mart 1328/April 2, 1912): 71.

52. İhsan Şerif, "Müze-i Hümayun'da Bir Ders," 211.

53. Quoted in "Müze-i Osmani Müdür-i Sabıkı Merhum Osman Hamdi Bey," 72.

54. See the essays by Çelik, Eldem, and Shaw in *The Scramble for the Past*.

55. "Hamdi Bey," *The Athenaeum*, no. 2994 (March 14, 1884), 353.

56. "House of Commons: Parliamentary Debate on the Purchasing of the Elgin Marbles" (1816), quoted in Siegel, *The Emergence of the Museum*, 54–55.

57. For public transportation in London in 1894, see Baedeker, *London and Its Environs*, 27.

58. Baedeker, *Berlin and Its Environs*, 70–72, 78, 82–83, 85–86, 96. For a discussion on the Pergamon Museum, see Bilsel, *Antiquity on Display*, 117–138.

59. Burrows and Wallace, *Gotham*, 790–791.

60. The literature on Central Park is vast. For a thorough overview, see, for example, Rosenzweig and Blackmar, *The Park and the People*.

61. *The Metropolitan Museum of Art*, 7; Howe, *History of the Metropolitan Museum*, 138.

62. Howe, *History of the Metropolitan Museum*, 138, 153, 156; *The Metropolitan Museum of Art*, 8–9.

63. "A Metropolitan Museum: The Opening of the Institution to Take Place Today," *New York Times*, March 30, 1880.

64. Howe, *History of the Metropolitan Museum*, 231, 265; *The Metropolitan Museum of Art*, 10–11.

65. For the development of the Imperial Museum, see also Shaw, "From Mausoleum to Museum," 425–430.

66. "Müzemizin Kıymet ve Ehemmiyeti," 4472–4473.

67. E. A. Wallis Budge, "The Imperial Ottoman Museum and the Fine Arts School at Constantinople," *The Athenaeum*, no. 3220 (July 13, 1889): 72.

68. "Müzemizin Kıymet ve Ehemmiyeti," 4473.

69. Ibid., 4472–4473, 4475.

70. Ibid., 4473.

71. Ibid., 4475.

72. Duyun-u Umumiye Mektupçusu [Mehmed] Vahid, "Osmanlı Müzesi ve Tarihçesi," *Servet-i Fünun* 38, no. 984 (1 Nisan 1326/April 14, 1910): 343.

73. "Gülhane Parkı," *Servet-i Fünun* 47, no. 1208 (17 Temmuz 1330/July 30, 1914): 181.

74. Topuzlu, *32 Sene Evvelki, Bugünkü, Yarınki Istanbul*, 132–134.

75. H. S., "İstanbul ve Şehremini Cemil Paşa: Cemil Paşa'nın İstanbul Halkını Medeni Bir Cemiyet Haline Getirmek için Çabaları," *İçtihad* 4, no. 87 (2 Kanunsani 1329/ January 15, 1914): 1931–1933.

76. For Auric, see Pierre-Yves Saunier, "La ville et la ville: les homes et les organismes municipaux de l'aménagement urbain 19e et 20e siècles," *Recherches contemporaines*, no. 3 (1995–1996): 131. For the urban interventions of the 1860s, see Çelik, *The Remaking of Istanbul*, 55–67.

77. *Guide to Greece*, 122.

78. "Müzemizin Kıymet ve Ehemmiyeti," 4472.

Two • *Scholarship and the Imperial Museum*

1. Smith, *Assyrian Discoveries*, 138.

2. Salomon Reinach, "Le vandalisme moderne en Orient," *Revue des deux mondes* 56 (March 1, 1883): 155, 161, 163–166.

3. Salomon Reinach, "Marble Heads in Tchinly Kiosk Museum," *American Journal of Archaeology* 2, no. 3 (July–September 1886): 320.

4. Salomon Reinach, "Loi sur les antiquités," *Revue archéologique* 1 (1884): 335–336. For the law, see pages 336–345. As indicated in this journal, the French translation had already been printed in *La Turquie*, a French-language paper published in Istanbul.

5. Salomon Reinach, "Archaeology and the Turkish Officials," *The Nation* 39, no. 993 (July 10, 1884): 30–31.

6. Reinach, *Conseils aux voyageurs archéologues*, 85–86.

7. J. Theodore Bent, "Hamdi Bey," *The Living Age* 64, 5th series (October, November, December 1888): 616–618.

8. See, for example, Emerson, *An Account of Recent Progress*, 18. It is noteworthy that

Peters included in the appendix to *Nippur* a complete "Translation of the Turkish Law on Archaeological Excavations," as well as the full text of the imperial permission that granted the team the permission to excavate; see Peters, *Nippur*, Appendix C and Appendix D, 1:301–309.

9. T. Hayter Lewis, "The Sarcophagi of Sidon," *The Builder* 53, no. 2240 (December 10, 1887): 803.

10. F. Max Müller, "The New Museum and the Sidon Sarcophagi," *The New Review* (London) 10, no. 56 (January 1894): 19.

11. "Letters from Constantinople," *The Literary News* 18, no. 4 (April 1897): 104.

12. For an overview of these debates, see the epilogue in this book.

13. Vahid, "Osmanlı Müzesi ve Tarihçesi," 346.

14. Radcliffe, *Schools and Masters of Sculpture*, 498, 532–533.

15. Professor J. P. Mahaffy, M.A., of the University of Dublin, Ireland, "Constantinople," *The Chautauquan* 21, no. 6 (September 1895): 722.

16. "The Museum of Constantinople," *New York Times*, April 24, 1897.

17. "The Late Hamid [*sic*] Bey, the Ottoman Museum He Founded and One of Its Own Greek Treasures," *New York Times*, December 18, 1910.

18. Hamdy-Bey, "Mémoire sur une nécropole royale découverte à Saïda," *Revue archéologique*, 3rd series, 10 (July–December 1887): 138–150.

19. Hamdy-Bey, "Sur une nécropole royale découverte à Saida," *Revue d'ethnographie* 6 (1889): 444–456.

20. Théodore Reinach, "Les sarcophages de Sidon au Musée de Constantinople," *Gazette des Beaux-Arts* 7, 3e période (1892): 104.

21. Brinkmann, "The Prince and the Goddess," 71.

22. Quatremère de Quincy, *Le Jupiter olympien*, 31–32.

23. Ibid., xxii.

24. Hittorff, *Restitution du temple d'Empédocle*, ix, xvi, xxi, and 4. Hittorff noted that the reconstitution drawings were printed thanks to the recently introduced technique of chromolithography, which seemed to have been invented for the reproduction of applied polychromy in architecture and sculpture. See Hittorff, *Restitution*, xvii.

25. Fenger, *Dorische Polychromie*.

26. "The Sepulchral Chambers and the Sarcophagi of Sidon," *The British Architect* (July 29, 1887): 94. Osman Hamdi's possessive attitude toward the sarcophagi and his unwillingness to show them to European colleagues after the discoveries had been a sore issue. For example, according to the "Report of the Executive Committee" of the Palestinian Exploration Fund, Osman Hamdi acted like a "Turkish man-of-war in order to secure the things for the Imperial Museum." The committee hoped that permission would be granted "to procure for the Society plans, drawings, figures, measurements, and the description of these objects, which are described as being the finest sarcophagi in the world." See *Palestine Exploration Fund Quarterly Statement for 1886*, 254.

27. Lewis, "The Sarcophagi of Sidon," 802–803.

28. W. K. Eddy, "Letters from Sidon, Phoenicia," *American Journal of Archaeology* 3, nos. 1–2 (1887): 97–101.

29. "The Sarcophagus of Alexander," *The American Architect and Building News* 23, no. 638, 132.

30. E. A. Wallis Budge, "The Imperial Ottoman Museum and the Fine Art School at Constantinople," *The Athenaeum*, no. 3220 (July 13, 1889): 72.

31. John P. Peters, "The Sidon Sarcophagi—I," *The Nation* 52, no. 1332 (January 8, 1891): 28–29.

32. T. Reinach, "Les sarcophages de Sidon au Musée de Constantinople," 178.

33. Ibid., 101–102.

34. Ibid., 178, 186–190.

35. Maxime Collignon, "La polychromie dans la sculpture grecque," *Revue de deux mondes*, no. 2 (1895): 835.

36. Gardner, *Sculptured Tombs of Hellas*, 244–259.

37. Mahaffy, *A Survey of Greek Civilization*, 235–237.

38. Fowler and Wheeler, *A Handbook of Greek Archaeology*, 274–276.

39. *Museum of Fine Arts Bulletin* (Boston) 1, no. 3 (July 1903): 13.

40. "İstanbul Postası: Müze-i Osmaniye," *Servet-i Fünun* 1, no. 13 (30 Kanunisani 1306/November 30, 1890): 84–85.

41. "Asar-ı Atika," *Servet-i Fünun* 2, no. 90 (19 Teşrinisani 1308/December 2, 1893): 42.

42. "Cümle-i Müessesat-ı İlmiye-i Cenab-ı Padişahiden Müze-i Hümayun," *Servet-i Fünun* 26, no. 673 (4 Mart 1320/March 17, 1904): 358.

43. Ibid., no. 674 (11 Mart 1320/March 24, 1904): 375–378.

44. Ibid., no. 676 (25 Mart 1320/April 7, 1904): 411.

45. "İstanbul Osmanlı Müzesinde Sidon Taş Lahidleri," *Servet-i Fünun* 1, no. 49, 266–269.

46. "Sarcophage dit 'd'Alexandre,'" *Malumat* 1, no. 5 (1311/1895): 98, 113–114.

47. [Mehmed] Vahid, "Müze-i Hümayun'da İskender Lahdi," *Darülfünun Edebiyat Fakültesi Mecmuası* 1, no. 2 (1925): 155–158.

48. Ibid., 158–169.

49. [Mehmed] Vahid, "Lahd-i İskender," *Darülfünun Edebiyat Fakültesi Mecmuası* 1, no. 3 (1925): 281–285.

50. "The Sepulchral Chambers and the Sarcophagi of Sidon," *The British Architect* (July 29, 1887): 94.

51. T. Reinach, "Les sarcophages de Sidon au Musée de Constantinople," 178–179.

52. For an analysis of the concept, see Neville Morley, "Decadence as a Theory of History," *New Literary History* 35, no. 4 (Autumn 2004): 573–585, esp. 574–577.

53. For a thorough analysis of the discourse in Germany, see Marchand, *Down from Olympus*, esp. 104–115.

54. Michaelis, *A Century of Archaeological Discoveries*, 282–283.

55. "L'art du moyen age: Est-it d'origine orientale?," *Revue de deux mondes* 50, période 5, (1909/03–1909/04): 655, 658.

56. Eugène Guillaume, "Les ruines de Palmyre et leur recent explorateur," *Revue de deux mondes* 142, période 4 (1897/07, 1897/08): 395, 399.

57. A. H. Sayce, "Letter from Constantinople," *The Academy* 16, no. 385, new series (September 20, 1879): 214.

58. Salomon Reinach, "Marble Statues of Artemis in the Museum at Constantinople," *American Journal of Archaeology* 1, no. 4 (October 1885): 319, 321–322.

59. S. Reinach, "Marble Heads in Tchinly Kiosk Museum," 314–317.

60. Paul F. Perdrizet, "Archaistic Reliefs," *The Annual of the British School at Athens*, no. 11 (1896–1897): Seminars 156–157.

61. "Babylonia," *Free Museum of Science and Art, Department of Archaeology and Palaeontology, University of Pennsylvania, Bulletin*, no. 1 (May 1897): 31–33.

62. Rogers, *A History of Babylonia and Assyria*, 243.

63. Ward, *Report on the Wolfe Expedition*, 31–33.

64. Harper, "Introduction," xxiv.

65. Ward, *Report on the Wolfe Expedition*, 6–7.

66. BOA, İ. HR Dosya 310, Gömlek 19769 (29 Şubat 1305/July 9, 1888). This document is the translation of the original in English by the Ottoman Office of Translation.

67. BOA, BEO Dosya 1083, Gömlek 81176 (13 Şubat 1313/February 26, 1898).

68. BOA, MF.MKT Dosya 429, Gömlek 8 (8 Şaban 1316/December 22, 1898).

69. BOA, DH.MKT Dosya 803, Gömlek 71 (1 Kanunievvel 1319/December 14, 1903).

Three • The Imperial Museum and Its Visitors

1. Zola, *L'assommoir*, 86–90.

2. Wharton, *The Age of Innocence*, 308–309, 344.

3. Kemal Tahir, *Esir Şehrin İnsanları*, 292.

4. "Album of Egyptian and Turkish photographs, assembled by Rudolf H. and Lulu Reinhart in 1906 on their wedding trip," The Metropolitan Museum, Thomas J. Watson Library, 2 vols.

5. "Seyyah Tercümanları ve Antikacılar," *Servet-i Fünun* 32, no. 811 (26 Teşrinievvel 1322/November 8, 1906): 67.

6. "Les Touristes," *Kalem*, no. 28 (24 Şubat 1324/February 27, 1909): 14–15. The satirical poem is in French. The curious choice of Bremen is due to the rhyming sound of "Brême" with "carême" at the end of the previous line.

7. T. Reinach, "Les sarcophages de Sidon au Musée de Constantinople," 89–90.

8. G. Müller, *Letters from Constantinople*, 131–132, 135.

9. F. M. Müller, "The New Museum and the Sidon Sarcophagi," *New Review*, v. X, no. 56 (January 1894), 18, 20.

10. Bourquelot, *Promenades en Égypte*, 366–367.

11. Hutton, *Constantinople*, 334–336.

12. Grosvenor, *Constantinople*, 1:vii.

13. Ibid., 2:772–786.

14. Barth, *Constantinople*, 164, 165, 174.

15. Gower, *Records and Reminiscences*, 474–475.

16. Paul Eudel, *Constantinople, Smyrne et Athènes: Journal de voyage* (1885); Frances Elliot, *Diary of an Idle Woman in Constantinople* (1893); John Lawson Stoddard, *John L. Stoddard's Lectures* (1897); Alexander Van Millingen, *Constantinople* (1906); Harry Griswold Dwight, *Constantinople, Old and New* (1915). This list could easily be extended.

17. G. Müller, *Letters from Constantinople*, 131–132.

18. Godins de Souhesmes, *Guide to Constantinople and Its Environs*, 76.

19. Roussé, *De Paris à Constantinople*, 260–267.

20. Montmarché, *De Paris à Constantinople*, 36–317.

21. Coufopoulos, *A Guide to Constantinople*, 88–90, 93–113.

22. Ibid., 91–92.

23. G. S. Hillard, quoted in the introduction to Gretton, *A Guide to the Microfiche Edition of Murray's Handbooks for Travellers*, viii–ix.

24. Ibid., ix.

25. *Handbook for Travellers*, 69–74.

26. Baedeker, *Konstantinopel*, 105–118.

27. Baedeker, *London and Its Environs*, 242–243.

28. Baedeker, *The United States, with an Excursion into Mexico*, 45.

29. *Guide to Greece*, 124–128.

30. Ibid., 128–134.

31. Cervati, *Guide horaire général international*, 101–102.

32. Centering on the collaboration between Osman Hamdi and Istanbul's famous photographer Pascal Sebah, as well as Gustave Mendel's three-volume *Catalogue des sculptures grecques, romaines et byzantines*, the catalogues published by the Imperial Museum have been the topic of an exhibition at the Istanbul Archaeological Museum and its accompanying publication. See Eldem, *Mendel-Sebah*.

33. Albert Dumont, "Le musée de Sainte-Irène à Constantinople: Antiquités grecques, gréco-romaines et byzantines." *Revue archéologique* 18, no. 1 (Nouv. ser. A9, 1868): 237–263.

34. Goold, *Catalogue explicatif*.

35. S. Reinach, *Ministère de l'Instruction publique*, "Avis" and 7.

36. Musée Impérial Ottoman, *Monuments funéraires*, viii–xi.

37. Musée Impérial Ottoman, *Monuments funéraires*, 1909 reprint, 2–16. Also see Musées Impériaux Ottomans, *Catalogues des poteries byzantines*. As announced in *Catalogues des poteries*, the catalogues could be bought at the museum ("En Vente au Musée Impérial").

38. Musée Impérial Ottoman, *Catalogue des sculptures grecques, romaines, byzantines et franques*.

39. Musée Impérial Ottoman, *Antiquités himyarites et palmyriennes*; Musée Impérial Ottoman, *Monuments égyptiens*; Musée Impérial Ottoman, *Bronzes et bijoux*.

40. See the introduction by André Joubin in Musée Impérial Ottoman, *Bronzes et bijoux*, n.p.

41. Musées Impériaux Ottomans, *Catalogue des figurines grecques de terre cuite*, v–vii.

42. Mendel, *Catalogue des sculptures grecques, romaines et byzantines*.

43. See, for example, İsmail Galib, *Takvim-i Meskukat-ı Osmaniye* (Istanbul: Mihran, 1307/1899); İsmail Galib, *Takvim-i Meskukat-ı Selçukiye* (Istanbul: Mihran, 1309/1891); İsmail Galib, Mübarek Galib, Ahmed Techid, and Halil Edhem, *Müze-i Hümayun Meskukat-ı İslamiye Kısmından Meskukat-ı Türkmaniye Kataloğu* (Istanbul: Mihran, 1312/1894); in French: *Catalogue des monnaies turcomanes Beni Ortok, Beni Zengui, Frou*

Atabeqyéh et Meliks Eyoubites de Meïyafarikin (Constantinople: Mihran, 1894). The list of catalogues on sale at the museum in 1904 included four volumes in this collection, with the fifth on Fatimid, Ayyubid, and Mamluk coins, noted as in preparation. See Müze-i Hümayun, *Kurşun Mühür Kataloğu*. A similar list from 1910 still mentioned the fifth volume as in preparation; see Musées Impériaux Ottomans, *Catalogues des poteries*, n.p.

44. Müze-i Hümayun, *Kurşun Mühür Kataloğu*, 4.

45. For Halil Edhem's engagement with the Islamic heritage, see chapter 4 herein.

46. O. Hamdy Bey and T. Reinach, *Une nécropole royale à Sidon*; Osman Hamdi Bey and Osgan Efendi, *Le tumulus de Nemroud-Dagh*.

47. The Metropolitan Museum of Art's publications can be accessed through the website of the Thomas J. Watson Library in the museum: library.metmuseum.org.

48. Valentier, *Catalogue of a Loan Exhibition*, ix.

49. "Havadis-i Dahiliye: Prens Ferdinand Hazretleri," *Servet-i Fünun* 11, no. 286 (19 Ağustos 1312/August 25, 1896): 36.

50. "Asar-ı Atik," *Servet-i Fünun* 3, no. 55 (19 Mart 1308/March 31, 1892): 189.

51. S. Reinach, "Le vandalisme moderne en Orient," 163.

52. Kemal, "Müzelerden İstifade," *Servet-i Fünun* 10, no. 238 (21 Eylül 1311/October 3, 1895): 55–58.

53. The museum hours were: 8:30 a.m.–4:30 p.m. in 1895, 11:00 a.m.–4:00 p.m. in 1900, 10:00 a.m.–5:00 p.m. (with the exception of Friday) in 1905, 10:00 a.m.–4:00 p.m. in winter and 9:30 a.m.–3:30 p.m. in summer in 1909 (all with the exception of Friday), and 10:00 a.m.–4:00 p.m. in winter and 9:30 a.m.–4:30 p.m. in summer (with the exception of Friday throughout the year and Sunday in summer) in 1912. Coufopoulos, *A Guide to Constantinople*, 88; *Handbook for Travellers*, 160; Baedeker, *Konstantinopel*, 77; Cervati, *Guide horaire général international*, 101; Montmarché, *De Paris à Constantinople*, 305. These hours are comparable to the schedules of other great museums. For example, in 1894, the British Museum was open on every weekday from 10:00 a.m. to 4:00 p.m., 5:00 p.m., and 6:00 p.m., depending on the season. However, some sections were also open 8:00 to 10:00 p.m. on certain days of the week. There was no admission fee. See Baedeker, *London and Its Environs*, 242.

54. İAMA, Müze-i Hümayun, nos. 36 and 37 (19 Mart 1338/March 19, 1922). That meant signing in a notebook every morning at 11:00 a.m. and signing out at 4:00 p.m., with a lunch break between noon and 1:00 p.m. Although the document dates from 1922, it also casts light on the Directorate's endeavors to keep to a strict schedule from the 1890s on.

55. BOA, MF.MKT, Dosya 994, Gömlek 19 (11 Ramazan 1925/April 24, 1907); BOA, MF.MKT, Dosya 1002, Gömlek 6 (11 Cemaziyelahir 1325/June 22, 1907; BOA, MF.MKT, Dosya 1151, Gömlek 62 (12 Ramazan 1328/September 16, 1910); BOA, MF.MKT, Dosya 1197, Gömlek 19 (24 Cemaziyelahir 1332/April 20, 1914).

56. "Müzeyi Ziyaret Meselesi," *Tedrisat Mecmuası* 4, no. 26 (15 Haziran 1330/June 28, 1914): 93.

57. Şerif, "Müze-i Hümayun'da Bir Ders," 210–212. The transcription in *Tedrisat Mecmuası* did not include the information given on the objects inside the museum.

58. Joubin, *Asar-ı Heykeltraşi Kataloğu; Luhud ve Mekabir-i Atike Kataloğu*, 1310 (1894) and 1317 (1900).

59. Müze-i Hümayun, *Asar-ı Misriyye Kataloğu*.

60. Joubin, *Luhud ve Mekabir-i Atike Kataloğu*, 1310 (1894), 3–4, 7.

61. Although Osman Hamdi wrote in his introduction to Joubin's 1898 catalogue on bronze objects and jewels that a Turkish edition was forthcoming, this project seems to have been dropped. See Musée Impérial Ottoman, *Bronzes et bijoux*.

62. Mehmed Vahid, *Rehnüma*, 1337 (1919). The earlier editions date from 1319 (1903), 1325 (1909), and 1330 (1914).

63. Nazmi Ziya, Sanayi-I Nefise: "Müzeler ve Meşherler," *Şehbal* (year 5) 4, no. 79 (15 Temmuz 1329/July 28, 1913): 138. The author may have not been aware of the European painting collection, intended for the students of the Fine Arts School (see chapter 1), as he had been in Paris for several years.

64. S. Reinach, "Le vandalisme moderne en Orient," 163–164.

65. Çelik, *Empire, Architecture, and the City*, 180.

66. İAMA, Müze-i Hümayun, letter from Sungurlu Kaymakamı (17 Cemaziyelevvel 1325 and 15 Temmuz 1323/July 28, 1907).

67. *Moniteur Oriental*, January 26, 1897, quoted in Young, *Corps de droit ottoman*, 2:389 as a note to Art. 3 of the 1884 Law of Antiquities.

68. BOA, DH.MKT, Dosya 2222, Gömlek 77 (9 Ramazan 1317/January 11, 1900).

69. İAMA, Müze-i Hümayun, letter from Hazine-i Hassa-i Şahane, Emlak-i Hümayun İdaresi (Mosul), to Müze-i Hümayun Müdiriyet-i Aliyesine (13 Zilhicce 1308 ve 8 Temmuz 1307/July 20, 1891).

70. İAMA, Müze-i Hümayun, letter to Nazir-i Hazine-i Hassa from Müze-i Hümayun Müdiri Hamdi (20 Muharrem 1309 ve 12 Ağustos 1307/August 24, 1891). The reason for Hamdi Bey's request was that the museum budget did not have sufficient funds to pay Bedri Bey the extra salary he merited.

71. See, for example, *Actes de la Société du Chemin de Fer Ottoman de la Syrie*, 13 (art. 22).

72. Bent, "Hamdi Bey," 617.

73. *Charter of the Metropolitan Museum of Art*, 27.

74. *The Metropolitan Museum of Art*, 10; Howe, *A History of the Metropolitan*, 239–245; Burrows and Wallace, *Gotham*, 1082.

75. "Art Museum's Progress: Twenty-Fifth Annual Report of the Trustees," *New York Times*, March 8, 1895.

76. *Charter of the Metropolitan Museum of Art*, 27.

77. "Cooperation of the Museum and the Public Schools," *The Metropolitan Museum of Art Bulletin* 1, no. 1 (November 1905): 5.

78. "Cooperation with the Schools," *The Metropolitan Museum of Art Bulletin* 4, no. 3 (March 1909): 42.

79. "What the Museum Is Doing for Public Schools," *The Metropolitan Museum of Art Bulletin* 3, no. 9 (September 1908): 174.

80. Edwin White Gaillard, "The Public Library, the Schools, and the Museums of the City," *The Metropolitan Museum of Art Bulletin* 1, no. 11 (October 1906): 142.

81. "What the Museum Is Doing for Public Schools," 174.

82. "Help Offered by the Museum to Teachers in High Schools," *The Metropolitan Museum of Art Bulletin* 2, no. 11 (November 1907): 181.

83. For the "museum schools," see Howe, *A History of the Metropolitan*, 202–205.

Four • *The Ottoman Reading Public and Antiquities*

1. "Muhasebe-i İlmiye (İlm-i Asar-ı Atika)," *Servet-i Fünun* 23, no. 579 (16 Mayıs 1318/ May 29, 1902): 108–109.

2. "Asar-ı Atika," *Servet-i Fünun* (Year 2) 4, no. 102 (11 Şubat 1308/February 23, 1893): 378–379.

3. "Milet Harabelerinde Yeni Hafriyat," *Servet-i Fünun* 35, no. 887 (10 Nisan 1324/ April 23, 1908): 36.

4. "Muhasebe-i Tarihiye—Babil Şehri," *Servet-i Fünun* 23, no. 579 (16 Mayıs 1318/ May 29, 1902): 102.

5. "Asar-ı Atika—Sard Harabeleri," *Şehbal* 5, no. 86 (15 Teşrinisani 1329/December 8, 1913): 268.

6. "Mısır'da Asar-ı Atika Keşfiyatı," *Servet-i Fünun* 7, no. 161 (31 Mart 1310/April 12, 1894): 70.

7. "Timgad Harabeleri," *Servet-i Fünun* 29, no. 732 (21 Nisan 1321/May 4, 1905): 50.

8. B. Mustafa Rıza, "Mütevvia Acaib Şeba-i Alem," *Hamiyet* 1, no. 9 (15 Ağustos 1302/ August 27, 1886): 71.

9. Kadri, "Muhasebe-i Tarihiye—Babil Şehri," *Servet-i Fünun* 23, no. 579 (16 Mayıs 1318/May 29, 1902): 102.

10. "Tedmür Harabeleri," *Maarif* 2, no. 28 (13 Şubat 1307/February 25, 1892): 19.

11. "Asar-ı Atika Kısmı: Balbek," *Musavver Malumat-ı Nafia* 1, no. 12 (1 Mayıs 1330/ May 14, 1914): 180.

12. "Ceras Harabeleri," *Servet-i Fünun* 34, no 882 (6 Mart 1323/March 19, 1907): 372–373.

13. "Asar-ı Atika: Suriye Vilayetinde," *Servet-i Fünun* 2, no. 45 (15 Teşrinisani 1327/ October 28, 1911): 416.

14. Müze-i Humayun Muhafızlarından Mendel, "Asar-ı Atika: Sard Harabeleri," *Şehbal* (Year 5) 4, no. 86 (15 Teşrinisani 1329/December 8, 1913): 268.

15. Cemal, "Asar-ı Atika: Truva Şehr-i Kadimi," *Şehbal* (Year 4) 3, no. 68 (1 Kanunisani 1328/January 14, 1913): 394.

16. "Asar-ı Atika—Sard Harabeleri," 268; "Asar-ı Atika Kısmı: Balbek," 81.

17. "Bergama," *Servet-i Fünun* 4, no. 66 (4 Haziran 1308/June 16, 1892): 220.

18. "Bergama Kasabası Kenarında Asar-ı Atika," *Servet-i Fünun* (Year 2) 4, no. 83 (1 Teşrinievvel 1308/October 13, 1892): 84.

19. Kadri, "Muhasebe-i Tarihiye—Babil Şehri," 103.

20. B. Mustafa Rıza, "Mütevvia Acaib Şeba-i Alem," 71.

21. Kadri, "Muhasebe-i Tarihiye—Babil Şehri," 102–103.

22. "Ceras Harabeleri," 373–374.

23. "Milet Harabelerinde Yeni Hafriyat," 36–37.

24. Mendel, "Asar-ı Atika: Sard Harabeleri," 268–269.

25. M. Sadık, "Balbek'te Bir Gece," *Servet-i Fünun* 5, no. 119 (28 Mayıs 1325/June 10, 1909): 232–234.

26. For extended analyses of these developments in late-Ottoman cities, see Çelik, *The Remaking of Istanbul* and *Empire, Architecture, and the City*.

27. "Tedmür Harabeleri," 19.

28. "Asar-ı Atika Kısmı: Balbek," 181.

29. M. Sadık, "Balbek'te Bir Gece," 231.

30. Ibid., 232–234.

31. Ibid., 231, 234.

32. For some of the photographs publicizing the inauguration ceremony, see Bahrani, Çelik, and Eldem, *Scramble for the Past*, 270–271. These were also printed in *Servet-i Fünun* at the time.

33. Cemal, "Asar-ı Atika: Truva Şehr-i Kadimi," 394.

34. See Schliemann, *Trojanische Alterthümer*. Clearly, the author of the article in *Şehbal* was not aware of this work, as he did not use any information from it.

35. "Asar-ı Atika," *Servet-i Fünun* 5, no. 106 (11 Mart 1308/March 23, 1892): 31.

36. "Asar-ı Atika," *Servet-i Fünun* (Year 2) 4, no. 91 (26 Teşrinisani 1308/December 8, 1892): 203.

37. "Asar-ı Atika," *Servet-i Fünun* (Year 2) 4, no. 92 (3 Kanunisani 1308/December 15, 1892): 220.

38. "Asar-ı Atika," *Servet-i Fünun* 6, no. 143, 208.

39. "Şuunat-i Asar-ı Atika," *Servet-i Fünun* 7, no. 168 (19 Nisan 1310/May 1, 1894): 191.

40. "Asar-ı Atika," *Servet-i Fünun* 8, no. 202 (12 Kanunisani 1310/January 24, 1895): 320.

41. "Mısır'da Asar-ı Atika Keşfiyatı," 70–71.

42. "Resimlerimiz: Pompei Harabeleri," *Servet-i Fünun* 44, no. 1129 (10 Kanunisani 1328/January 23, 1913): 261–262.

43. "Müze," *Servet-i Fünun* 3, no. 57 (2 Nisan 1308/April 14, 1892): 74.

44. "Luvr Müzesi," *Servet-i Fünun* 6, no. 134 (23 Eylül 1309/October 5, 1893): 59.

45. Ahmed İhsan, *Avrupa'da Ne Gördüm*, 6, 19–20.

46. Ibid., 94–99.

47. Ibid., 236–238.

48. Shaw, *Possessors and Possessed*, 46–58; Mehmed Raif, *Topkapı Saray-ı Hümayunu*, 27.

49. Ahmed İhsan, *Avrupa'da Ne Gördüm*, 349–350.

50. Marchand, *Down from Olympus*, 94–95. See also Bilsel, *Antiquity on Display*, 91–100.

51. Duchéne, "Les musées royaux enrichis," 141.

52. Ahmed İhsan, *Avrupa'da Ne Gördüm*, 499–505.

53. "Asar-ı Atika: Arkadyus Sütunu Bakiyesi (Avrat Taşı)," *Şehbal* (Year 5) 4, no. 91 (15 Şubat 1329/February 28, 1914): 367.

54. Nazmi Ziya, "Sanayi-i Nefise: Müzeler ve Meşherler."

55. Halil Edhem, "Asar-ı Atika: Sinan Paşa Köşkü," *Şehbal* (Year 4) 3, no. 60 (1 Eylül 1328/September 14, 1912): 224–225.

56. Halil Edhem, "Asar-ı Atika: Kayıkhane Ocağı," *Şehbal* (Year 5) 4, no. 75 (1 Mayıs 1329/May 28, 1913): 147–148.

57. Mehmed Ziya, "Asar-ı Atika: Şimdiye Kadar Tedkik Olunmamış Bir Şehzade Mezarı," *Şehbal* (Year 4) 3, no. 58 (1 Ağustos 1912/August 14, 1912): 194.

58. Halil Edhem, "Asar-ı Atika: Yine Konya," *Şehbal* (Year 4) 3, no. 59 (15 Ağustos 1328/August 28, 1912): 212–213.

59. Halil Edhem, "Asar-ı Atika: Asar-ı Atika-i Milliyemiz Nasıl Mahvoluyor?" *Şehbal* (Year 2), no. 36 (15 Mart 1327/March 30, 1911): 226.

60. Ibid., 226–227.

61. Ibid., 227.

62. Ibid., 227–228.

63. Mukbil Kemal, "Memalik-i Osmaniye'de Asar-ı Atika ve Nefise-i İslamiye Hırsızlığı," *Bilgi Mecmuası* 1, no. 5 (Mart 1329/March–April 1913): 535–537.

64. Ibid., 537–539.

65. For a discussion of Salomon Reinach's "Le vandalisme moderne en Orient," see chapter 3.

66. Ahmed Süreyya, "Evkaf-ı İslamiye Müzesi," 1112–1113.

67. Diaz-Andreu, *A World History of Nineteenth-Century Archaeology*, 21.

68. Ahmed Süreyya, "Evkaf-ı İslamiye Müzesi," 1113–1116.

69. Seymour, *Legend, History and the Ancient City*, 2.

70. The classic text for this interpretation is Linda Nochlin, "The Imaginary Orient," 118–131, 187–191.

71. Lord Byron, *Sardanapalus: A Tragedy*. Michael Seymour suggests that Aeschylus's *Persians* may have been the original text to attribute a "decadent hedonism" to Sardanapalus and provide a "template for what was to become the modern literary and artistic trope of the oriental despot." See Seymour, *Legend, History and the Ancient City*, 64–65.

72. For Abdülhak Hamid's references to history, see Uğurcan, *Abdülhak Hamid Tarhan'in Eserlerinde Tarih*.

73. Erginün, "Byron ve Hamid'in Sardanapal Piyesleri Üzerinde Mukayeseli Bir Araştırma," 13–44. www.journals.istanbul.edu.tr/tr/indexphp/turkdili/article/viewfile /17616/16859.

74. For a discussion of Kean's production, see Bohrer, *Orientalism and Visual Culture*, 178–180.

75. *Lord Byron's Historical Tragedy of Sardanapalus*, iii.

76. Ibid., iv.

77. Ibid., 1.

78. Ibid., 22.

79. Ibid., 25.

80. For the deconstruction of the myth of scholarship in Layard's famous drawing, see Bahrani, "History in Reverse," 15–28. As examined by Frederick Bohrer, *Sardana-*

pal, Historische Pantomime, staged in Berlin in September 1908, was similarly based on the recent archaeological discoveries. An accompanying brochure described how the sets were copied from scholarly reconstructions of Mesopotamian monuments. The inspiration clearly went back to Byron's play. See Bohrer, *Orientalism and Visual Culture*, 198–299. It is most likely that Calvert's instructions for Byron's *Sardanapalus* served as inspiration for the *Historische Pantomime*.

81. According to Erginün, the lack of unity in space and time, as compared with the tight structure of Byron's play, is a sign of the fragmented nature of Abdülhak Hamid's play. See Erginün, "Byron ve Hamid'in Sardanapal Piyesleri," 27–28.

82. Abdülhak Hamid, *Sardanapal: Bir Facia-i Tarihiye*, 9, 18, 30.

83. Ibid., 66.

84. Ibid., 75, 99.

85. Ibid., 109, 118, 128.

86. Ibid., 132, 149.

Five • *The Landscape of Labor*

1. Quirke, *Hidden Hands*, 9.

2. Cesnola, *Cyprus*, 68, 128, 135, 143, 146, 255, 277.

3. Michaelis, *A Century of Archaeological Discoveries*, 30, 34, and 36.

4. Layard, *Nineveh and Its Remains*, 1: 44–45, 122, 126, 267–270.

5. J. T. Wood, *Discoveries at Ephesus*, 24, 26, 226, 228–230, 246.

6. Rassam, *Asshur and the Land of Nimrod*, 198–199.

7. Koldewey, *Excavations at Babylon*, v, 24.

8. UPMAAA, Near East, Nippur I/II. Peters's Field Notes. I. Expedition, 1889. Journal of Excavations, February 8–March 16.

9. UPMAAA, Near East. Peters, Journal II. Expedition. 1890. I Journal, January 14–January 29.

10. UPMAAA, Near East. Daily Work Reports by Mrs. John Henry Haynes, 30th Report, September 2, 1899.

11. Clarke, *Report on the Investigations at Assos*, 23–25.

12. Butler, *Sardis: The Excavations*, 1:39, 68.

13. Eldem, *Le voyage à Nemrud Dağı*, 39, 63, 64.

14. O. Hamdy Bey and T. Reinach, *Une nécropole royale à Sidon*, 14, 26.

15. Rassam, *Asshur and the Land of Nimrod*, 13.

16. Koldewey, *Excavations at Babylon*, 24.

17. Peters, *Nippur, or Excavations and Adventures*, 2: 88–89, 110–111. Peters gives the exchange rate as 3 piasters = 12 cents.

18. SPHC, James Andrew Meyer, Diary (1894), June 4, 1894. Hilprecht described Meyer as "eminently qualified," as he had studied monuments in Europe, the Middle East, and Turkey and he was an "accurate draughtsman … enthusiastically devoted to his subject." Meyer died of dysentery and malaria in December 1894 in Baghdad, where he was taken a month before. See Hilprecht, *The Babylonian Expedition*, 1: 351–353.

19. SPHC, Meyer, Diary, July 7, 1894.

20. UPMAAA, Near East. Peters, Journal II, Expedition, 1890. I Journal, February 1–February 5.

21. PUAA, Howard Crosby Butler Archive, Howard Crosby Butler, *Journal of Excavation at Sardis* (1910), 1, 11.

22. Ibid., 7.

23. Peters, *Nippur, or Excavations and Adventures*, 2:111–112.

24. Ibid., 2:89–90.

25. O. Hamdy Bey and T. Reinach, *Une nécropole royale à Sidon*, 26, 35, 96.

26. PUAA, Butler Archive, Howard Crosby Butler, *Journal of Excavation at Sardis* (1910), 1–2.

27. Aristarchi Bey (Grégoire), *Législation ottomane*, Troisième Partie: Droit Administratif, Règlement sur les antiquités, Article 9, 163.

28. Young, *Corps de droit ottoman*, 392 (article 21). The salaries of these officers were fixed by the government and paid by the excavating agency.

29. Bent, "Hamdi Bey," 617.

30. "Americans in Babylonia," *New York Times*, July 3, 1897.

31. BOA, DH.MKT, Dosya 2222, Gömlek 77 (9 Ramazan 1317/January 11, 1900).

32. PUAA, Butler Archive, Howard Crosby Butler, *Journal of Excavation at Sardis* (1910), 13, 76.

33. "Asar-ı Atika Hafriyat ve Harabiye Mevaki Bekçilerine Ait Talimname," articles 6 and 7, *Maarif Vekaleti Mecmuası* 1, no. 2 (1 Mayıs 1341/May 1, 1925): 80. Even though this regulation dates from the 1920s, it reflects a reiteration of the previous practice, which did not change during the early decades of the Turkish Republic.

34. *Salname-i Nezaret-i Maarif-i Umumiye*, 1321 (1903), 53–92.

35. SPHC, Meyer, Diary, March 29, 1894. Meyer reported that the officer was treated to a "swell dinner" with the Americans, while his men consumed their entire stock of "chicken and rice."

36. Kuklick, *Puritans in Babylon*, 49.

37. BOA, DH. İD, Dosya 28, Gömlek 2-39 (14 Ramazan 1332/August 6, 1914).

38. BOA, DH. İD, Dosya 28, Gömlek 2-39 (8 Şevval 1332/August 30, 1914).

39. Cesnola, *Cyprus*, 255–256; for the image, see p. 272.

40. Ibid., 138.

41. Koldewey, *Excavations at Babylon*, 40, figure 25.

42. Butler, *Sardis*, 68.

43. Ibid.

44. The relationship between archaeology and ethnography and anthropology dates from the early decades of the history of the disciplines, calling attention to similarities between ancient objects and those in use at the time of the excavations around the same locations. Ethnology was seen as especially conducive to an association with archaeology, as it dealt with the past and the present. See Stocking, *Victorian Anthropology*, 173, 245.

45. Hilprecht, *Excavations in Assyria and Babylonia*, 1:438.

46. The photographs of the Nemrud Dağı expedition have been published in Eldem, *Le voyage à Nemrud Dağı*; for typical poses, see, for example, plates 29, 31, 32, 39, and 40.

47. Layard, *Nineveh and Its Remains*, 51, 65–66, 78.

48. The drawing is among the plates at the end of J. T. Wood's *Discoveries at Ephesus*. This section is not paged.

49. See, for example, Hilprecht, *Excavations in Assyria and Babylonia*, 1:154, 222, and 298.

50. Layard, *Nineveh and Its Remains*, 98, 100.

51. Ibid., 98–99.

52. Ibid., 99.

53. Ibid.

54. Cesnola, *Cyprus*, 126–127.

55. Ibid., 193.

56. Clarke, *Report on the Investigations at Assos*, 18, 20.

57. Peters, *Nippur, or Excavations and Adventures*, 2:82–83, 90.

58. Hilprecht, *The Babylonian Expedition*, 314–315, 317, 324.

59. Rassam, *Asshur and the Land of Nimrod*, ix.

60. Ibid., 69.

61. Ibid., 284.

62. Ibid., 131–132.

63. Eldem, *Un Ottoman en Orient*, 2010.

64. Eldem, *Le voyage à Nemrud Dağı*, 30–33.

65. O. Hamdy Bey and T. Reinach, *Une nécropole royale à Sidon*, 21, 96, 63.

66. Eldem, *Le voyage à Nemrud Dağı*, 34.

67. M. Wood, "The Question of Shakespeare's Prejudices," 62.

68. J. T. Wood, *Discoveries at Ephesus*, 234, 257.

69. Hilprecht, *Excavations in Assyria and Babylonia*, 446.

70. Butler, *Sardis*, 52.

71. Garstang, *Land of the Hittites*, 12.

72. UPMAAA, Near East, Nippur I/II. Peters's Field Notes. I. Expedition, 1889, February 20, 1889.

73. Peters, *Nippur, or Excavations and Adventures*, 2:185, 326.

74. Hamilakis, "Indigenous Archaeologies in Ottoman Greece," 49–69.

75. Peters, *Nippur, or Excavations and Adventures*, 2:81–82.

76. O. Hamdy Bey and T. Reinach, *Une nécropole royale à Sidon*, 59.

77. Ibid., 84.

78. Peters, *Nippur, or Excavations and Adventures*, 2:305.

Six • Dual Settlements

1. Volney, *Voyage en Syrie et en Égypte*, 2:264.

2. Wightman, *The Wonders of the World*, 111, 112–113. See R. Wood, *The Ruins of Palmyra*.

3. Addison, *Damascus and Palmyra*, 2:300–302, 334.

4. Kelman, *From Damascus to Palmyra*, 224.

5. Eugène Guillaume, "Les ruines de Palmyre," *Revue de deux mondes* (Période 4) 142, (1897): 395.

6. Kelman, *From Damascus to Palmyra*, 225.

7. Peters, *Nippur, or Excavations and Adventures*, 2:349.

8. İsmail Fazıl Pasha, "Asar-ı Atika: Suriye Vilayetinde," *Şehbal* 2, no. 45 (15 Teşrinisani 1327/October 28, 1911): 417.

9. Michaelis, *A Century of Archaeological Discoveries*, 36.

10. On Layard's involvement in British imperialism, see Malley, "The Layard Enterprise," 99–123.

11. Layard, *Nineveh and Its Remains*, 1:44–45, 122, 126, 267–270.

12. Clarke, *Report on the Investigations at Assos*, 364.

13. Butler, *Sardis*, 38.

14. PUAA, Howard Crosby Butler Archive. Howard Crosby Butler, *Journal of Excavation at Sardis* (1910), 76, 87, 88.

15. Butler, *Sardis*, 58, 86.

16. Ibid., 58–60.

17. Ibid., 60.

18. For a discussion on this topic, see Çelik, *Empire, Architecture, and the City*, chapters 3 and 4. In that book, I examined the late-Ottoman proto-regionalist experiments in the Arab provinces. The phenomenon, although not studied, applies to other areas of the Ottoman Empire.

19. *Aydın Vilayetine Mahsus Salname*, 582; Karpat, *Osmanlı Nüfusu (1830–1914)*, 212.

20. Peters, *Nippur, or Excavations and Adventures*, 1:432.

21. Ibid., 1:227.

22. Eroğlu, Babuçoğlu, and Özdil, *Osmanlı Vilayet Salnamelerinde Bağdat*, 119–121. This publication brings together information from the Baghdad *salname*s (yearbooks) of 1309 (1892), 1312 (1895), 1313–1314 (1896), and 1315 (1897).

23. Peters, *Nippur, or Excavations and Adventures*, 1:212.

24. Eroğlu, Babuçoğlu, and Özdil, *Osmanlı Vilayet Salnamelerinde Bağdat*, 121–124.

25. Peters, *Nippur, or Excavations and Adventures*, 1:222.

26. Ibid., 2:54, 60.

27. İAMA, Müze-i Hümayun, no. 1566 (3 Nisan 1315/April 15, 1899). American archaeologists paid for the security forces. According to Meyer, in 1894, the team was protected by four Turkish "zaptiehs" and six Arab guards, equipped with guns and pistols. He adds that "they are quite faithful in putting in an appearance and we always have two of them at the excavations." See SPHC, Meyer, Diary, July 1, 1894.

28. Peters, *Nippur, or Excavations and Adventures*, 1:228.

29. Hilprecht, *The Babylonian Expedition*, 1:304–306, 315, 317; Peters, *Nippur, or Excavations and Adventures*, 1:234–235, 284.

30. Hilprecht, *The Babylonian Expedition*, 1:322.

31. Peters, *Nippur, or Excavations and Adventures*, 1:64–65, 74.

32. UPMAAA, The Diary of Mr. J. H. Haynes (1899–1900), Expedition IV, July 29, 1899.

33. Peters, *Nippur, or Excavations and Adventures*, 1:65.

34. Hilprecht, *The Babylonian Expedition*, 1:315; Peters, *Nippur, or Excavations and Adventures*, 1:65.

35. Peters, *Nippur, or Excavations and Adventures*, 2:74, 87–88.

36. SPHC, Meyer, Diary, June 10, 1894.

37. UPMAAA, J. H. Haynes, Expedition III, Report (transcribed copy), 177.

38. Hilprecht, *The Babylonian Expedition*, 1:349.

39. UPMAAA, J. H. Haynes, Expedition III, Report (transcribed copy), 178.

40. UPMAAA, J. H. Haynes, Expedition III, Report (transcribed copy), 177–179. The solution to the water problem was addressed during the following expedition by digging three more wells in the garden. The last one was the source of "excellent" water, which was conducted to the court of the Castle by subterranean pipes. See Hilprecht, *The Babylonian Expedition*, 1:434–435.

41. UPMAAA, The Diary of Mr. J. H. Haynes (1899–1900), Expedition IV, June 4, 1899, and July 14–15, 1899; Hilprecht, *The Babylonian Expedition*, 1:435.

42. UPMAAA, J. H. Haynes, Expedition III, Report (transcribed copy), 178–179.

43. SPHC, Meyer, Diary, May 29, June 2, and June 3, 1894.

44. SPHC, Meyer, Diary, June 15, 1894.

45. Ibid.

46. UPMAAA, J. H. Haynes, Expedition III, Report (transcribed copy), 179.

47. UPMAAA, The Diary of Mr. J. H. Haynes (1899–1900), Expedition IV, June 11, 1899.

48. Ibid., October 15, 1899.

49. Ibid., June 29, 1899.

50. UPMAAA, J. H. Haynes, Expedition III, Report (transcribed copy), 179.

51. UPMAAA, Diaries or daybook of Mr. Joseph Meyer, May 29, 1894.

52. Ibid., June 12, 1894.

53. Hilprecht, *The Babylonian Expedition*, 1:427–428. Bruce Kuklick found it "difficult" to understand Mrs. Haynes and the nature of the marriage. Although she kept the house well and treated the guests and the team members to "a table" that drew compliments, she had a strong temper, which she seems to have expressed often. See Kuklick, *Puritans in Babylon*, 84–87.

54. UPMAAA, The Diary of Mr. J. H. Haynes (1899–1900), Expedition IV, February 7, 1899.

55. For the indigenous villages in world's fairs, see Çelik, *Displaying the Orient*, especially chapters 1 and 2.

56. Peters, *Nippur, or Excavations and Adventures*, 1:231, 237, 252, 324, 326–326. The Ottoman yearbooks describe these huts, named *sarifas*, in a similar manner and add that the tribal chiefs use a larger version, called *muzif*, as *selamlık* (men's quarters) and for entertaining their guests. It is also noted that when the tribes are at war with each other, they take refuge in small castles, or *meftuls*. See Eroğlu, Babuçoğlu, and Özdil, *Osmanlı Vilayet Salnamelerinde Bağdat*, 119.

57. Peters, *Nippur, or Excavations and Adventures*, 2:370–371.

58. UPMAAA, Letter from G. Brown Goode to William Pepper, March 13, 1889.

59. UPMAAA, The Diary of Mr. J. H. Haynes (1899–1900), Expedition IV, February 12, 1899.

60. SPHC, Meyer, Diary, June 15, 1894.

61. Meyer, "Joseph Andrew Meyer, Jr., Architect at Niffer," 138.

62. UPMAAA, Diaries or daybook of Mr. Joseph Meyer, May 29 and June 13, 1894. See also SPHC, Meyer, Diary, June 14, June 15, and June 18, 1894.

63. UPMAAA, Nippur 1899–1900, Expedition IV. Pictures taken by John Henry Haynes, Series "C," No. 143.

64. SPHC, Meyer, Diary, June 15, 1894.

65. UPMAAA, Nippur 1899–1900, Expedition IV. Pictures taken by John Henry Haynes, Series "C," No. 144.

66. Hilprecht, The Babylonian Expedition, 1:322.

67. Ibid., 1:434.

68. SPHC, Meyer, Diary, June 9, 1894.

69. SPHC, Meyer, Diary, June 15, 1894.

Epilogue • Enduring Dilemmas

1. Parts of this section are derived from Zeynep Çelik, "Archéologie, politique et histoire en débat," Perspective, no. 2 (2010–2011), 271–276.

2. Cuno, Who Owns Antiquity?, xviii–xix; and Whose Culture?, 37.

3. MacGregor, "To Shape the Citizens," 39.

4. Cuno, Who Owns Antiquity?, xix.

5. Cuno, "Art Museums, Archaeology, and Antiquities," 16, 22.

6. Cuno, Who Owns Antiquity?, 11.

7. Nationalism and historic heritage has been the topic of several studies recently. Among them, for Turkey, Egypt, Iran, and Iraq, see Goode, Negotiating for the Past; for Greece, see Hamilakis, The Nation and Its Ruins.

8. Cuno, Who Owns Antiquity?, xxxiv; Rhodes, "Introduction" in Rhodes, The Acquisition and Exhibition of Classical Antiquities, 8. Their target is not only the legislation against the exportation of antiquities but also the archaeologists who insist on the protection of the sites from looting because they maintain that relevant information on history "can only be extracted from objects in context." On this point, see Rosenberg, "Response to James Cuno," 29.

9. Hugh Eakin, "The Great Giveback," New York Times, January 27, 2013, 12.

10. See chapter 3 for a discussion of this article.

11. Goode, Negotiating for the Past, 5.

12. Rhodes, "Introduction," in Rhodes, The Acquisition and Exhibition of Classical Antiquities, 7.

13. Cuno, "Art Museums, Archaeology, and Antiquities," 11, 23–25, 55, 154.

14. Doordan, "Response to Malcolm Bell," 44–45.

15. Michael Kimmelman, "Who Draws the Borders of Culture?" New York Times, May 5, 2010.

16. Ibid.; Beard, The Parthenon, 199–200.

17. Beard, *The Parthenon*, 199.

18. Dan Bilefsky, "Seeking Return of Art, Turkey Jolts Museums," *New York Times*, September 30, 2012.

19. "Herakles'in İki Yarısı Buluştu," *Milliyet*, October 10, 2011.

20. "Türkiye Bu Eserlerin Peşinde," *Milliyet*, April 1, 2012. The article referred to is Jason Felch, "Turkey Asks U.S. Museums for Return of Antiquities," *Los Angeles Times*, March 30, 2012.

21. "Türkiye Bu Eserlerin Peşinde," *Milliyet*.

22. Rose and Acar, "Turkey's War on the Illicit Antiquities Trade," 49; "Yorgun Herakles'e Yoğun İlgi," *Milliyet*, July 14, 2014.

23. "Yorgun Herakles'e Yoğun İlgi," *Milliyet*.

24. For an overview of the situation, see Tom Mashberg and Graham Bowley, "As ISIS Destroys Treasures, Debate over Antiquities Renews," *New York Times*, March 31, 2015.

25. Nicholas Pelham, "ISIS and the Shia Revival in Iraq," *New York Review of Books* 62, no. 10 (June 4, 2015): 30–32.

BIBLIOGRAPHY

Archives

Başbakanlık Osmanlı Arşivi (Prime Minister's Archives, BOA)
BEO (Bab-ı Ali Evrak Odası)
DH.İD (Dahiliye İdare)
DH.MKT (Dahiliye Mektubi Kalemi)
İ.HR (İrade Hariciye)
MF.MKT (Maarif Mektubi Kalemi)
İstanbul Arkeoloji Müzeleri Arşivi (Istanbul Archaeological Museums Archives, İAMA)
İstanbul Üniversitesi Merkez Kütüphanesi, Nadide Eserler (Istanbul University Central Library, Rare Works Collection, İÜMK)
Pierpont Morgan Library Archives
Princeton University Archaeological Archives (PUAA)
Special Collections, Haverford College, Haverford, PA (SPHC)
University of Pennsylvania Museum of Archaeology and Anthropology Archives, Manuscript collections (UPMAAA)

Periodicals

The Academy
The American Architect and Building News
American Journal of Archaeology
Ankara Üniversitesi Hukuk Fakültesi Dergisi
The Annual of the British School at Athens
The Athenaeum
Bilgi Mecmuası
The British Architect
The Builder
The Century: Illustrated Monthly Magazine
The Chautauquan
Darülfünun Edebiyat Fakültesi Mecmuası

Free Museum of Science and Art,
 Department of Archaeology
 and Palaeontology, University of
 Pennsylvania, Bulletin
Gazette des Beaux-Arts
Hamiyet
İçtihad
İslam Mecmuası
Kalem
The Literary News
Littell's Living Age
The Living Age
Maarif
Maarif Vekaleti Mecmuası
Malumat

The Metropolitan Museum of Art Bulletin
Milliyet
Musavver Malumat-ı Nafia
Museum of Fine Arts Bulletin (Boston)
The Nation
The New Review
The New York Times
Osmanlı Ressamlar Cemiyeti Gazetesi
Recherches contemporaines
Revue archéologique
Revue des deux mondes
Revue d'ethnographie
Şehbal
Servet-i Fünun
Tedrisat Mecmuası

Books and Articles

Abdülhak Hamid. *Sardanapal: Bir Facia-i Tarihiye*. Istanbul: Matbaa-i Amire, 1335 (1919).

Actes de la Société du Chemin de Fer Ottoman de la Syrie. Akka à Damas. Constantinople: Imprimerie du journal "Stamboul," 1891.

Addison, Charles G. *Damascus and Palmyra: A Journey to the East*. Vol. 2. London: Richard Bentley, 1838.

Ahmed İhsan. *Avrupa'da Ne Gördüm*. Istanbul: Alem Matbaası, 1891.

Ahmed Refik. *Büyük Tarih-i Umumi*. Istanbul: Kütüphane-i İslam ve Askeri—İbrahim Hilmi, AH 1328 (1910).

Aristarchi Bey (Grégoire). *Législation ottomane, ou Receuil des lois, réglements, ordonnances, traités, capitulations et autres documents officiels de l'Empire ottoman*. Constantinople: Demétrius Nicolaïdes, 1874.

Aydın Vilayetine Mahsus Salname. Aydın: Matbaa-i Vilayet, 1308 (1891).

Baedeker, Karl. *Berlin and Its Environs*. 3rd ed. Leipzig: Karl Baedeker, 1908.

————. *Konstantinopel, Balkanstaaten, Kleinasien Archipel, Cypern*. Leipzig: Karl Baedeker, 1915.

————. *Konstantinopel und das Westliche Kleinasien*. Leipzig: Karl Baedeker, 1905.

————. *London and Its Environs*. Leipzig: Karl Baedeker, 1894. (Figure 1.5 is from the 1911 edition.)

————. *Paris et ses environs*. Leipzig: K. Beadeker; and Paris: P. Ollendorff, 1900.

————. *The United States, with an Excursion into Mexico*. 3rd ed. Leipzig: Karl Baedeker; and New York: Charles Scribner's Sons, 1908. (Figure 1.7 is from the 1904 edition.)

Bahrani, Zainab. "History in Reverse: Archaeological Illustration and the Invention of Assyria." In *Historiography in the Cuneiform Word*, ed. Tzivi Abush et al., 15–28. Bethesda: CDL Press, 2001.

Bahrani, Zainab, Zeynep Çelik, and Edhem Eldem. "Introduction: Archaeology and Empire." In Bahrani, Çelik, and Eldem, *Scramble for the Past*, 13–43.

———, eds. *Scramble for the Past: A Story of Archaeology in the Ottoman Empire, 1753–1914.* Istanbul: SALT/Garanti Kültür, 2011.

Barth, H. *Constantinople.* Paris: Librairie Renouard, 1903.

Beard, Mary. *The Parthenon.* Rev. ed. Cambridge, MA: Harvard University Press, 2010.

Bilsel, Can. *Antiquity on Display: Regimes of the Authentic in Berlin's Pergamon Museum.* Oxford: Oxford University Press, 2012.

Bohrer, Frederick N. *Orientalism and Visual Culture: Imagining Mesopotamia in Nineteenth-Century Europe.* Cambridge: Cambridge University Press, 2003.

———. *Photography and Archaeology.* London: Reaktion Books, 2011.

Bourquelot, Émile. *Promenades en Égypte et à Constantinople.* Paris: Challamel ainé, Librairie Coloniale, 1886.

Brinkmann, Vinzenz. "The Prince and the Goddess: The Rediscovered Color on the Pediment Statues of the Aphaia Temple." In Brinkmann and Wünsche, *Gods in Color,* 70–97.

Brinkmann, Vinzenz, and Raimund Wünsche, eds. *Gods in Color: Painted Sculpture of Classical Antiquity.* Munich: Stiftung Archäologie, 2007.

Burrows, Edwin G., and Mike Wallace. *Gotham: A History of New York City to 1898.* Oxford: Oxford University Press, 2000.

Butler, Howard Crosby. *Sardis: The Excavations, Part I (1910–1914).* Vol. 1. Leyden: Late E. J. Brill, 1922.

Byron, Lord. *Sardanapalus: A Tragedy.* London: John Murray, 1821.

Caillard, Vincent. "The Imperial Ottoman Museum." In Cornwallis-West, *Anglo-Saxon Review,* 132–150.

Casey, Christopher. "'Grecian Grandeurs, and the Rude Wasting of Old Time': Britain, the Elgin Marbles, and Post-Revolutionary Hellenism." *Foundations* 3, no. 1 (Fall 2008): 30–62.

Çelik, Zeynep. "Archéologie, politique et histoire en débat." *Perspective,* no. 2 (2010–2011): 271–276.

———. "Defining Empire's Patrimony: Late Ottoman Perceptions of Antiquities." In Bahrani, Çelik, and Eldem, *Scramble for the Past,* 443–477.

———. *Displaying the Orient: Architecture of Islam at Nineteenth-Century World's Fairs.* Berkeley: University of California Press, 1992.

———. *Empire, Architecture, and the City: French-Ottoman Encounters, 1830–1914.* Seattle and London: University of Washington Press, 2008.

———. *The Remaking of Istanbul: Portrait of an Ottoman City in the Nineteenth Century.* Seattle and London: University of Washington Press, 1986.

Cervati, R. C. *Guide horaire général international illustré pour le voyageur en Orient.* Constantinople: R. C. Cervati, 1909.

Cesnola, Luigi Palma di. *An Address on the Practical Value of the American Museum, delivered at Round Lake, N.Y., July 12, 1887.* Troy, NY: The Stowell Printing House, 1887.

———. *Cyprus: Its Ancient Cities, Tombs, and Temples.* New York: Harper and Brothers, 1878.

Charter of the Metropolitan Museum of Art and Laws Relating to It. New York: The Metropolitan Museum of Art, 1901.

Clarke, Joseph Thacher. *Report on the Investigations at Assos, 1882, 1883, Part I.* New York: Macmillan Company, 1898.

Cornwallis-West, Mrs. George, ed. *The Anglo-Saxon Review: A Quarterly Miscellany* 7 (December 1900). New York: G. P. Putnam's Sons; London: Mrs. George Cornwallis-West, 1900.

Coufopoulos, Demetrius. *A Guide to Constantinople.* London: Adam and Charles Black, 1895.

Cuno, James. "Art Museums, Archaeology, and Antiquities in an Age of Sectarian Violence and Nationalist Politics." In Rhodes, *The Acquisition and Exhibition of Classical Antiquities,* 9–26.

———. *Who Owns Antiquity? Museums and the Battle over Our Ancient Heritage.* Princeton, NJ: Princeton University Press, 2008.

———, ed. *Whose Culture? The Promise of Museums and the Debate over Antiquities.* Princeton, NJ: Princeton University Press, 2009.

Davis, Natalie Zemon. *Fiction in the Archives: Pardon Tales and Their Tellers in Sixteenth-Century France.* Palo Alto: Stanford University Press, 1987.

deJong Ellis, Maria, ed. *Nippur at the Centennial: Papers Read at the 35e Rencontre Assyriologique Internationale, Philadelphia, 1988.* Philadelphia: The University Museum, 1992.

Diaz-Andreu, Margarita. *A World History of Nineteenth-Century Archaeology: Nationalism, Colonialism, and the Past.* Oxford: Oxford University Press, 2007.

Doordan, Dennis P. "Response to Malcolm Bell." In Rhodes, *The Acquisition and Exhibition of Classical Antiquities,* 43–45.

Duchéne, Hervé. "Les musées royaux enrichis de maints trésors." In Krings and Isabelle Tassignon, *Archéologie dans l'Empire Ottoman autour de 1900: Entre politique, économie et science,* 141–196.

Dwight, Harry Griswold. *Constantinople, Old and New.* London: Longmans, Green, 1915.

Edwards, Edward. *Memoirs of Libraries.* London: Trübner, 1859.

Eldem, Edhem, ed. *Le voyage à Nemrud Dağı d'Osman Hamdi Bey et Osgan Efendi (1883).* Istanbul and Paris: L'Institut Français d'Études Anatoliennes—Georges Dumézel, 2010.

———. *Mendel-Sebah: Müze-i Hümayun'u Belgelemek/Mendel-Sebah: Documenting the Imperial Museum.* Istanbul: Istanbul Archaeological Museums, 2014.

———. *Un Ottoman en Orient, Osman Hamdi Bey en Irak.* Paris: Sindbad, 2010.

Elliot, Frances. *Diary of an Idle Woman in Constantinople.* London: John Murray, 1893.

Emerson, Alfred. *An Account of Recent Progress in Classical Archaeology, 1875–1889.* Cambridge, MA: John Wilson and Son, 1889.

Erginün, İnci. "Byron ve Hamid'in Sardanapal Piyesleri Üzerinde Mukayeseli Bir Araştırma." *Türk Dili ve Edebiyatı Dergisi* (2012): 13–44.

Eroğlu, Cengiz, Murat Babuçoğlu, and Orhan Özdil, eds. *Osmanlı Vilayet Salnamelerinde Bağdat.* Ankara: Global Strateji Enstitüsü, 2006.

Eudel, Paul. *Constantinople, Smyrne et Athènes: Journal de voyage.* Paris: E. Dentu, 1885.

Fenger, Ludvig Peter. *Dorische Polychromie.* Berlin: A. Asher, 1886.

Fowler, Harold North, and James Rignall Wheeler (with the collaboration of Gorham

Phillips Stevens). *A Handbook of Greek Archaeology*. New York, Cincinnati, Chicago: American Book Company, 1909.

Gardner, Percy. *Sculptured Tombs of Hellas*. London and New York: Macmillan, 1896.

Garstang, John. *The Land of the Hittites: An Account of Recent Explorations and Discoveries in Asia Minor, with Descriptions of the Hittite Monuments*. New York: E. P. Dutton, 1910.

Ginzburg, Carlo. *The Cheese and the Worms: The Cosmos of a Sixteenth-Century Miller*. Translated by John and Anne Tedeschi. Baltimore: Johns Hopkins University Press, 1980.

Godins de Souhesmes, G. des. *Guide to Constantinople and Its Environs*. Constantinople: A. Zellich, 1893.

Goode, James F. *Negotiating for the Past: Archaeology, Nationalism, and Diplomacy in the Middle East, 1919–1941*. Austin: University of Texas Press, 2007.

Goold, Edward. *Catalogue explicatif, historique et scientifique d'un certain nombre d'objets contenus dans le Musée impérial de Constantinople fondé en 1869 sous le grand vésirat de Son Altesse A'ali Pacha*. Constantinople: Imprimerie Zellich, 1871.

Gower, Lord Ronald Sutherland. *Records and Reminiscences selected from "My Reminiscences" and "Old Diaries."* London: John Murray, 1903.

Gretton, John R. *A Guide to the Microfiche Edition of Murray's Handbooks for Travellers*. N.p.: University Publications of America, 1993.

Grosvenor, Edwin Augustus. *Constantinople*. 2 vols. Boston: Roberts Brothers, 1895.

Guide to Greece, the Archipelago, Constantinople, the Coasts of Asia Minor, Crete, and Cyprus. London: Macmillan, 1908.

Gutron, Clémentine. *L'archéologie en Tunisie (XIXe–XXe siècles): Jeux généalogiques sur l'Antiquité*. Paris: Karthala, 2010.

Habel, Dorothy Metzger. *"When All of Rome Was under Construction": The Building Process in Baroque Rome*. University Park: Pennsylvania State University Press, 2013.

Halil Edhem. *Elvah-ı Nakşiye Koleksiyonu*. Istanbul: Matbaa-i Amire, 1924. Reprinted in transliterated and simplified Turkish in 1970 (Istanbul: Milliyet Yayınları, 1970). All citations refer to the 1970 edition.

Hamilakis, Yannis. "Indigenous Archaeologies in Ottoman Greece." In Bahrani, Çelik, and Eldem, *Scramble for the Past*, 49–69.

———. *The Nation and Its Ruins: Antiquity, Archaeology, and National Imagination in Greece*. Oxford: Oxford University Press, 2007.

Handbook for Travellers in Constantinople, Brûsa, and the Troad. London: John Murray, 1900.

Harper, Robert Francis. "Introduction." *Assyrian and Babylonian Literature: Selected Translations*. New York: D. Appleton, 1901.

Hilprecht, Hermann Volrath, ed., *The Babylonian Expedition of the University of Pennsylvania*. Philadelphia: Department of Archaeology, University of Pennsylvania, 1896.

———. *The Excavations in Assyria and Babylonia*. Philadelphia: A. J. Holman, 1904.

Hittorff, Jacques-Ignace. *Restitution du temple d'Empédocle à Sélinonte, ou L'architecture polychrome chez les Grecs*. Paris: Librairie de Firmin Didot Frères, 1851.

Holod, Renata, and Robert Ousterhout, eds. *Osman Hamdi Bey and the Americans.* Istanbul: Pera Museum, 2011.

Howe, Winifred E. *A History of the Metropolitan Museum of Art.* New York: Metropolitan Museum of Art, 1913.

Hutton, William Holden. *Constantinople: The Story of the Old Capital of the Empire.* London: J. M. Dent, 1900.

Jasanoff, Maya. *Edges of Empire: Conquest and Collecting in the East, 1750–1850.* London: Harper Perennial, 2006.

Jockey, Philippe. "The Venus de Milo: Genesis of a Modern Myth." In Bahrani, Çelik, and Eldem, *Scramble for the Past,* 237–255.

Joubin, André. *Asar-ı Heykeltraşi Kataloğu: Kadim Yunan, Roma, Bizanten ve Frank Devirleri.* Istanbul: Mihran, 1311 (1894).

———. *Luhud ve Mekabir-i Atike Kataloğu.* Constantinople (Konstantinye): Mihran Matbaası, 1310 (1894). Reprint, Constantinople: Mahmud Bey Matbaası, 1317 (1900).

Karpat, Kemal. *Osmanlı Nüfusu (1830–1914): Demografik ve Sosyal Özellikleri.* Istanbul: Tarih Vakfı Yurt Yayınları, 2003.

Kelman, John. *From Damascus to Palmyra.* London: Adam and Charles Black, 1908.

Kemal Tahir. *Esir Şehrin İnsanları.* Istanbul: Ithaki, 2005. First ed., 1956.

Kohl, Phillip, and Clare Fawcett. *Nationalism, Politics and the Practice of Archaeology.* Cambridge: Cambridge University Press, 1995.

Koldewey, Robert. *The Excavations at Babylon.* Translated by Agnes S. Jones. London: Macmillan, 1914.

Krings, Véronique, and Isabelle Tassignon, eds. *Archéologie dans l'Empire ottoman autour de 1900: Entre politique, économie et science.* Brussels: Institut historique belge de Rome, 2004.

Kuklick, Bruce. *Puritans in Babylon: The Ancient Near East and American Intellectual Life, 1880–1930.* Princeton, NJ: Princeton University Press, 1996.

Layard, Austen Henry. *Nineveh and Its Remains.* 2 vols. New York: George P. Putnam, 1849.

Lord Byron's Historical Tragedy of Sardanapalus, Arranged for Representation in Four Acts by Charles Calvert. London, 1876.

MacGregor, Neil. "To Shape the Citizens of 'That Great City, the World.'" In Cuno, *Whose Culture?,* 39–54.

Mahaffy, J. P. *A Survey of Greek Civilization.* New York, Cincinnati, and Chicago: The Chautauqua Century Press, 1896.

Malley, Shawn. "The Layard Enterprise: Victorian Archaeology and Informal Imperialism in Mesopotamia." In Bahrani, Çelik, and Eldem, *Scramble for the Past,* 99–123.

Marchand, Suzanne L. *Down from Olympus: Archaeology and Philhellenism in Germany, 1750–1970,* Princeton, NJ: Princeton University Press, 1996.

Mehmed Raif. *Topkapı Saray-ı Hümayunu ve Parkının Tarihi.* Istanbul: Matbaa-i Hayriye ve Şürekası, 1332 (1916).

Mehmed Vahid. *Rehnüma.* Istanbul: Ahmed İhsan, 1337 (1919).

A Memorial of George Brown Goode Together with a Selection of His Papers on Museums. Washington, DC: Government Printing Office, 1901.

Mendel, Gustave. *Catalogue des sculptures grecques, romaines et byzantines.* 3 vols. Constantinople: Musées Impériaux Ottomans, 1914.

The Metropolitan Museum of Art: A Brief Record of Development, 1870–1922. New York, 1923.

Meyer, Charles F., Jr. "Joseph Andrew Meyer, Jr., Architect at Niffer." In deJong Ellis, *Nippur at the Centennial: Papers Read at the 35e Rencontre Assyriologique Internationale, Philadelphia, 1988,* 15–19.

Michaelis, Adolf. *A Century of Archaeological Discoveries.* Translated by Bettina Kahnwerter. London: John Murray, 1908.

Montmarché, Marcel. *De Paris à Constantinople.* Paris: Librairie Hachette, 1912.

Morley, Neville. "Decadence as a Theory of History." *New Literary History* 35, no. 4 (Autumn 2004): 573–585.

Müller, Georgina Adelaide. *Letters from Constantinople by Mrs. Max Müller.* London, New York, and Bombay: Longman, Green, 1897.

Musée Impérial Ottoman. *Antiquités himyarites et palmyriennes: Catalogue sommaire.* Constantinople: Mihran, 1895.

———. *Bronzes et bijoux: Catalogue sommaire.* Constantinople: F. Loeffer, 1898.

———. *Catalogue des sculptures grecques, romaines, byzantines et franques.* Constantinople: Mihran, 1893.

———. *Monuments égyptiens: Notice sommaire.* Constantinople: Mihran, 1898.

———. *Monuments funéraires: Catalogue sommaire.* Constantinople: Mihran, 1893. Reprint, Constantinople: Ahmed İhsan, 1909.

Musées Impériaux Ottomans. *Catalogue des figurines grecques de terre cuite.* Constantinople: Ahmed İhsan, 1908.

———. *Catalogues des poteries byzantines et anatoliennes du Musée de Constantinople.* Constantinople: Ahmed İhsan, 1910.

Müze-i Hümayun. *Asar-ı Misriyye Kataloğu.* Istanbul: Mihran, 1317 (1899).

———. *Kurşun Mühür Kataloğu.* Istanbul: Mahmud Bey Matbaası, 1321 (1904).

Nochlin, Linda. "The Imaginary Orient." *Art in America* 71, no. 5 (May 1983): 118–131, 187–191.

Osman Hamdi Bey and Osgan Efendi. *Le tumulus de Nemroud-Dagh.* Constantinople: F. Loeffler, 1883.

O. Hamdy Bey and Théodore Reinach. *Une nécropole royale à Sidon: Fouilles de Hamdy Bey.* Paris: Leroux, 1892.

Oulebsir, Nabila. *Les usages du patrimoine: Monuments, musées et politique coloniale en Algérie (1830–1930).* Paris: Maison des Sciences de l'Homme, 2004.

Ousterhout, Robert G. *John Henry Haynes: A Photographer and Archaeologist in the Ottoman Empire, 1881–1900.* Istanbul: Kayık Yayıncılık; Hawick: Cornucopia Books, 2011.

Palestine Exploration Fund Quarterly Statement for 1886. London: Society's Office and Richard Bentley and Son, 1886.

Papers Relating to the Foreign Relations of the United States, Transmitted to Congress. December 3, 1888, Part II. Washington, DC: Government Printing Office, 1889.

Pelham, Nicholas. "ISIS & the Shia Revival in Iraq." *New York Review of Books* 62, no. 10 (June 4, 2015): 30–32.

Perdrizet, Paul F. "Archaistic Reliefs." *Annual of the British School at Athens*, no. 11 (1896–1897): Seminars 156–157.

Peters, John Punnett. *Nippur, or Excavations and Adventures on the Euphrates: The Narrative of the University of Pennsylvania Expedition to Babylonia in the Years 1888–1890.* 2 vols. 2nd ed. New York and London: J. P. Putnam's Sons, 1898.

Preyer, David C. *The Art of the Metropolitan Museum of New York.* Boston: L. C. Page, 1909.

Quatremère de Quincy, Antoine. *Le Jupiter olympien, ou L'art de la sculpture antique considéré sous un nouveau point de vue, ouvrage qui comprend un essai sur le goût de la sculpture polychrome, l'analyse explicative de la toreutique, et l'histoire de la statuaire en or et ivoire [...].* Paris: Firmin Didot, 1814.

Quirke, Stephen. *Hidden Hands: Egyptian Workforces in Petrie Excavation Archives, 1880–1924.* London: Duckworth, 2011.

Radcliffe, Abigail G. *Schools and Masters of Sculpture.* New York: D. Appleton, 1894.

Rassam, Hormuzd. *Asshur and the Land of Nimrod.* Cincinatti: Curts and Jennings; New York: Eaton and Maris, 1897.

Reid, Donald Malcolm. *Whose Pharaohs? Archaeology, Museums, and Egyptian National Identity from Napoleon to World War I.* Berkeley, Los Angeles, and London: University of California Press, 2002.

Reinach, Salomon. *Conseils aux voyageurs archéologues.* Paris: Ernest Leroux, 1886.

———. *Ministère de l'Instruction publique: Catalogue du Musée impérial des antiquités.* Constantinople: Imprimerie Levant Times, 1882.

Rhodes, Robin F., ed. *The Acquisition and Exhibition of Classical Antiquities: Professional, Legal, and Ethical Perspectives.* Notre Dame, IN: University of Notre Dame Press, 2007.

Rogers, Roger William. *A History of Babylonia and Assyria.* New York: Eaton and Mains; Cincinnati: Jenning and Pye, 1900.

Rona, Zeynep, ed. *Osman Hamdi Bey ve Dönemi.* Istanbul: Tarih Vakfı Yurt Yayınları, 1993.

Rose, Marc, and Özgen Acar. "Turkey's War on the Illicit Antiquities Trade." *Archaeology* 48, no. 2 (March–April 1995): 45–56.

Rosenberg, Charles. "Response to James Cuno." In Rhodes, *The Acquisition and Exhibition of Classical Antiquities,* 27–30.

Roussé, Léon. *De Paris à Constantinople.* Paris: Librairie Hachette, 1892.

Rosenzweig, Roy, and Elizabeth Blackmar. *The Park and the People: A History of Central Park.* Ithaca, NY: Cornell University Press, 1992.

Salname-i Nezaret-i Maarif-i Umumiye. Istanbul: Matbaa-i Amire, 1318 (1900). Rev. ed. Istanbul: Asır Matbaası, 1321 (1903).

Schliemann, Heinrich. *Trojanische Alterthümer: Berichte über die Ausgrabungen in Troja.* Leipzig: In Commission bei F. A. Brockhaus, 1874.

Schnapp, Alain. *La conquête du passé: Aux origines de l'archéologie.* Paris: Carré, 1993. English edition: *The Discovery of the Past.* London: British Museum Press, 1996.

Serbestoğlu, İbrahim, and Turan Açık. "Osmanlı Devleti'nde Modern Bir Okul Projesi: Müze-i Hümayun Mektebi." *Akademik Bakış* 6, no. 12 (Summer 2013): 157–172.

Seymour, Michael. *Legend, History and the Ancient City: Babylon.* London and New York: I. B. Tauris, 2014.

Shaw, Wendy M. K. "From Mausoleum to Museum: Resurrecting Antiquity for Ottoman Modernity." In Bahrani, Çelik, and Eldem, *Scramble for the Past,* 425–430.

———. *Possessors and Possessed: Museums, Archaeology, and the Visualization of History in the Late Ottoman Empire.* Berkeley: University of California Press, 2003.

Siegel, Jonah, ed. *The Emergence of the Museum: An Anthology of Nineteenth-Century Sources.* New York: Oxford University Press, 2008.

Smith, George. *Assyrian Discoveries: An Account of Explorations and Discoveries on the Site of Nineveh during 1873 and 1874.* New York: Scribner, Armstrong, 1876.

Sterrett, J. R. Sitlington. *A Plea for Research in Asia Minor and Syria.* Ithaca, NY: Cornell University, 1911.

Stocking, George W., Jr. *Victorian Anthropology.* New York: The Free Press, 1987.

Stoddard, John Lawson. *John L. Stoddard's Lectures.* Boston: Balch Brothers, 1897.

Topuzlu, Cemil. *32 Sene Evvelki, Bugünkü, Yarınki Istanbul.* Istanbul: Ülkü, 1944.

Trigger, Bruce. "Alternative Archaeologies: Nationalist, Colonialist, Imperialist." *Man* 19, no. 3 (1983): 355–370.

———. *A History of Archaeological Thought.* Cambridge: Cambridge University Press, 1989.

Trümpler, Charlotte, ed. *Das Grosse Spiel: Archäologie und Politik zur Zeit des Kolonialusmus.* Essen and Köln: Dumont, 2008.

Uğurcan, Sema. *Abdülhak Hamid Tarhan'in Eserlerinde Tarih.* İzmir: Akademi Kitabevi, 2002.

Valentier, Wilhelm M. R. *Catalogue of a Loan Exhibition of Early Oriental Rugs.* New York: Metropolitan Museum of Art, 1910.

Van Millingen, Alexander. *Constantinople.* London: A. and C. Black, 1906.

Volney, Constantin-François. *Voyage en Syrie et en Égypte, pendant les années 1783, 1784 et 1785.* Vol. 2. Paris: Chez Desenne, 1787.

Ward, William Hayes. *Report on the Wolfe Expedition to Babylonia.* Papers of the Archaeological Institute of America, 1884–1885. Boston: Cupples, Upham; London: N. Trübner, 1886.

Wharton, Edith. *The Age of Innocence.* New York: Charles Scribner's Sons, 1968. First ed., 1920.

Wightman, Julia P. *The Wonders of the World.* Dublin: Brett Smith, 1825.

Wood, J. T. *Discoveries at Ephesus.* Boston: James R. Osgood, 1877.

Wood, Michael. "The Question of Shakespeare's Prejudices." *New York Review of Books* 58, no. 20 (December 22, 2011).

Wood, Robert. *The Ruins of Palmyra, Otherwise Tedmor.* London: Robert Wood, 1753.

Young, George. *Corps de droit ottoman: Receuil des codes, lois, réglements, ordonnances et actes les plus importants du droit intérieur, et d'études sur le droit coutumier de l'Empire ottoman.* Vol. 2. Oxford: Clarendon Press, 1905–1906.

Zola, Émile. *L'assomoir.* Translated by Atwood H. Townsend. New York: Signet Classics, 1962. First ed., 1877.

INDEX

Note: Italic page numbers refer to figures.

Abdel Hamid, castle of, 197
Abdülaziz (sultan), 129
Abdülhak Hamid, *Sardanapal*, 8, 95, 129, 131–133, 237n81
Abdülhamid II (sultan), 4, 19, 35, 63, 64, 109, 129, 188
Addison, Charles G., 176
Aegina, Aphaia Temple in, 49, 50
Aeschylus, *Persians*, 236n71
Ahi Yunus, mausoleum of, 121
Ahmed Cemal, 127
Ahmed Fethi Pasha, 116
Ahmed İhsan, *Avrupa'da Ne Gödüm*, 112, 113–118, *115*
Ahmed III (sultan), 74
Ahmed Refik, 20
Ahmed Süreyya, 17
Ahmed Usta, 124
Alaeddin Kiosk, 124–125
Alaeddin Mosque, 74, 121–122
Alexander the Great, 54, 57, 98, 99. *See also* Sarcophagus of Alexander
Ali Pasha, 33–34
American Archaeological Institute, 144, 152

American Architect and Building News, 51
American Journal of Archaeology, 51, 62
American Museum of Natural History, 92
American museums: and artifacts from source countries, 215, 216, 218–219; democratic agenda of, 22–23, 87; educational mission of, 86. *See also* Metropolitan Museum of Art, New York; *and other specific museums*
American Presbyterian Mission, 51
American Sabbath Union, 91
American Secular Union, 91
American Society for the Excavation of Sardis, 180
Anatolia: agglomeration of ancient sites in, 6; ancient theaters in, 104; archaeological explorations of, 18, 83; Ottoman heritage in, 121–124, *125*; tourism of historic sites in, 220
Antalya Museum, 219–220
Antiochus (Syrian king), 99
antiquities: debates on, 1, 9, 43, 46, 215–217; destruction of, 221; ethics of transportation of, 28; and guidebooks,

95, 108–109, 113–118; leaving in situ, 46; looting of, 20, 96, 100, 111, 117, 126, 127, 218, 219, 242n8; meanings for local people, 3, 4, 220; and nationalism, 215–216; nineteenth-century cultural and artistic productions appropriating, 2, 8; Ottoman Empire's claims to, 7, 24–25, 43–44, 46–47, 64, 86, 127; Ottoman perceptions of, 8, 96; and Ottoman press, 25, 98–104, 106–119; ownership of, 220, 221; repatriation of, 217–220, 221; and retentionist cultural property laws, 215, 216, 217, 242n8; storage of antiquities from Ottoman provinces, 89–90; transportation by railroads, 2, 4, 91

antiquities laws: American reaction to, 18, 45–46; antiquities defined by, 24–25; British reaction to, 43–44; as diplomatic concern, 18, 43, 45; effect on archaeological science, 46–47; enforcement of, 3, 45, 63, 91, 154–155, 215; and European museums, 18, 19, 47; exportation restricted or banned by, 24, 44, 46, 63, 89, 90–91, 96, 110, 117; and Imperial Museum, 23–24, 33, 47, 61, 77, 84, 117, 152; Ottoman evaluation of, 47; Ottoman supervision of archaeological sites, 150, 152–153, 215; Peters on, 227–228n8; and smuggling of antiquities, 45, 47, 63–64, 91, 96, 110, 117, 154–155, 178; writing of, 3. See also specific laws

Apollo torso, in Imperial Museum, 71
Arab objects, in Imperial Museum, 83
Arcadius (Roman emperor), 117
Archaeological Institute of America (AIA), 19, 21
archaeological sites: and continuity of past and present, 170, 172, 175–176, 178; and daily life, 136, 204, 208, 209, 209, 210, 211–213, 211; history of, 98–104, 106–110; organization of workforce, 8–9, 135, 144, 146–148, 148, 153–

154; Ottoman officers supervising, 8, 9, 150, 152–155, 167, 168, 238n28; quarters of archaeologists compared with quarters of workers, 178–181, 183–187; and railroads, 100, 107, 156–157, 157, 181, 186–187; reports of, 139; similarities between contemporary and historic objects, 170, 171; size of sites, 144; size of workforce at, 139–141, 143–144, 146, 148, 149; social history of, 137; tools and technology of, 137, 138, 140, 141, 142, 146–147, 147, 150, 151, 155–157, 168; transportation of earth in baskets, 146, 155; and transportation of statues, 141, 142; workers' perspective of, 11, 137. See also archaeologists; workers; and specific sites

archaeologists: accounts of, 139, 158; Americans on antiquities laws, 18, 45–46; civilizing mission of, 157–158; credentials of, 21; Europeans on antiquities laws, 47; on Imperial Museum, 43–48; Ottoman officers supervising, 8, 9, 150, 152–155, 167, 168, 189, 194, 238nn28, 33; perspective on workforce of archaeological sites, 135–136; quarters of, 178–181, 181, 182, 183–187, 189–190, 191, 192–198, 193, 194, 195, 211, 212, 241n40; relationships with workers, 8–9, 143, 147–148, 150, 154, 155, 157–158, 159, 160–167, 169–170, 172–173, 193. See also specific archaeologists

archaeology: categories of alternative archaeologies, 4–5; collaboration with other disciplines, 97; establishment as academic discipline, 1; and ethnography, 1, 157–158, 160–167, 161, 162, 170, 171, 179, 186, 199–202, 201, 203, 204, 205, 206, 207, 208, 209, 209, 210, 211–213, 211, 238n44; history of, 2–3, 4, 6, 61, 96–99, 128, 135, 136–137; impact of antiquities laws on, 46–47; imperialism linked to, 1–2, 135, 137, 157–158,

180, 216; Ottoman press on, 56, 99; political and ideological undertones of, 4–5, 11, 216

Archaic Greek art, 62

architecture: history of, 3; of Imperial Museum, 22, 36–37, 75, 76, 84; in Ottoman Empire, 3–4, 107, 184, 240n18; polychromy in Greek architecture, 49–50

Artemis statue, 45, 62

Assos site, excavations in, 21, 144, 164, 180

Assyria, reliefs of, 53

Assyrian objects: in European museums, 130; in Imperial Museum, 17, 35, 55, 70; and ISIS, 221; pillaging of, 154–155

Athenaeum, The, 52

Athenaeum Club, 46

Athens: acropolis of, 57; excavation of, 139; Periclean Athens, 60; Temple of Dionysus, 111; Temple of Theseus, 56, 57

Athens Museums: Central Museum, 56; Imperial Museum compared to, 48; National Archeological Museum, 57

Attic family groups, 53

Augustus (Roman emperor), 62

Augustus (ruler of Palmyra), 98

Auric, André Joseph, 40

Austria, 13, 14

Aydın Province, excavations in, 97

Baalbek: general view of, *108*; and Orientalism, 61; origins of, 98, 100, 106; Temple of Jupiter, 106, 109; Temple of the Sun, 106; Temple of Venus, 106; travel to site, 107–108

Babylonia, Wolfe Expedition to, 63

Babylonian collection, in Imperial Museum, 63

Babylon site: excavations in, 97, 101, 137, *138*, 150, 152, 156, 167; gardens of, 101, *102*; history of, 98, 101–102; Ishtar Gate excavation, 156; literary works on, 128, 129–133; workers of, 144, 146

Baedeker's guidebooks, 73–74, 75, 77, 78, 117

Bahrani, Zainab, 3, 4

Balkans, Ottoman wars in, 14

Beard, Mary, 6, 218

Beato, Antonio, 67–68

Bedreddin, mausoleum of, 124

Bedri Bey, 10, 11, 90–91, 189, 194, 233n70

Beethoven, Ludwig van, 2

Bent, James Theodore, 45–46

Berlin Museums: Ahmed İhsan on, 116–117; Altes Museum, 29, 116–117; Imperial Museum compared to, 48; Kaiser Friedrich Museum, 30–31; Museum Island in, 28–29, *29*; National Gallery, 30; Neues Museum, 29; organization of, 31; Pergamon Museum, 30, 57; site plan of, *30*; urban context of, 28–29, *30*

Berlioz, Hector, 128

Beyhekim Mosque, Konya, 124

Blunt, Anne, 165

Blunt, Wilfrid Scawen, 165

Bohrer, Frederick, 5, 223–224n11, 236–237n80

Bonfils, Félix, 67–68

Botta, Paul-Émile, 140

British Architect, The, 50

British Library, 116

British Museum: Ahmed İhsan on, 114–115; and antiquities laws, 43–44; Assyrian artifacts in, 130; Baedeker's guide to, 75; building additions to, 28; collection of, 21, 63; Elgin Marbles in, 28, 69, 115, 218, 221; Ethnography Gallery, 115, 116; funding of Layard's excavations, 140; hours of, 232n53; Imperial Museum compared to, 48; Mesopotamian artifacts in, 129, 133; mission of, 215; Montagu House, 28; organization of, 31; Reading Room, 28, *116*; site plan of, *29*; statue of Heracles in, 57; urban context of, 28, *29*; White Wing, 28

Burckhardt, John Lewis, 99
Butler, Howard Crosby, 13, 97, 99, 148, 152, 180–181
Byron, George Gordon, Lord, *Sardanapalus*, 2, 8, 95, 129–131, 237nn80, 81
Byzantine objects, in Imperial Museum, 70, 79, 81, 83

Caillard, Vincent, 19, 24–25
Calvert, Charles, 130–131, 237n80
Cape Bon, Tunisia, 220
Caucasus, excavations in, 110
Cemal Bey, 109–110
Cemil Pasha, 38, 40
Central Labor Union, 91
Central Park, New York, 31, 33
Cesnola, Luigi Palma di: accounts of fieldwork, 139, *140*, 155, 163–164, 169, *170*; acquisitions of, 34, 85; excavation permits from Ottoman Empire, 20; on goal of American museums, 22–23; rumors of illegal smuggling of antiquities to London, 20
Choate, Joseph H., 22
chromolithography, 228n24
cities. *See* urban context
civilization: Egyptian civilization, 97; European civilization based on classical antiquities, 43, 44, 45; Islamic civilization, 16; Ottoman concepts of, 4
Clarke, Joseph Thacher, 164, 180
Cleveland Museum of Art, 218
Çoban Mustafa Pasha Mosque, Gebze, 124
Cockerell, Charles Robert, 49
Collection of Antique Weapons (Mecma-i Asar-ı Atika), 116
Collignon, Maxime, 53
Column of Constantine, 107
Coufopoulos, Demetrius, 73
Crete, archaeological explorations of, 18
Croessus (king of Lydia), 99

cultural heritage, protection of, 217, 218, 220
Cuno, James, 217, 221
Curtis, Canon C. G., 86
Cypriote objects: in Imperial Museum, 34, 62, 70, 72, 85; in Metropolitan Museum of Art, 76, 85
Cyprus, excavation in, 155

Darfur, sculptures from, 62
Davis, Natalie Zemon, 11
Dawkins, Robert, 175
decadence, as aesthetic term, 60
Delacroix, Eugène, 2, 128
Déthier, Philipp Anton, 34, 61
Diaz-Andreu, Margarita, 2, 5
Diwaniyah, and Nippur site, 187–188, 189
Doordan, Dennis, 217
Downing, Andrew Jackson, 31
Dumont, Albert, 79
Duvernoy, Victor-Alphonse, 129
Düyun-u Umumiye (Public Debt Administration), 47
Dwight, Harry Griswold, 72

early Christian objects, in Imperial Museum, 79
Eddy, W. K., 51
Egypt: excavations in, 111–112; Napoleon I's occupation of, 2; Petrie's excavations of, 6
Egyptian museums, 97
Egyptian objects: in Imperial Museum, 17, 35, 55, 70, 80, 88; in Louvre, 113; in Metropolitan Museum of Art, 85
Egyptology, 97
Eldem, Edhem, 3, 4, 166, 167, 239n46
Elgin, Thomas Bruce, Lord, 1, 2, 28, 139
Elgin Marbles, 1, 28, 46, 69, 115, 139, 218, 221
Elliot, Frances, 71
England, 18, 21, 73. *See also* British Museum

Enlightenment, 215

Ephesus site: workers of, 169; workmen with superintendents, *143*

Erdoğan, Recep Tayyip, 219

Erginün, İnci, 129, 237n81

Eshmunazar II, 58

ethnography: and archaeology, 1, 157–158, 160–167, *161, 162,* 170, 171, 179, 186, 199–202, *201, 203, 204, 205, 206, 207, 208, 209, 209, 210,* 211–213, *211,* 238n44

Eudel, Paul, 71

European museums: and antiquities laws of Ottoman Empire, 18, 19, 44; and artifacts from source countries, 215, 216; and art theft, 126; charged histories of, 216; in city centers, 26, 28–31; collection methods of, 127; educational mission of, 86; Imperial Museum compared to, 6–7, 17, 20, 21–22, 41, 48; Islamic artifacts in, 126, 127; Mesopotamian objects in, 128; Metropolitan Museum of Art compared to, 6–7, 17, 20–21, 23; in Ottoman press, 112, 113–119; parks surrounding, 26, 28, 29; and reputation of Imperial Museum, 21; urban contexts of, 7, 26, 28–31, *30*

Evliya Çelebi, 6

Fenger, Ludvig Peter, 50

Ferdinand, Prince of Bulgaria, 86

France, 4, 18, 21

French Revolution, 26

Funerary Complex of Dahshur, 111

Gardner, Percy, 53–54

Garstang, John, 169–170, *171*

Gazette des Beaux-Arts, 21, 56

George West Museum of Art and Archaeology, Round Lake, New York, 22

Gerasa: continuity of past and present in, 178; history of, 98–99, 102–103, *103*

Germany, 13, 14, 18. *See also* Berlin Museums

Ginzburg, Carlo, 11

Glyptothek of Munich, Imperial Museum compared to, 48

Golgoi site: drawings of modern priest and stone head, *170;* excavation of tombs, 139, *140,* 167

Goode, George Brown, 23, 86–87, 200, 202, 211

Goode, James F., 217

Goold, Edward, 34, 79–80, *79*

Gower, Ronald Sutherland, 71

Greco-Roman objects: artists of Renaissance era interpreting, 96; in Imperial Museum, 79, 81, 128

Greco-Roman sites: European claims to, 44, 45; interpretation of, 60–61; reports on, 8

Greek objects: in Imperial Museum, 70, 79, 81; in Metropolitan Museum of Art, 76

Grenfell, E. C., 13–14

Grosvenor, Edwin Augustus, 70–71

Grynium, necropolis of, 144, 146

guidebooks: and antiquities, 95, 108–109, 113–118; and tourism, 72–77, *78,* 84, 89

Günay, Ertuğul, 218

Gutron, Clémentine, 5

Habel, Dorothy Metzger, 11

Hadrian (Roman emperor), 62

Hagia Eirene, 33, 34, 79, 80, 116

Hagia Sophia Square, 38, 40, 107

Halil Edhem, 16, 83, 119, 121–128, 224–225n10

Halil Edib, 16

Hallerstein, Carl Haller von, 49, 179

Hamilakis, Yannis, 3, 172

Hamiyet, 101, 102

Harris, Clarence O., 21

Harvard University, Dumbarton Oaks

Research Library and Collection, 218–219

Haussmann, Georges-Eugène, 28

Haynes, Cassandria, 198, 212–213, 241n53

Haynes, John Henry: ethnography of Nippur, 199, 200, 201, *201*, 202, 204, 207, 209, 211–213, 224n11; on Nippur excavations, 10, 63, 64, 146, 187, 189, 190, 192, 193–194, 196–197, 198; Orientalism of, 5; and Osman Hamdi, 6

Hayter Lewis, T., 46, 50–51

Hellas, tombs of, 53

Heracles statue, 57

Herodotus, 101

Hillah, and Nippur site, 187–188, 192, 194

Hilprecht, Hermann Vollrat: account of fieldwork, 144, 161, 164, 169, 187, 198, 212; and antiquities laws, 154; and Bedri Bey, 10; on colonial civilizing mission, 157–158; on cuneiform, 62–63; on Meyer, 237n18; Orientalism of, 5; and Osman Hamdi, 6

Himyarite antiquities, in Imperial Museum, 80

Hisarlık, collection from, 62

historical surveys, 54, 95, 96

Hittite objects, in Imperial Museum, 17, 35, 63, 90

Hittorff, Jacques-Ignace, 49–50, 51, 228n24

Holod, Renata, 5

Hormuzd Rassam, 5, 137, 144, 146, 158, 164–166, 199

Hoskins, Franklin Evans, 99

humanism, 215, 216

Humann, Carl, 117

Hungary, excavations in, 111

Hunt, Richard Morris, 33

Hutton, William Holden, 69–70

İbrahim Pasha, mausoleum of, 125

Ihne, Ernst Eberhard von, 30–31

İhsan Şerif, 17

imperialism: archaeology linked to, 1–2, 135, 137, 157–158, 180, 216; and physical structure of colonial cities, 179

Imperial Museum of Antiquities, Istanbul: Ahmed İhsan's familiarity with, 115; archaeological and preservation administration responsibilities of, 14; archaeologists on, 43–48; architecture of, 22, 36–37, 75, 76, 84; archives of, 9; catalogues published by, 78–81, *79*, *82*, 83–84, 88, 89, 231n32, 232n43; Çinili Köşk, 15, *15*, 16, 34, 35, 36, *38*, 44, 55, 61, 62, 68, 69, 71, 72, 73, 74, 75, 76, 77, 80, 81, 84, 88; collaboration with scholars, 61–64; and collection and exhibition of artifacts, 14–15, 16, 17, 18, 67; construction history of, 35, 36, 72, 77, 80; educational mission of, 86, 88, 89, 91, 93; European painting collection in, 16–17, 224–225n10, 233n63; funding of, 6, 14, 17–18, 20; growth in collections, 15–17, 18, 34, 43, 48, 63, 84, 96, 131; in guidebooks, 72–77, 84, 89; Halil Edhem as director of, 83, 119, 121–128; Hercules statue in, 71, 72–73; and history of archaeology, 2–3, 6; hours of, 87, 232n53; and interest in Metropolitan Museum of Art, 20; interior photographs of, 10–11, *14*, *15*; Islamic objects in, 55, 81, 83, 84, 127, 128; library of, 36, 37, 115–116; in literature, 65, 66–67; local visitors to, 10–11, 67, 69, 84, 86–91; Mesopotamian artifacts in, 129, 131, 133; Metropolitan Museum of Art, New York, compared to, 6–7, 17, 84–85, 91–93; mission of, 7, 14–15, 16, 17, 23–25, 41, 43, 86, 88, 91, 93; new museum buildings opening, 3, 7, 15–16, 17, 34–35, 72, 73, 75, 76, 77, 81, 84, 86, 112, 215; Osman Hamdi as director of, 5–6, 7, 9–10, 14, 19–20, 22, 25, 26, 35, 41, 46, 47, 48, 51, 63, 69, 71, 77, 80, 84, 86, 87, 88–91, 115, 127–128,

152, 225n25, 233n70; and Ottoman heritage, 119, 121–128; and Ottoman modernity, 25–26, 84; photographs of, 67–68, 70; plan of museum building with extension, *15*, *55*; public of, 7–8, 41, 44; reputation of, 21–22, 43, 45, 51, 54, 61–64, 68; and rumored sale of contents of, 13–14, 17, 19–20, 21; Sarcophagus of Alexander in, *14*, 48, 51, 52, 57–58; and Sardis site grave artifacts, 106; scholarly recognition of, 19, 46–48, 68, 83; School of Fine Arts in, 16–17, 24, 35, 59–60, 71, 233n63; School of the Imperial Museum, 24; Sidon sarcophagi in, 52, 54, 61, 68–72, 74, *75*, 76, 77, 80, 86, 89, 215; significance in cultural consciousness, 17; Siloam Inscription in, 76; site plan of, *39*; staff responsibilities, 87, 232n54; student visits to, 87–88, 91; torso of Apollo in, 71; transportation of antiquities to, 2, 10, 16; urban context of, 7, 33–34, 37–38, *39*, 40–41; value of holdings, 76, 80; view of North Wing, *38*; Western visitors to, 67–79, 84, 86

Iraq, 217

Iraqi objects, in Imperial Museum, 83

İslahat-ı Turuk Komisyonu (Commission for Road Improvement), 40

Islam: on antiquities, 48; on representation of living creatures, 71

Islamic heritage: reports on, 8. *See also* Ottoman heritage

Islamic objects: in European museums, 126, 127; in Imperial Museum, 55, 81, 83, 84, 127, 128

Islamic State (ISIS or ISIL), 221

İsmail Fazıl Pasha, 178, *179*

İsmail Galib, 81, 83

Istanbul, Turkey: Column of Constantine, 107; guidebooks to, 72–77; Gülhane Park, 38, 40, *40*; Hagia Sophia Square, 38, 40; Hippodrome, 107;

periodicals published in, 8; and postcard industry, 77–78; public transportation in, 40; Sultan Ahmed Park, 38, 40; Taksim Park, 38; Tepebaşı Park, 38; as travel destination, 68–72; urban planning in, 38, 40, 107

Istanbul Archaeological Museum. *See* Imperial Museum of Antiquities, Istanbul

Istanbul University, 58, 59–60

janissary corps, 116

Jasanoff, Maya, 5

Jockey, Philippe, 1

Johnson, Boris, 221

Joncières, Victorin de, 128–129

Joubin, André, 80–81, 88, 233n61

J. Paul Getty Museum, 218, 219

Judeo-Christian heritage, 5

"Jupiter à Olympie," 49

Justinian (Byzantine emperor), 98

Kadri Bey, 16

Kalaa-Shirgat site, 146

Karamanoğlu İbrahim Bey, mausoleum of, 124

Kean, Charles, 129–130

Kemal Bey, 86–87

Kemal Tahir, *Esir Şehrin İnsanları* (*People of the Captive City*), 66, 67

Khorsabad site, 154, 179–180

Koldewey, Robert, 144, 146, 156

Konya Citadel, 124

Koyuncuk site, 144

Kuklick, Bruce, 5, 241n53

labor landscape: and history of archaeology, 3, 135; technology of, 137, *138*, *140*, 141, *142*, 146, 146–147, *147*, 150, *151*, 155–157, *168*; and wages, 6, 223–224n11. *See also* archaeological sites; archaeologists; workers

Ladies' Christian Union, 91

Lakina, Ottoman excavation of, 16

Law of Antiquities (Asar-ı Atika Nizam-namesi, 1906), 14, 18
Layard, Austen Henry: account of fieldwork, 137, 139–141, 143, 163, 179, 199; house at Khorsabad, 180; and imperialism linked to archaeology, 2, 158; *Nineveh and Its Remains*, 129, 130, 131, 139–141, *141*, *142*, 143, 158, *161*, *162*, *163*; on Oriental women, 161–163, *163*; and Rassam, 5; relationship with workers, 158, 160–163; and Sayce, 61
Legation of the United States, 18
Lehmann, Karl, 152
Leonardo da Vinci, 71
Lesbos, 62, 144, 180
Levy, Leon, 219
Libbey, William, 99
Libya, 14
Liszt, Franz, 128
Literary News, 47
literature: classic references in, 95; Imperial Museum in, 65, 66–67; literary works on Mesopotamia, 2, 128, 129–133
local people: meanings of antiquities for, 3, 4, 220; as visitors to Imperial Museum, 10–11, 67, 69, 84, 86–91
Los Angeles Times, 218
Louvre Museum: Artemis-statues of Praxiteles in, 62; buildings of, 26; bust of Alexander in, 57; collection of, 21; general view, 1851, *27*; growth of, 67; Imperial Museum compared to, 48; in literature, 65–67; metope of Temple of Zeus from Olympia in, 56; organization of, 31; Ottoman press on, 112–113, 114, *115*, 118–119; site plan of, *27*; and Tuileries Garden, *27*, 28; urban context of, 26, *27*; Venus de Milo in, 57; visibility of, 28
Ludovisi Medusa in Rome, 62
Lycée de Galatasaray, 79
Lydia, 99, 106
Lysippos, 219

Macmillan guidebooks, 75–77
Macridi Bey, 81, 90
Madame Tussauds museum, London, 114
Magnesia, German excavation of, 30
Mahmud (sultan), 119
Malumat, 56–58, *56*
Manisa region, excavation of, 35
Marchand, Suzanne, 5
Mariette, Auguste, 111
Marmaris, antiquities discovered in, 16
Marquand, Henry G., 23
Maspero, Gaston, 111
medieval objects, in Imperial Museum, 70
Medusa sculptures, in Imperial Museum, 62
Mehmed Şerif Efendi, 58
Mehmed Vahid, 37, 58–60
Mendel, Gustave, 81, 82, 99, 231n32
Mesopotamia: archaeological sites of, 5, 10, 63, 76, 133, 139, 144, 187, 211; literary works on, 2, 128, 129–133
Messel, Alfred, 30
Metropolitan Museum of Art, New York: administrative system of, 23; Annual Reports of the Trustees, 84–85; archaeological excavations sponsored by, 180; archives of, 9; Baedeker's guide to, 75; buildings of, 33, 78–79; catalogues published by, 85; and Central Park, 31; Cesnola as director of, 20; Cesnola Collection purchased by, 20, 33, 34, 66, 75, 85, 139; and contraband trade in antiquities, 63; East Wing of, 77; educational mission of, 91–93; funding of, 6–7, 17, 18; growth of, 33, 67; hours of, 91–92; Imperial Museum compared to, 6–7, 17, 84–85, 91–93; and interest in Imperial Museum, 20; library of, 85; in literature, 65, 66–67; Lydian Hoard, 219; mission of, 7, 22, 23, 91–93; Norbert Schimmel Collection, 218, 219; North

Wing of, 23, 33; origins of, 22; and postcard industry, 77–78, 78; public of, 7–8, 22; publishing activities of, 84–85; and rumored sale of contents of Imperial Museum of Antiquities, Istanbul, 13–14; site plan of, 32; student visits to, 92–93; temporary quarters of, 33; urban context of, 7, 31, 32, 33, 34; view from Fifth Avenue, 34

Metropolitan Street Railway System, 92

Mexico, ruins of Aztec settlement in, 111

Meyer, Joseph Andrew: "Arab forts," sketches of, 196, 197, 198; documentation of Nippur site, 136, 146–147, 147, 148, 194–195, 195, 196, 196, 197–198, 197; ethnography of Nippur, 200–202, 201, 204, 207, 209, 212; Hilprecht on qualifications of, 237n18; on security forces, 240n27

Michaelis, Adolf, 139

Middle East, 3, 4, 6, 60–61, 218, 221

Miletus, history of, 103–104, 104

Military Museum, Istanbul, 128

Milliyet, 218

Minister of Culture and Tourism, 218

Ministry of Education, 16, 24, 64, 152, 153, 154

Ministry of Interior Affairs, 154–155, 188

Ministry of Pious Foundations, 124, 128

Mohammed, Ahmed Kamel, 221

Morgan, Jacques Jean Marie de, 111

Morgan, J. Pierpont, 13–15, 17, 21, 78

Mosque of Olive Trees (Zeytinli Camii), 121

Mould, Jacob Wrey, 33

M. Sadık, 106, 108–109

Mukbil Kemal, 126–127

Müller, F. Max, 46–47, 69

Müller, Georgina Adelaide, 68–69, 72

Murray's Handbooks for Travellers, 73, 74–75, 77

Museum of Fine Arts, Boston, 54, 219

Museum of Paintings and Sculptures, 224–225n10

Museum of Pious Foundations, 17, 83, 126, 127, 128

Muybridge, Eadweard James, 64

Nabil Yunus, 221

Naples Museum, 62, 112

Napoleon I (emperor of France), 2, 28

Napoléon III (emperor of France), 28

Nation, The, 45

nationalism, 128, 215–216, 217

National Museum of Iraq, Baghdad, 221

Nazmi Ziya, 89, 118–119

Nemrud Dağı site, 144, 158, 166, 167, 239n46

New Review, 47

New York East Conference of the Methodist Episcopalian Church, 91

New York Historical Society, 22

New York Public Library, 92

New York Times, 18–20, 33, 48, 152, 216, 217

Nicole, Georges, 81

Nimrud site: British excavation of, 43–44, 160; German excavation of, 90, 152; workers of, 144

Nineveh site: British excavation of, 43–44, 139–141; and imperialism, 2; and Layard's Nineveh and Its Remains, 129, 130, 131, 139–141, 141, 142, 143, 158, 161, 162, 163; lifting of the statues, 142; in literature, 95, 129–133; pillaging of, 154; transportation of statues, 142; workers at, 139–141, 141, 142, 143

Nippur site: American archaeologists in, 5, 10, 63, 64, 152; archaeologists' quarters in, 189–190, 191, 192–198, 193, 194, 195, 211, 212, 241n40; and continuity between past and present, 170, 172; excavations in, 63, 64, 76, 136, 150, 154, 172–173; Haynes's ethnography of, 199, 200, 201, 201, 202, 204, 207, 209, 211–213, 224n11; Haynes's reports on, 10, 63, 64, 146, 187, 189, 190, 192, 193–194, 196–197, 198; Meyer's documentation of, 136, 146–147, 147, 148, 194–

195, *195*, 196, *196*, 197–198, *197*; Meyer's ethnography of workers, 200–202, *201*, 204, *207*, 209, 212; Meyer's sketch of tools used in excavation, *147*; Peters's drawing of excavation site, *148*; security forces for, 188, 189, *189*, 194, 240n27; and transportation, 188, *189*; workers' daily life, 204, *208*, *209*, 210, 211–213, *211*; workers of, 144, 145, 146–148, 150, 169, 170, *171*, 199; workers' village in, 190, 192, 198–202, *203*, 204, *205*, *206*, *207*, *208*, 209, *209*, 210, 211–213, *211*, 241n56

Nisroch, an Assyrian god, drawing, *132*

North Africa, architecture of, 4

Olmstead, Frederick Law, 31, 33

Orientalism, 5, 8, 61, 128, 143, 157–158, 160–167, 183, 199, 211

Osgan Efendi, 16, 83, 144, 158, 166–167

Osman Hamdi: accounts of fieldwork, 137, 144, 146, 150, 166–167, 172–173, 199; American archaeologists' interactions with, 5–6, 7, 18; American press's image of, 25, 225n25; archaeological scholarship of, 127; and catalogues published by Imperial Museum, 80–81, 83, 88–89, 231n32, 233n61; death of, 16, 19–20, 48, 83, 119; as director of Imperial Museum, 5–6, 7, 9–10, 14, 19–20, 22, 25, 26, 35, 41, 46, 47, 48, 51, 63, 69, 71, 77, 80, 84, 86, 87, 88–91, 115, 127–128, 152, 225n25, 233n70; European archaeologists' interactions with, 7; excavations of, 73, 76, 137, 144, 146, 150, 158, *160*; foreign scholars' interaction with, 25–26, 67; goals for Imperial Museum, 7; on Lakina excavations, 16; legislation written by, 7, 24–25, 44, 45–46; *Une nécropole royale à Sidon*, 51–52, 58, 83, 155, *156*, 167; paintings of, 25; and Sidon sarcophagi, 7, 49, 51–52, 58,

73, 76, 88, 146, 150, 166–167, 172–173, 228n26

Osmanlı Ressamlar Cemiyeti Gazetesi (Journal of Ottoman Painters' Society), 25

Ottoman Bank, 57

Ottoman Empire: American archaeologists engaging in scientific work in, 18, 21; archaeological discourse of, 4, 24–25, 55, 99–100, 107; architecture of, 3–4, 107, 184, 240n18; claims to antiquities, 7, 24–25, 43–44, 46–47, 64, 86, 127; control of ethnic and religious groups, 11; funding of Imperial Museum, 17–18; and history of archaeology, 2–3; and modernity, 4, 25–26, 84, 89, 95, 100, 107, 127, 188; nature of primary sources on, 11; railroad network's function in, 2, 4, 57, 91; Second Constitutional Regime, 109, 119, 127; territory of, 18; transition to Turkish Republican era, 60

Ottoman heritage: in Aleppo, 126–127; in Anatolia, 121–124, *125*; Çoban Mustafa Pasha Mosque, Gebze, 124; and early mausoleums, 124; Halil Edhem's focus on, 119, 121–128; *imaret* in Karaman, 124; İnce Minareli Medrese, Konya, 122–123, *123*; in Konya, 121–123, 124; and looting, 126–127; Mosque of Olive Trees, 121; prince's tomb in Ezine, 121, *122*; and royal boathouses, 119, *121*; and Sinan Pasha kiosk, 119, *120*

Ottoman officials: archaeologists supervised by, 8, 9, 150, 152–155, 167, *168*, 189, 194, 238nn28, 33; in Gerasa, *179*

Ottoman periodicals, reports on museum collections and archaeological finds, 95, 96, 98–100

Ottoman press: and definition of objects of antiquity, 25; and foreigners' views of Imperial Museum, 86; on Louvre

Museum, 112–113, 114, *115*, 118–119; and mission of museums, 87; popular press's reporting on antiquities abroad, 110–119; popular press's reporting on local antiquities, 98–104, 106–110; and reputation of Imperial Museum, 21, 35, 88, 115; on Sidon sarcophagi, 54–58

Ottoman provinces: antiquities displayed in, 90; architecture of Arab provinces, 4; British interests in, 2; and Eastern territories, 4; investment in, 188; and Museum of Pious Foundations, 128; primitive populations destroying monuments, 46; storage of antiquities for Imperial Museum, 89–90; and surveillance of excavations, 91, 150, 152–155, 238n33

Oulebsir, Nabila, 5

Ousterhout, Robert, 5, 224n11

Palais Longchamps, Marseille, 113–114

Palestinian Exploration Fund, 228n26

Palmyra: and continuity of past and present, 175–176, 178; excavation of, *160*; history of, 98, 107; and Orientalism, 61; Temple of the Sun, 107, 175–176; village among ruins, 9, 175–176, *177*

Palymrian antiquities, in Imperial Museum, 80

Parker, Montague, 13

partage, practice of, 24, 47, 217

Parthenon: and Elgin Marbles, 2, 69, 139, 218; excavation of, 139; frieze of, 50; Panathenaic procession on exterior colonnade of, 49; and polychromy, 49, 50; reliefs of, 52; Sidon sarcophagi compared to, 60

Pelham, Nicholas, 221

Pepper, William, 200

Pera Museum, Istanbul, 6

Perdrizet, Paul, 62

Pergamon: Altar of Zeus, 30; and Bedri Bey, 10; German excavation of, 30, 101, 117; reconstruction of agora, 100–101, *100*; Sidon sarcophagi compared to examples from, 50

Periclean Athens, 60

Perrot, Georges, 72–73

Peters, John Punnett: accounts of fieldwork, 137, 144, 146, 147–148, 150, 161, 164, 170, 172, 173, 178, 187–189, 190, 193; on antiquities laws, 227–228n8; archaeological expeditions proposed by, 20–21; drawing of Nippur excavation site, *148*; ethnography of, 199–200; Orientalism of, 5; on Osman Hamdi, 225n25; on Sidon sarcophagi, 52; and transportation of illegal objects, 154, 178

Petra, history of, 99

Petrie, William Matthew Flinders, 6, 136

Philo, 101–102

philology, 97

Phoenician objects: in Imperial Museum, 63, 71, 73; in Metropolitan Museum of Art, 76

polychromy: and Sarcophagus of Alexander, 48, 51, 52, 53, 55, 59, 74; and Sarcophagus of the Mourning Women, 51, 74; uses in Greek antiquity, 7, 48, 49–50, 51, 52–53, 228n24

Pompeii, excavation of, 112

popular books, and historical topics, 95

postcard industry, 77–78

power relations, and workers' relationship with archaeologists, 8, 169–170, 193

Presbytery of New York, 91

Priene, German excavation of, 30

Protestant beliefs, and American archaeologists, 5

public transportation: and access to museums, 95; and urban context, 26, 28, 40

Qasr Amra, 198
Quatremère de Quincy, Antoine-
    Chrysostome, 49
Quirke, Stephen, 6, 135–137

racial hierarchy, 4, 61
Radcliffe, Abigail G., 48
railroads: and archaeological sites, 100,
    107, 156–157, 157, 181, 186–187; and
    looting, 127; of Ottoman Empire, 2,
    4, 57, 91
Reid, Donald Malcolm, 6
Reinach, Salomon, 44–45, 62, 80, 86, 89,
    127, 217
Reinach, Théodore: Une nécropole royale
    à Sidon, 51–52, 58, 83, 155, 156, 167; on
    Sarcophagus of Alexander, 52–53, 60;
    on Sidon sarcophagi, 49, 56, 68
Reinhart, Charles Stanley, The Copyist in
    the Louvre, 114
Renan, Ernest, 58
retentionist cultural property laws, 215,
    216, 217, 242n8
Revue archéologique, 45, 49, 51, 79
Revue des deux mondes, 44, 45, 53, 61
Revue d'ethnographie, 49
Rhodes, Robin F., 217
Rich, Claudius James, 2
Robinson, E., 13
Roman Forum, Ahmed İhsan on, 117–118,
    118
Rondanini Medusa in Munich, 62
royal boathouses, 119, 121

Sadık Bey, 69, 109
Sahib Ata, 122, 125–126
Sahibiye Medresesi, 125
Saleh (Salih) Bey, 194
Salihli village, and Sardis site, 150, 152, 181,
    183, 185, 186–187
Sarcophagus of Alexander: and an-
    tiquities laws, 19; attribution of, 54,
    57, 224n1; in catalogues of Imperial
    Museum, 89; Gardner on, 53; in Im-
perial Museum, 14, 48, 51, 52, 54, 70,
    71, 73, 74, 75, 76; Imperial Museum's
    rumored sale of, 13, 17, 19–20; Meh-
    med Vahid on, 59; in Ottoman press,
    54–58, 56; photographs of, 68, 69,
    70, 71; and polychromatic reliefs, 48,
    51, 52, 53, 55, 59, 74; preservation of,
    19; Théodore Reinach on, 52–53, 60;
    value of, 17
Sarcophagus of Satrap, in Imperial Mu-
    seum, 53, 73, 74, 75, 76
Sarcophagus of Tabnith, in Imperial
    Museum, 76
Sarcophagus of the Mourning Women:
    extraction from site, 155, 156; Gard-
    ner on, 53; in Imperial Museum, 48,
    54, 70, 72, 73, 74, 75, 76; Imperial
    Museum's rumored sale of, 20; inter-
    pretations of, 86; names for, 225n24;
    in Ottoman press, 55; photographs of,
    68, 69, 70, 71; and polychromy, 51, 74;
    south and north façades, 55
Sardanapalus (king of Assyria), 8, 128–
    133, 236n71
Sardis site: archaeologists' quarters at,
    180–181, 181, 182, 183–186; Butler's ac-
    count of, 148; excavation of, 97, 137,
    138, 150, 152; field house at, 181, 182,
    183–184, 183, 184, 185, 186; history of,
    99, 100, 104, 106, 107; railroads used
    in, 156–157, 157, 181, 186–187; security
    forces at, 151, 152–153, 181; views of
    the Temple of Artemis, 104, 105, 106;
    workers of, 144, 148, 149, 151, 158, 159,
    169, 185–186; workers' village, 181, 185–
    187; Yakub Efendi's visit to, 152, 153
Sayce, Archibald Henry, 61–62
Schinkel, Karl Friedrich, 29, 117
Schliemann, Heinrich, 62, 69, 76, 110
Sebah, Pascal, 231n32
Seetzen, Ulrich Jasper, 99
Şehbal: on column of Arcadius, 117; Halil
    Edhem's articles on Ottoman heri-
    tage, 119, 120, 121, 121, 122, 123–125, 123,

125; and Schliemann, 235n34; views of Temple of Artemis at Sardis, 105

Selinunte, Sicily, 50, 111

Semper, Gottfried, 49

Servet-i Fünun: on antiquities, 96, 99, 100–101, *100*; on antiquities abroad, 110; on Baalbek, 106, 107–109, *108*; on Babylon, 101–102; on Gerasa, 102, *103*; on Imperial Museum, 37, 86, 115; on Louvre, 112–113, 114, *115*; on Miletus, 103–104, *104*; on Sidon sarcophagi, 21, 54–56; on Versailles, 112

Seymour, Michael, 128, 236n71

Seyyid Mahmud, mausoleum of, 125

Shaw, Wendy, 4

Shelley, Percy Bysshe, 2

Shemtob, Joseph, 64

Sidon site: American Presbyterian Mission in, 51; excavation of, 55, 58, 150, 155, *156*, 172–173; Osman Hamdi's discovery of sarcophagi, 7, 58, 73, 76, 88, 172–173; Osman Hamdi's "jealousy" over sarcophagi, 51, 228n26; Osman Hamdi's report on sarcophagi, 49, 51; Osman Hamdi's workers in, 146, 150, 166–167, *168*, 172–173; sarcophagi of, 7, 21, 35, 46, 48, 49, 50–60, 68–72, 74, 80, 86, 88, 89, 228n26. *See also* Sarcophagus of Alexander; Sarcophagus of the Mourning Women

Siloam Inscription, 76

Sinan, 124

Sinan Pasha kiosk, 119, *120*

Sloane, Hans, 28, 114

Smirke, Robert, 28

Smirke, Sydney, 28

Smith, George, 43–44, 130

Smith, George Adam, 99

Smithsonian Institution, 23, 86–87, 200

Sofouk (sheik), 161–163

Solomon, King, 98

South Kensington Museum, 62

Stackelberg, Otto Magnus, 179

Sterrett, J. R. Sitlington, 21

Stoddard, John, 71

Straus, Oscar Solomon, 18

Strzygowski, Josef, 60–61

Stüler, Friedrich August, 29–30

Süleyman (sultan), 76

Süleymaniye Külliye, 128

Süleyman Nazif, 155

Switzerland, excavations in, 110

Syria: excavations in, 97, 106, 176; Roman invasion of, 98

Syrian objects, in Imperial Museum, 83

Tamerlane (Timur), 99

Tashkent, excavation in, 111

Tello, excavations of, 76

Temple of Apollo at Melitus, 104

Temple of Artemis at Sardis, 95, 104, *105*, 106

Temple of Baal at Nippur, 172

Temple of Bassae in Peloponnese, 179

Temple of Bel at Babylon, 62

Temple of Jupiter at Baalbek, 106, 109

Temple of Jupiter at Timgad, 97

Temple of the Sun at Baalbek, 106

Temple of the Sun at Palmyra, 107, 175–176

Temple of Venus at Baalbek, 106

textbooks, 54, 95, 96

Theodosius, 117–118

Timgad, excavation of, 97

Topkapı Museum, 128

Topkapı Palace, 15, 33–34, *36*, 38, 40, 119

Topuzlu, Cemil Pasha, 38, 40

tourism: of Anatolia, 220; and guidebooks, 72–77, 78, 84, 89; of Istanbul, 68, 230n6; and popular press, 107, 113–118; and postcard industry, 77–78; and railroads, 2, 107

Trajan (Roman emperor), 117

Trajan's Column, 117–118

Trigger, Bruce, 4–5

Troy, history of, 99, 109–110

Trümpler, Charlotte, 5

Tuckerman, Arthur L., 33

Tulane University, 21
Turkish Republic, 60, 218–219
Turkistan, 111
La Turquie, 227n4

universal expositions, 199
University of Pennsylvania: museum of, 62–64; and Nippur excavations, 187, 200
urban context: and European museums, 7, 26, 28–31, *30*; and Imperial Museum, 7, 33–34, 37–38, *39*, 40–41; of Istanbul, 38, 40, 107; and Metropolitan Museum of Art, 7, 31, *32*, 33, 34; and public transportation, 26, 28, 40

Valentier, Wilhelm M. R., 85
Vallaury, Alexandre, 15, *16*
Van Millingen, Alexander, 72
Vatican, Imperial Museum compared to, 48
Vaux, Calvert, 31, 33
Veli Pasha, 179
Venus de Milo: discovery of, 58; and identity of France, 1; in Louvre, 57, 69
Venus of Tralles, 57
Versailles, 112
Vienna, Austria, Belvedere, 57
Vitali, Philippe, 57
Volney, Constantin-François, 175–176

Walid (Umayyad caliph), 198
Ward, William Hayes, 63–64
Weary Herakles statue, 219–220
Weston, Theodore, 33
Wharton, Edith, *Age of Innocence*, 66, 67
White, Shelby, 219
Wilhelm II (emperor of Germany), 109
Wolfe Expedition, to Babylonia, 63
Wolff, Fritz, 30
Wood, James T., 143, 160–161, 169, 175, 199, 239n48
Woods, Michael, 169

workers: artifacts unearthed by, 139, *140*; at Ephesus site, 143, *143*; ethnicity of, 140–141, 143, 144, 148, 150, *151*, 154, 155, 158, 160–167, 169–170, *171*, 172, 180, 199; ethnography of, 1, 157–158, 160–167, *161*, *162*, 170, *171*, 179, 186, 199–202, *201*, *203*, *204*, *205*, *206*, *207*, 208, *209*, 210, 211–213, *211*, 238n44; at Golgoi site, 139, *140*; hierarchy of, 146, 147, 150, 158; horse carts used by, 150, *151*; at Nineveh site, 139–141, *141*, *142*, 143; of Nippur site, 144, *145*, 146–148, 150, 169, 170, *171*, 199; organization of workforce, 8–9, 135, 144, 146–148, *148*; and Ottoman officers, 154; in photographs of archaeological sites, 137, *137*, 150, 167; relationships with archaeologists, 8–9, 143, 147–148, 150, 154, 155, 157–158, *159*, 160–167, 169–170, 172–173, 193; residential areas of, 9, 137, *138*, 140, 143, 178–181, 183–187, 190, 192, 198–202, *203*, *204*, *205*, *206*, *207*, 208, *209*, *209*, *210*, 211–213, *211*, 241n56; seasonal migration of, 178–179; Sidon sarcophagi discovered by, 51, 58; at Sidon site, 146, 150, 166–167, *168*, 172–173; "silence" in documents, 11, 135, 211; size of workforce at sites, 139–141, 143–144, 146, 148, *149*, 157; statistics on, 139; tools used by, 137, *138*, *140*, 146–147, *147*, 150, *151*, 155–157; wages of, 6, 147, 150, 169, 212, 223–224n11; working conditions of, 139, 141, *142*, 150, 155, *156*, 158
World's Columbian Exposition in Chicago (1893), 199
World War I, 3, 154

Yakub Bey, 150, 152
Yeni Cami, model of, 74, 128
Young Turks, 14

Zenobia, Queen, 98
Zola, Émile, *L'assommoir*, 65–66, 67